CIVILIZATION AND MONSTERS

ASIA-PACIFIC: CULTURE, POLITICS, AND SOCIETY

Editors: Rey Chow, H. D. Harootunian, and Masao Miyoshi

A Study of the East Asian Institute, Columbia University

Civilization and Monsters

Spirits of Modernity in Meiji Japan

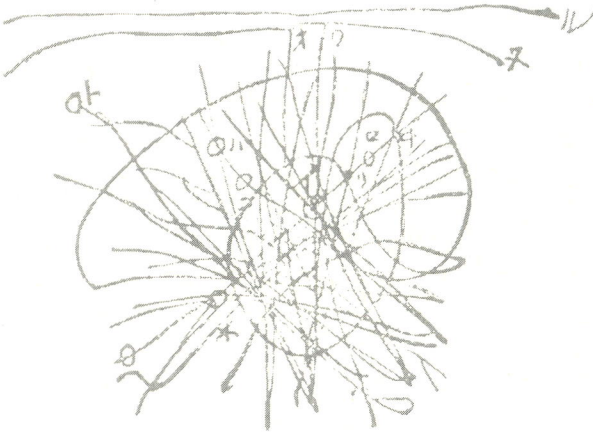

GERALD FIGAL

DUKE UNIVERSITY PRESS DURHAM AND LONDON 1999

2nd printing, 2007
© 1999 Duke University Press
All rights reserved
Printed in the United States of America on acid-free paper ∞
Designed by Amy Ruth Buchanan
Typeset in Bembo by Tseng Information Systems, Inc.
Library of Congress Cataloging-in-Publication Data appear
on the last printed page of this book.

Studies of the East Asian Institute, Columbia University
The East Asian Institute is Columbia University's center for
research, publication, and teaching on modern East Asia. The
Studies of the East Asia Institute were inaugurated in 1962 to
bring to a wider public the results of significant new research
on modern and contemporary East Asia.

To my fantastic folks, Judy and Gary Figal

CONTENTS

ACKNOWLEDGMENTS

I owe a fantastic amount of thanks to many folks. Let me first acknowledge the most distant and least obvious. Friends and common folks in Japan who have provided me tangible and intangible forms of support are too many to cite, but a few do merit special recognition. Unsung heroes of the everyday grind, Ms. Komugai of the Tōno City Museum and Mr. Murata of the library and archives at Tōyō University displayed rare kindness in aiding me to gather research materials. I must also, in spite of our disputes over theory and methodology, give credit to Harashida Minoru, ex-restaurateur and freelance scholar, for pointing me several years ago to sources that were the seed of my master's thesis and eventually blossomed into the dissertation on which this book is based. Although they would hardly believe it judging by my constant bickering and complaints, the faculty of the Inter-University Center for Japanese Language Studies earned my appreciation for their unflagging efforts to cut diamonds from the roughest of rocks. The friendship extended to me there by Tateoka Yōko, Aoki Sōichi, and Kishida Rie made an intensive program less tense. Yōko in particular has been a much-cherished friend, and I will be ever grateful to her and her husband Yasuo for putting me up (and putting up with me) in their home during one research trip.

The Mellon Fellowship in the Humanities that I received from the Woodrow Wilson National Fellowship Foundation and subsequent funding from the University of Chicago Humanities Division allowed me to complete the initial research for this book in relatively swift time with relatively little stress while a graduate student from 1985 to 1992. With a research fellowship from the University of Chicago's Center for East Asian Studies (and the Tateoka's hospitality) I was also able to carry out crucial research in Japan in autumn 1990.

All of the funding, research help, and language training in the world, however, would have been all for nought without the guidance and inspiration from the members of my thesis committee at the University of Chicago. Harry Harootunian, who first suggested to me the complexity and importance of questions of the "folk" in modern Japanese history, has never lagged in showing genuine enthusiasm and zeal for my project. If only a fraction of his intellectual energy remains with me I will consider myself well stoked for many years to come. Tetsuo Najita shares with him an ability gained only by experience to relate the particulars of any research to larger political, social, and cultural formations. Their analytical and critical attention as well as their open minds are what made a topic such as mine even thinkable. I only wish William Sibley's uncanny sensitivity to nuances of literary language—Japanese or otherwise—would somehow magically rub off on me. I thank him for introducing me to the eerie pleasure of Izumi Kyōka's prose and for getting me through the more tortuous passages. His wit and pleasant company often made more endurable the more tortuous passages of graduate school as well. I also thank Norma Field not only for teaching me something of classical Japanese language and literature but also for her always amicable and vibrant conversations on all topics great and small.

Above and beyond intellectual guidance, I owe all of my mentors heartfelt gratitude for the concern they have shown for me as a fellow human being plugging along in life. Since the first (and only!) history course I ever took from him in 1980 to the present, Hal Drake of the University of California at Santa Barbara has been a valued adviser and friend—and whether he approves of it or not, he is my role model for teaching. I would not be studying history today if it weren't for him, and I would not be studying Japanese history if it weren't for his then colleague at UCSB, Henry D. Smith II. Henry's undergraduate courses captured my interest in Japan, and the rest is history. His continuing concern and overall good-naturedness I will always hold in high esteem.

I must also credit Henry's fellow historian of Japan at Columbia University, Carol Gluck, for urging me to get this book out and for recommending the Studies of the East Asian Institute at Columbia University as a vehicle for that task. The Institute Publications Director Madge Huntington, in conjunction with Duke University Press Executive Editor J. Reynolds Smith and his Senior Editorial Assistant Sharon P. Torian, have made the publication process much more bearable than I imagined. To begin with, they secured three conscientious reviewers who characterized and clarified my project better than I ever could. The constructive comments and overwhelming encouragement I received from them eased some of the anxieties accompanying authorship. Stefan Tanaka's thorough pro bono reading of an early draft, too, worked wonders to help frame the project and bolster my confidence.

I could go on about the priceless intellectual stimulation that my peers from the Chicago days have provided, but I won't, since what must be acknowledged as having been at least as important is their down-to-earth camaraderie without which this life of the mind would be a very paltry thing indeed. That means all those things we did together which reminded us that there is also a life of the body, and we needed a lot of reminding. The "we" in this case includes Bob Adams, Noriko Aso, Susan Burns, Alan Christy, Yoshikuni Igarashi, Tom LaMarre, Tom Looser, Fukiko Ogisu, Walter Skya, and Kentarō Tomio. Once I crossed to the other side of the podium with my first job at Lewis and Clark College and then in the Department of History at the University of Delaware, I found invaluable collegiality and encouragement from persons too numerous to name, but you know who you are.

Finally, to the closest and most obvious: my parents, whose unwavering faith in all of my endeavors has been my secret catalyst; and my wife, Ruth Rogaski, whose spirited intellect, good humor, loving companionship, and unparalleled patience make it all worthwhile.

Monsters in the Twilight of Enlightenment

The ideal Kyōka twilightizes life.

> —Orikuchi Shinobu, cited in Miyata Noburu,
>
> "Kyōka to yōkai" [Kyōka and monsters]

I wonder how many people there are in the world who truly have a sense of taste for twilight? It seems to me that many people have lumped twilight and dusk together. When speaking of "dusk" the sensation of the color of night, the color of darkness, becomes dominant. However, twilight is neither the color of night nor the color of darkness. So saying, it is neither simply a sensation of day, nor of light. In the momentary world of entering night from day, at the momentary boundary of entering darkness from light, is that not where the twilight world lies? Twilight is neither darkness nor light, and nor is it a mixture of light and darkness. I think that twilight is a world of singularly subtle shades that exist solely in that momentary space of entering darkness from light, of entering night from day. Similar to the singularly subtle twilight world, existing in the space of entering darkness from light, there is a world of subtle shades called dawn on the boundary of entering light from darkness, in the momentary interval of moving to day from night. This too is a singularly subtle world that is neither darkness nor light nor a mixture of darkness and light. I consider it a great mistake that people in the world think as though there were no other worlds outside of night and day, darkness and light. It is my belief that there is certainly a singularly subtle world of the in-between outside of sensations that approach the two extremes of dusk and day-

break. I have been thinking that this taste for twilight, this taste for
dawn, is something I would like to impart to people in the world.

This taste for twilight, this taste for dawn, is not something that
exists merely in the relation of day with night. I believe that in
similar fashion among all things in the universe there are singularly
subtle worlds. For example, even when it comes to people, good
and evil is something like day and night, but in between this good
and evil there is in addition a singularly subtle place that we should
not destroy, that we should not extinguish. In the momentary space
of moving from good to evil, in the momentary space of entering
from evil to good, humans display singularly nuanced shapes and
feelings. I would like primarily to sketch and to transcribe such a
twilight-like world. I have been thinking too that I would like to
impart in my works a world of the singularly in-between, a taste of
the singularly in-between, which is on neither extremity of good
and evil, right and wrong, pleasure and displeasure. (Izumi Kyōka,
"Tasogare no aji" [The taste of twilight])

The above are words spoken in the twilight of Meiji enlightenment, at
the dawn of Japanese modernity.[1] Their spirit issued from a cusp in time
and space at which a tick and a step backward was the Old Japan and a
tick and a step forward was the New. Their utterance marked both the
singularity of an event and the commonality of a discourse—which is
merely an abstract way of stating that once upon a time at a certain place
there lived a man who used language to converse with his neighbors
about something.

The conversation in which Izumi Kyōka (1873–1939) participated revolved around the fragility of identity within a rapidly modernizing
Japan. He did not engage this topic philosophically as a problem of modern subjectivity per se; rather, with his aesthetics of twilight (*tasogare*), of
the in-between (*chūkan*), he dramatized a ceaseless interrogation of modern categories of identity in a form of fantastic fiction that seems fitting
in an era of fantastic change. The scene of Japanese society in the late
nineteenth and early twentieth centuries was nothing less than phantasmagoric; it was "a constantly shifting succession of things seen or imagined; a scene that constantly changes." Within such a scene the phrase
"Meiji settlement" takes on enhanced meaning, for it was the primary

work of Meiji rulers to set relations among individuals and between individual and the state, to settle on and to disseminate a normative definition of a modern civic identity for the masses of bodies living on the archipelago that had become known as the Japanese nation. If such a settlement—however urgent it may have been in the face of foreign pressure—entailed the curtailment of critical thought and creative potential by installing a fixity of black-and-white oppositions, Kyōka and other kindred spirits would keep the scene shifting by twilighting the Enlightened Rule ("Meiji") that Japan's new leaders had purportedly bestowed.

In Kyōka's articulation, the discussion of unsettled identity begins with the simplest question: Who is that? This question is built in the figure of twilight that Kyōka invoked specifically with the word *tasogare*, for this word's reputed origin is from the interrogative remark *tare so, kare wa*. The word for twilight is thus derived from the question one asks when the identity of an other whom one meets is difficult to distinguish. The same holds true for its synonym *kawatare*, derived from an inversion of the other's syntax: *kare wa tare*.[2] To insist on the artistic twilightization of human existence as Kyōka did in Meiji Japan (1868–1912) was thus to explore diffuse moments of uncertainty and islands of imagination within the eternity of light and totality of reason heralded by enlightenment thought.

I open this study with Kyōka's twilight first to signal both an epistemological and an ontological infirmity that arose in Meiji Japan from the rupture that the will to new forms of power had introduced at the "Restoration" of 1868. During the Restorers' ideological consolidation of a *kokumin*, a national Japanese people, the structures of local knowledges and identities were being demolished, and amid the rubble new surveyors staked often contestatory claims to new knowledges. Whether enlightenment ideologue, ethnographer, provincial bureaucrat, folklorist, or writer, each sought ways to inscribe the deep and diverse pockets of the population that were largely uninscribed. Representation of these little-known portions of the provinces by and for the center of economic, political, and intellectual activity that the new capital of Tokyo had become constituted a practice of knowledge and power over them, often with the accompanying right to define the essence of "Japanese culture," the standard of "the ordinary Japanese," and the role of both in the constitution of "Modern Japan."

Second, I offer twilight to evoke the uncertain atmosphere that enveloped the deployment of "reason" and containment of "imagination" in the formation of a modern Japanese state. My scare quotes around these two terms are themselves marks of the indeterminate or at least relative status of the notions they respectively dare to signify. Although usually presented as antagonistic, they are by no means necessarily mutually exclusive terms, for as operations of mind they could very well work in concert. Yet when questions of human knowledge and power, of social and political order, are at stake, Plato exiles the poets from the Republic and Confucius banishes the spirits from discussion. Why such treatment of fantasizers and their prodigies? Perhaps because, not bound to rules drawn from a measurable material world, the caprice of imagination disconcerts the precision of the ratio, the root of reason. It can become a threat to order. True, an imaginatively inspired reformation of a present reality might furnish a tactical pretense for a political overthrow, but the strategic ordering of a new settlement will more often than not end up dividing the daylight of reason, of enlightened rule, from the darkness of unreason, of the unruly. If it cannot be reasonably altered and co-opted to serve apparatuses of state order, imagination and the modes of thought that it encourages become cast as murky cousins of unreason and their partisans are put under virtual house arrest.

Given the rapidity of its thrust into modernity, Meiji Japan offers, I believe, a concentrated case of this kind of clash in which a program to rule by "modern reason" entailed recasting past "reason" as well as past and present "imagination" as folly. Consequently, local ways of mapping the world and living in it—however fantastic these beliefs and practices might seem from the eye of modern reason—were scientifically nominated as "superstition." After the successful overthrow of the Tokugawa shōgunate, the dismantling and reorganization of what could be conveniently labeled "folk knowledges" was among the most pressing ideological concerns to the fabricators of modern Japanese citizens. How this pitched battle between the "facts" of reason and the "fictions" of imagination was played out in a discourse centered on the fantastical aspects of these disparate folk knowledges is my prime interest.

As anyone familiar with Japanese folk motifs knew, to invoke twilight was also to invite *bakemono* (monsters, literally "changing things") onto the stage of discourse. Yanagita Kunio (1875–1962), an admirer of Kyōka and undoubtedly familiar with the latter's theory of twilight, took the question of twilight to the folk of the Japanese provinces. In "Kawatare-doki" (Twilight time, 1930), Yanagita demonstrated that words used to refer to twilight in certain provinces were also used as a greeting when encountering at twilight a figure whose identity was indiscernible. He then took this interpretation further with examples of words related to twilight used when encountering any unfamiliar passerby, stranger, or potential monster.³ Six years later, Yanagita made more explicit the association between these regional words for twilight and the presence of monsters in "Yōkai dangi" (Discourse on monsters, 1936). In this piece, he argued for a linguistic connection that concurs with the belief that twilight was the time when monsters appeared at specific places (in contrast to ghosts, *yūrei,* who, according to Yanagita, appeared after midnight to haunt specific people). This conjunction of twilight with unforeseen monsters led Yanagita to conclude that "the mutual exchange of words between people who travel at twilight was not only a common courtesy. It was identical to a license, so to speak, that proves one is not a monster."⁴ In Yanagita's interpretation, the phenomenon of twilight was indeed conducive to the appearance of monsters, whereas the verbalization of "twilight" within twilight was a warning against them.

Or, more generally and less elegantly: A time and space betwixt and between determinate categories creates the conditions of possibility for unfamiliar and perhaps fearful changes, whereas mediating this time and space with language could foreclose on the same unforeseeable (and unwanted) apparitions. The strategic reinvention and use of language qua reason to represent a new and exclusive modern knowledge was key in mediating and thereby controlling the monsters of superstition that might waylay the Meiji settlement. Indeed, it was, as this study sets out to demonstrate, a principal task of Meiji ideology to fashion from disparate beliefs in spirits a modern and unified Japanese Spirit of certain, albeit mystified, form. For Kyōka's and Yanagita's part, they both described twilight as a time of uncertain identities and indistinct forms. As such, it could give rise to monstrous transformations. Through their joint conjuration of twilight, the specter of a chronotope—a "time-space"—of *fushigi* (the mysterious, the supernatural, the fantastic) materialized, which questioned creeds of reason and disclosed the nation-state's own imaginary foundations. In this turn, Kyōka and Yanagita both stirred the same cauldron, but they took to the potion differently.

Yanagita described and interpreted the meaning of twilight among the folk throughout Japan. He did not use the image of twilight and its connotations to any apparent end other than to explain folk beliefs and practices. In his explanation, the words for twilight were implicated in a demonstration of how demons, strangers, and other undesirables were kept out of (and how fellow locals were kept in) a particular locality. The proper greeting to a passing figure in twilight was a license, a kind of passport guaranteeing that one was not a shifty *bakemono* but a human of local origins and fixed identity. The mouth and ears (and at other times the heart) are thus treated as temporary substitutes for the eye, the organ that normally oversees the production of, and access to, knowledge.[5] Through this procedure of description and interpretation, Yanagita in effect ended up replicating the conservative gesture of reaffirming identity and divisions at moments of indeterminacy. And who could blame him? It is the safest thing to do when confronting the unknown.

In comparison, Kyōka put twilight, this chronotope of *fushigi,* to critical use. He seized (or was seized by) the indeterminacy of twilight to defer if not deconstruct the night-and-day logic grounding the bureaucratic reason that seemingly conducted modern civilization and enlightenment in Meiji Japan. He sought to enhance, not diminish, the twilight effect in human society. He therefore worked to sharpen perceptions of the in-between, of the indistinct, of that which resists rational grids and rules, without sharpening—and thereby denaturing—the twilight entities themselves. In spinning modern tales of monsters and mysteries spawned in the twilight of enlightenment, Kyōka was implicitly experimenting with possibilities of alternative forms of being and knowing in a modernizing Japan. He was also risking the charge of madness.

I, too, perhaps risk respectability by suggesting, contrary to common sense, that objects of fantasy and folk belief—ghosts, goblins, monsters, and mysteries of every sort—played fundamental roles in the constitution of modernity in Meiji Japan. Admittedly, monsters are not usually the first things that come to mind in discussions of Japanese modernity, even though they preoccupied the thoughts of many modern writers and intellectuals in late-nineteenth- and early-twentieth-century Japan.

When they do appear, it is likely as a sign of the irrationality of pre-modern mentalities, as an obstacle to a modern trajectory anchored by a scientific understanding of the natural world. In this instance, they are conceived as pests to the modern project, targeted for extermination through education and even state legislation. They are made outlaws. Or perhaps they arise as curios, quaint relics of "traditional Japan" for native nostalgia and foreign orientalism to capitalize on. In that instance, they are incorporated into modern capitalist and libidinal economies as commodities to soothe psychic needs, fascinate desires, and line the pockets of entrepreneurs. In either case and others, they are reduced to passive objects, temporally and spatially distanced from the modern subject in order to put its own progress into perspective. Monsters are thus rendered inconsequential, or at best a sideshow, to the positive pursuit and serious study of Japan's modernity.

Studies of Japan's modernity have largely told the story of the development—complete or not—of economic, political, and social institutions away from anything smacking of the "feudal." Doctrinaire Marxist analyses of Japan's aborted transition from feudal structures such as the emperor system, progressive modernist laments over an underdeveloped bourgeoisie, and modernization theorists' laudations of Japan's relative success at a putatively Western game, have all tended to cast feudal forms as the bugbear to be overcome. Popular beliefs in monsters and things supernatural are ipso facto considered feudal forms and are thus relegated to a villain's role in the drama of a modernizing Japan. Education and legislation against particular supernatural beliefs and practices labeled feudal in Meiji Japan have been, for example, cited as elements in Japan's program for civilization and enlightenment (*bunmei kaika*), but that a discourse on the supernatural, the mysterious, and the fantastic—what I refer to as *fushigi*—was *constitutive* of Japan's modern transformation has been, until this study, unheard of. Even when the study of such beliefs by Japan's first folklorists has been recognized as a modern phenomenon, the form and content of their research have rarely been connected to Japanese modernity in an active and sustained way. In short, contemporary scholars of Japan's modernity have not yet taken monsters as seriously as Japan's modernizers did.

This is not to say that *fushigi na genshō* (mysterious phenomena) associated with the menagerie of Japanese monsters and apparitions—what are most commonly referred to collectively as *yōkai* or *bakemono*—have not been objects of academic and popular interest in contemporary Japan.[6] On the contrary, a veritable *bakemono* boom comparable to that which blossomed in the late nineteenth century has possessed the late twentieth. From comics, cartoons, movies, department store museum exhibits, and expanding "occult studies" sections in bookstores to a revived interest in prewar pioneers of *yōkai* research and a proliferation of new publications by Japanese scholars, there has been no lack of presence of the supernatural across the spectrum of contemporary Japanese society, rural and urban alike.[7] The range—if not commercial volume—of interest is not unlike that of dinosaurs in post–*Jurassic Park* America, where toddlers can learn and play with a friendly purple T-rex on TV, Junior can be enthralled by the pictures in *The Big Book of Dinosaurs,* everyone can be terrified and entertained by *The Lost World,* and then edified (and entertained) by the natural history museum exhibit that is down the street from the university where preeminent paleontologists debate the latest evidence of dinosaur death by comets. In other words, much as was the case in late-nineteenth- and early-twentieth-century Japan, monsters have appeared conspicuously across the contemporary Japanese scene in "lowbrow" entertainments, "middlebrow" edification, and "highbrow" scholarship. And, whether as amusement or academic topic, they have invariably been associated with "the folk's" lore.[8]

There is an immense literature on the Japanese folk and an ever growing bibliography on its lore about Japanese monsters and apparitions, but nothing that conceives of them as principal figures in a widespread *fushigiron,* or discourse on the fantastic, that was at the very heart of the historical configuration of Japanese modernity. Though in most cases aptly fulfilling stated goals and producing valuable guides to Japan's literary and folkloric supernatural landscape, Japanese scholarship has tended to be divided up and narrowly circumscribed within cultural anthropology/folklore and literary studies. Typically taking the paradigmatic folklore studies (*minzokugaku*)[9] associated with Yanagita Kunio and to a lesser degree the rediscovered "monsterology" (*yōkaigaku*) of Inoue Enryō (1859–1919) as starting points, these works have exhaustively identified, catalogued, and characterized Japanese monsters, have mapped the dissemination of supernatural folklore across the time and space of modern Japan, have marked regional differences and similarities among folk

tales, beliefs, and practices, and have offered social, historical, and psychological explanations for the mentalities that have spawned such stories,
beliefs, and practices among the folk.[10] Yet they have rarely attempted
to situate rigorously within broader historical and discursive formations
their supernatural object of study or the discipline that purports to study
it best. Even among the more historically minded folklorists who, for
example, have correlated changes in supernatural beliefs with changes in
modern living space, there lingers a sense that essential features of the
folk and the fantastic in modern Japan transcend the historicity of Japanese modernity and abide as aspects of timeless tradition. In this sense,
Yanagita has cast a long shadow, despite thoughtful critiques of his view
of *yōkai*. Indeed, until a generation of scholars began from the late 1970s
to home in on the weaknesses and limitations of Yanagita's work,[11] histories of folk studies and analyses of its methodology have, in their best
moments, produced useful chronologies and compendiums in the "man
and his work" genre of intellectual biography; in their worst moments
they have been little more than hagiographies of Yanagita and promo-
tions of his "uniquely Japanese" discipline. At the same time, folk studies
have tended to fetishize the *fushigi* of the folk as novelty items that display the novelty of Japan itself.

In addition to the pioneering efforts of Miyata Noboru and Komatsu
Kazuhiko in the history and ethnology of monsters, there are a few notable exceptions to this trend which have made some headway in theorizing and historicizing the folk and the fantastic in Japanese modernity.
The interpretive force and originality of Yoshimoto Takaaki's theoretical
interventions into Yanagita's writings, noting in them the construction
of a *kyōdō gensō* (collective imaginary) of what Yanagita dubbed *jōmin*
(abiding folk),[12] has made its effects known throughout a generation of
commentators whether or not they have agreed with his interpretations.
Literary critic Karatani Kōjin, intellectual historian Akasaka Norio, and
social theorist Uchida Ryūzō, building on the insights of Yoshimoto,
have all offered in their own ways critical analyses of the place of fiction
and the fantastic in the formation of Yanagita's style of folk studies.[13]
At a basic level, this work has recognized the formation of folk studies
as a historically specific discursive activity, exploring its representational
practices in relation to scientific, literary, and historical discourses. It has
gone beyond a naive acceptance of folk studies as innocent empirical

or literary pursuit and has provoked questions about the political and ideological place of folk studies within Japan's modernity. Akasaka and Uchida in particular have focused their efforts on Yanagita's abstraction of a homogeneous *jōmin* in the context of his earlier preoccupation with a heterogeneous *yamabito* (mountain people) and "other world" filled with fantastic beings and supernatural happenings. As a result, more serious attention has been brought to bear on the role of the fantastic, in its many forms, within the historical formation of modern Japanese folk studies. This present study seeks to develop this discourse on the fantastic in Japanese modernity beyond Yanagita's folk studies while complicating the historical "origins" of the discipline he putatively founded.

Useful to this endeavor is recent Japanese scholarship on the social and cultural history of rumors and superstitions, especially during the late Tokugawa and Meiji periods. While sometimes drawing on the work of folk studies, this research is not bounded by it and is thus free to take a wider view of what constitutes "the folk" and "the fantastic." Kawamura Kunimitsu's study of popular beliefs about physical and mental disease and the subsequent management of such beliefs to the advantage of modern nation-state building offers an approach by which to consider the fantastic crucial to the ideological and institutional construction of "modern Japan."[14] Although not as concerned with state ideology, Matsuyama Iwao has similarly written an ambitious "history of the mentality of the modern masses" from the point of view of rumors associated with, among many other things, the early Meiji cholera and "blood-tax" riots; late Meiji exhibitions of the exotic and occultism; the Great Kantō Earthquake; the military, the war, and defeat; and popular beliefs concerning social customs and hygiene, regional identities, and Japanese ethnic origins.[15] Just as recent reexaminations of Yanagita's oeuvre have helped historicize folk studies, Kawamura's and Matsuyama's work has helped historicize the fantastic in modern Japan, removing it from the realm of abstract metaphor and literary imaginings and placing it within modern nation building and everyday life.

Critical engagements with Japanese folk studies and with the idea of the fantastic in modern Japan have not been the exclusive purview of scholars in Japan. After Ronald A. Morse's dissertation on the Japanese folklore movement and translation of Yanagita's *Tōno monogatari* (as *The Legends of Tōno*) in the mid-1970s, an international group of scholars at

Cornell University produced in 1985 a volume of essays that represent the first concerted introduction and critical overview of Yanagita's work published in English.[16] At about the same time, a cohort of graduate students (including myself) under Harry Harootunian and Tetsuo Najita began its own interrogation of *minzokugaku* at the University of Chicago from the mid-1980s, and Harootunian himself has since written on Yanagita's project in relation to Tokugawa period nativism.[17] I went on to write a master's thesis in 1987 on literary and scientific discourse in Yanagita's *Tōno monogatari* and his view of written representation, which became part of one chapter of the 1992 dissertation on which this book is based.[18]

Since my dissertation two important studies dealing with aspects of fantasy and modernity in Japan have been published in English. One is Susan J. Napier's wide-ranging and welcome study of modern Japanese fantastic literature. Napier surveys the field of better and lesser known examples of the genre in Japan to demonstrate how the fantastic mode of writing carries within it varying potential to escape, critique, reverse, and subvert modern paradigms. Privileging the fantastic as the genre "that has shown both the positive and negative sides of modernity on the deepest and most archetypal level," she writes: "What the fantastic is subverting in modern Japanese literature, then, is not so much 'Westernization' as modernity itself, a modernity in which Japan has participated at least as fully and wholeheartedly as any Western country. To study the fantastic in modern Japanese literature is, therefore, to find a kind of mirror image of modern Japanese history, the reverse side of the myths of constant progress, economic miracle, and social harmony; stereotypes which have dominated the thinking not only of those outside Japan but among the Japanese themselves."[19] Her argument, which I generally endorse, is similar to that presented for the Western context by Rosemary Jackson, whose work has also informed my approach in chapter 5 to the fantastic tales of Izumi Kyōka as forms of critique. Our work differs, however, in that Napier is concerned predominantly with a mode of literary writing spread across the twentieth century, whereas I see the fantastic as an object of interest and mode of thought that manifests itself across literary, scientific, educational, medical, religious, and even legal discourses in a particular historical conjuncture. As such, in my view, it becomes not so much a "mirror image of modern Japanese history" as a part of mainstream Japanese modernity itself, even as it might work to subvert modernity from the margins or to support it from the center. Our different emphases could largely be attributed to our respective disciplinary orientations, hers being literary criticism (with an eye to history) and mine being cultural and intellectual history (with an eye to literature), but we are also working with concepts of the fantastic on different levels of analysis.

In an ethnographic and cultural studies vein, Marilyn Ivy has written an equally wide-ranging and exceedingly provocative book about the phantasms of modernity haunting sites of national-cultural production throughout Japan. I am very sympathetic with Ivy's approach to "the modern uncanny"; indeed, her third chapter, "Ghastly Insufficiencies: *Tōno monogatari* and the Origins of Nativist Ethnology," uncannily tracks a set of texts and arguments similar to that which appeared in both my graduate work and Uchida's 1995 book *Yanagita Kunio to jiken no kiroku*.[20] Characterizing *Tōno monogatari* as Yanagita's inscription of "the uncanny remainder of capitalist modernity," Ivy argues that the ghostly and ghastly "present-day facts" of Tōno that Yanagita relates in 1910 indicate "not so much a resistance to the modern as the product of Japanese modernity, its uncanny counterpart. . . . Far from sheerly indicating a timeless Japan somehow preserved intact within the space of modernity, the tales became, through Yanagita's writing, modernity's uncanny other." For Ivy, this "uncanny other," this "remainder of modernity," marks a kind of return of the repressed: what was marginalized for the foundations of "civilization and enlightenment" (*bunmei kaika*) and the formation of the modern subject during the Meiji period comes back as an evil but necessary twin, objectified in folk studies as "the most essentially traditional."[21]

There is much in Ivy's interpretation of *Tōno monogatari* that is compelling as a meditation on modernity, but it leaves much to be desired as an investigation into the historical conjunctures surrounding the formation of Japanese folk studies and the dynamics of the fantastic in Japanese modernity. By repeating the canonical assertion that *Tōno monogatari* is *the* founding text of an "originary discipline," she unwittingly shares in reducing "the origins of nativist ethnology" to one work by one man, pruning away an important tangle of textual and contextual underbrush that crisscrosses within and without Yanagita and his work. As Alan S. Christy has persuasively argued in a wonderfully nuanced and thickly

documented study of Japanese native ethnology, "To portray the formation of a field merely through the texts of one person who formulates it is
to risk resorting to notions of influence as the operative mode by which
the field disseminates. If, as one recent account of native ethnology's origins stated, 'there was no doubt that it was [Yanagita's] discipline' [Ivy,
94], then the history of the field is reduced to the task of measuring how
closely anyone else approximated Yanagita's design. We are also left profoundly in the dark as to why anyone else would take up 'his' project."[22]
In short, the discursive, personal, practical, and institutional relations involved in the formation of Japanese folk studies are far more vast than
what Ivy portrays, although in her defense I would recognize that it is
not her principal concern to delve into that history. Still, her engaging
foray into Tōno (the text and the place) does leave the impression of a
discipline sprouting from a single seed in a stark historical field.

Though I would not presume to restore all of the rich complexity of
that field with this study (as if that could ever be achieved), I would like
to present a modest attempt to complicate a picture that appears far too
clear-cut in previous scholarship. Christy has gone far in this direction,
broadening the theoretical and historical view of Japanese folk studies in
a way that will hopefully put to rest the mythic grip that Yanagita has
had as *the* founder and *Tōno monogatari* has had as *the* birthplace of that
discipline.[23] For my part, I aim to enlarge that context in other directions
with approaches drawn from the fields of history, literary studies, and
contemporary theory. My principal goal is threefold: first, to foreground
relations among persons and texts that have largely been underappreci-
ated if not consciously silenced in the history of modern Japanese folk
studies; second, to demonstrate that these relations were formed around
figures of the fantastic (*fushigi* in a broad sense) to the extent that one
can speak of a widespread discourse on the fantastic from which a variety
of disciplinary and critical practices historically emerged; and third, to
argue that this discourse on the fantastic was part and parcel of the production of modernity in Meiji Japan.

This last point is where I share a close affinity with, yet subtle difference from, Ivy's theoretical configuration of "the rhetoric of phantasm
and its operations within Japanese modernity."[24] Where I differ is in shifting the emphasis of Ivy's description of the uncanny as a remaindered
product of Japanese modernity, an "excess of the 'real.'" My discussions

of the folk and modern national-cultural identity places the uncanny qua fantastic as a crucial element within the very *production* of Japanese modernity. Rather than stubborn residue of modern rationalist knowledge, the fantastic as I conceive of it is the constant condition of Japanese modernity in all its contradictions and fluidity. I would even extend this argument to suggest that to some degree modernity in general is born of fantasy and that any "doubling" perceived within it is between modernity as "reality" and modernity as "imaginary." Whether configured as negative impediment to national-cultural consolidation or as positive site of alternative new worlds, the fantastic allows the modern to be thought. In a sense, modernity itself is phantasmagoric; it ceaselessly generates that which is à la mode by consciously imagining difference from things past. Embodying transformation, a change of modes, modernity is akin to the root definition of *bakemono,* "a thing that changes form."

By associating something "fantastic" and "supernatural" with the production of modernity in Japan, I run the risk of becoming an accomplice to the cultural chauvinism associated with *nihonjinron,* the popular and academic discussions of Japanese cultural origins and identity that began to inundate the media from the 1970s. Nothing could be further from my intentions. Rather, one secondary aim of this study is to indicate how the shaping of Japanese modernity around discussions of the fantastic in the form of supernatural beings and inexplicable happenings cultivated early on conditions of possibility for discussions of Japanese uniqueness that later underwrite *nihonjinron.* In this respect, I am excavating sources of *nihonjinron,* not endorsing them. There should be no confusion between asserting an ahistorical and unique "Japanese Spirit" that produced a modernity that is uniquely Japanese on the one hand and tracing historical conjunctures of persons and texts that took up the question of "Japanese spirit(s)" in the context of Japan's modernity on the other. I have no patience for the former and have great interest in the latter. Assertions of national character or spirit in the modern state-building process are, of course, not unique to Japan. In fact, Inoue looked to the London Society of Psychical Research to form his brand of folk studies, and Yanagita cited foreign models of national character studies as his rationale for the study of the spiritual realm of the Japanese people. The scientific study of the supernatural and the emergence of folk studies as a discipline indeed appear to be universal phenomena of modernity. Whether Japan's modernity is particularly distinguished from that of other nations in its preoccupation with the fantastic, however, is a question left for future comparative studies.

Japan's modern discourse on the fantastic entailed both a negative repression and management of beliefs in monsters and spirits and a positive identification of "Japanese" mentality with their production. In either case, it resulted in an overdetermination of "spirit" in Japanese modernity that has persisted since Meiji. Indeed, the drive to forge a homogeneous national citizenry from disparate regional populations throughout the archipelago was accompanied by an effort to displace or identify diverse spirits with a Japanese Spirit. In the case of efforts by government authorities and leading intellectuals, this Japanese Spirit was ultimately embodied by the newly constituted emperor, a modernized supernatural being. The imperial myth was one prominent fantastical element of the past that was meticulously maintained and deployed throughout Japan's modernizing process.[25] The Meiji emperor, who as a manifest deity was perhaps the most fantastic creature of all in Japan, became a kind of ideological lightning rod to rechannel, focus, galvanize, and control the outlet of worldly thoughts and sentiments as well as otherworldly fantasies and desires that coursed through Japanese bodies: from that of the urban dandy in his cutaway to that of the rural peasant in her straw raincoat. The origin of their spirits was to be located in the same *Yamato-damashii,* the Spirit of Imperial Japan. This high-profile example forces us, at the very least, to reconsider the proposition that *all fushigi* was recast as premodern folly and recognize the positive role that the fantastic had in fashioning modern Japan. When necessary, modern reason had its imaginary allies.

While officials and public intellectuals worked to center a modern national citizenry on a supernatural emperor, folklorists were sympathetically studying "outmoded" forms of supernatural beliefs throughout the Japanese populace. Despite cataloguing variations in material practices among regional folks, this diverse group of writers and researchers tended to define an underlying temporal if not spatial continuity of common spiritual sentiment in the national folk. Often critical of modern state policies destructive of a rural habitus, the work of folklorists in "psychoanalyzing" the spirit of the people could nevertheless be used to facilitate the execution of state policies. In any case, uncovering fantastic spirits was at the same time an occulting of a fantastic Japanese Spirit, not unlike that which occurs in *nihonjinron*. The late-twentieth-century *bake-mono* boom implicitly connects, in this instance, *nihonjinron* with an earlier *fushigiron*. This present study works toward making this historical connection between *nihonjinron* and *fushigiron* more explicit, but its primary concern lies in establishing that a *fushigiron* existed as a constitutive force in Japanese modernity and connecting through it what have largely been viewed as unrelated discursive activities during a period of vast transformation. This effort is necessarily selective in the authors it chooses and the texts it plunders, but it endeavors in good faith to open up rather than misrepresent a field of inquiry into the shaping of Japanese modernity.

I begin this project by first surveying in chapter 1 the reserve of supernatural beings and their social significations on the eve of the Meiji Restoration (1868). Against this backdrop, chapter 2 brings forth mid- to late-Meiji approaches to the fantastic appearing in the works of Inoue Enryō and Minakata Kumagusu (1867–1941). Their lectures, letters, and essays represent separate scientistic efforts to define the limits of positive knowledge while preserving the presence of wonder in the world. Both offered forms of folk studies before and outside the Yanagita mold. Minakata, in his typically iconoclastic fashion, also presented in this context an against-the-grain conceptualization of evolution and human culture that hinges on a multivalent understanding of *fushigi*. From this discussion I move on in chapter 3 to the status and role of folk beliefs (Inoue's *meishin*, superstitions) within two important sites of ideological production for the transformation of local bodies into a Japanese national body: elementary schools and medical institutions. Here the Meiji state's interests in Inoue's folk studies and his involvement in the reform of late Meiji education of "the benighted folk" appear alongside attempts to take the care of the body away from local folk practitioners and place it in the hands of state-supported professionals trained in modern science and medicine.

After having established this early intersection of the folk, the fantastic, and Japan's modern nation building, I present in chapter 4 Yanagita's early folk studies as part of a fad for things *fushigi* as well as a conscious attempt to counter Inoue's work while containing Minakata's. It is here where I also join in the longstanding debate over Yanagita's shift of focus from the *fushigi*-filled mountains of *yamabito* (mountain people) to the cultivated plains of *jōmin* as the imagined heartland of Japanese national-cultural identity. The extent and limits of Yanagita's interest in the fantastic then become further apparent in his relations with writers of fantastic literature, most notably Izumi Kyōka, whose works I take up in chapter 5 as a connection to and critical departure from Yanagita's folk studies. I conclude in chapter 6 by suggesting some of the implications of these epiphanies of the fantastic for the formation of modern Japan and beyond.

My invocation of Kyōka's twilight to open this prologue serves, finally, to signal a metaphorical periodization in which the "events" in the textual space of historical discourse and their "meanings" slip the linear notches of chronology. A chronology fading in from about the 1860s, focusing on the period 1905–1912, and then fading out into the 1930s could surely be drawn from the chapters that follow, but that particular narrative phenomenon is less important than the generation of the dialogues — on reason, imagination, the folk, and the fantastic — that it frames. Twilight, as a figure of transition and ambiguity, concurrently conjures up the sense of an ending and of a beginning and thus denotes a particular period of possibilities and panic in Japanese history. But apart from any particular time or place, it also denotes a more general problematic that indiscriminately plagues modernity in other places at other times: the tensions, anxieties, ambiguities, contestations, crises, and critiques that foment in between old and new forms of knowledge and in between the social and cultural orders to which they are attached.

By the end of this book, the particular historical and critical status of the folk and the fantastic in Japanese modernity should become clear; whether or not we must then radically reconsider the "Japaneseness" of this modernity or the idea of modernity in general is not so clear. The ambiguity of this position can be considered as another nod to Kyōka's concept of twilight and the in-between, but not one intended to mystify conclusions or timidly withhold them. Rather, it is a gesture of humility in recognizing the provisional nature of any conclusions about a topic as monstrous as modernity, Japanese or other.

PART I

SUPERNATURAL SIGNIFICATIONS

CHAPTER 1

Bakumatsu Bakemono

The entire square to the other side of these teahouses was occupied by the Muraemon-za Theater, the "Three Sisters" female kabuki, peep shows of *Chūshin-gura, Naniwa-bushi* chanting (also known as *chobokure*), *uta-saimon* beggar's opera (also called *deroren*), raconteurs, archery booths, barbershops, massage healers, and around them peddlers of toys, loquat leaf broth, chilled water, "white jade" and "Dōmyōji" confectionery, chilled and solidified agar-agar jelly, *sushi* vinegar rice, tempura, dumplings, stuffed Inari fritters, fried eel livers, insects, lanterns, as well as wandering masseurs and Shinnai balladeers, peddlers of all sorts, blowgun booths, *dokkoi-dokkoi-dokkoi* [snatches of a refrain], fortune-sellers with lanterns dangling from their collars, vendors of "streetwalker" noodles, drunks, quarrels, pests, public urination.

—Kajima Manbei, *Edo no yūbae* (The evening glow of Edo)

Monsters share more than the root word with the verb "to demonstrate"; monsters signify.

—Donna Haraway, *Simians, Cyborgs, and Women*

In 1922, Kajima Manbei offered the above recollection of what the scene at Ryōgoku Bridge in Edo looked like circa 1865, about three years prior to the Meiji Restoration. Located on the lower Sumida River between Nihonbashi and Honjo, Ryōgoku Bridge was the site of the most famous late-Tokugawa-period form of popular entertainment and entrepreneurship, known as *misemono* (exhibitions, sideshows). Kajima's marvelous yet ultimately subdued sampling here fails to mention the more ghastly category of attractions for which the Ryōgoku carnival had become famous: freaks and monsters. A whale washed ashore and advertised as a monster sunfish, a hideously ugly "demon girl," a scale-covered reptile child, the fur-covered "Bear Boy," the hermaphroditic "testicle girl," giants, dwarfs, strong men (and women), the famous "mist-descending flower-blossoming man" who gulped air and expelled it in "modulated flatulent arias," and the teenager who could pop out his eyeballs and hang weights from his optic nerve, all attest to a libidinal economy in which a fascination with the strange and supernatural conditioned and sustained the production, consumption, and circulation of sundry monsters as commodities in "the evening glow of Edo."[1]

Bakemono of the *bakumatsu* (literally, "end of the shōgunal government," i.e., late Tokugawa) and early Meiji periods did not exist simply as quaint rural throwbacks or captivating commodities at urban *misemono*. They manifested themselves in numerous forms among commoner and intellectual cultures where their use value was found not in procuring an economic profit at a carnival, but in signifying social and political protest in a crisis. The explosion of *bakemono* in various cultural productions of the mid-1800s occurred amid a period of social, economic, and political unease, a coincidence that has led the cultural anthropologist Komatsu Kazuhiko to suggest a fundamental link between "times of crisis" and the prodigious appearance of monsters in narrative, visual, and performative art. In his analysis, power and authority in Japan had, from imperial rule in the seventh century to the founding of the military government of the Tokugawa clan in the seventeenth century, relied not only on the conquest of real enemies, but subsequently on the maintenance of symbolic control over surreal "demon" enemies posited beyond the borders of the central realm (usually in the largely undeveloped regions to the north) and concentrated in special sacred and mysterious areas within the realm. Magicoreligious ceremonies directed at such sites were devised to draw an aura of awe and authority from these objects of fear thus controlled. If such symbolic management appeared inadequate—for example, in times of famine, epidemics, and other natural catastrophes or even in the invasion of strangers from overseas—these outside demons would be tied to elements within society, usually those that for whatever reason could be seen as a threat to order. Those stigmatized elements could then be controlled, thereby indirectly controlling the demons on the outside in a scapegoat mechanism rigged to uphold the integrity of a rule whose authority rested on calming the fears of its subjects, whether those fears be of natural or supernatural origin.[2]

This hypothesis lends a double edge to Komatsu's general theory of the symbolic use of the supernatural throughout Japanese history. From the Nara period to modern times, the representation and magicoreligious management of an "other world" of symbolic demon-enemies and the dark outer regions of the country associated with it has been used by emperors as well as shōguns to secure and display power and authority; it has also been used by discontented factions (peasants, disgruntled samurai, religious groups, opposition parties) as a means to protest authority through carnivalesque reversal and parody (in which monsters become champions of the common folk), or by directly designating the authorities themselves as evil monsters. In such instances, *bakemono* were consciously being used as signifiers in a discourse while they were being produced as commodities to gratify morbid fascinations in the marketplace.[3] There are some doubts about the general applicability of Komatsu's paradigm, but it does offer a way other than the grossly economic to explain, for example, the licensing of pleasure quarters, the strict regulation of itinerant travel, and the increasing number of sumptuary laws applied during the last part of the Tokugawa reign, when the means of central government control rapidly decayed. At the very least, Komatsu's suggestion that an inordinate appearance of the weird seems to coincide with periods of crisis and transition in Japanese history provides a point from which to begin an examination of the proliferation of supernatural signs that spread from late Tokugawa into early Meiji Japan.

From the array of disruptive events of *bakumatsu* Japan—earthquakes, fires, rice riots, disease epidemics, the arrival of Commodore Perry's "blackships," and the civil wars leading to and in the wake of the Meiji Restoration—catastrophic change itself was often portrayed as a monster to be feared. The development of an economically potent but politically neutered merchant class and of a thriving but officially disdained popular culture had also contributed to a social existence among the populace that had become increasingly disjointed from the official representation of social order and the organization of society informed by this representation (crudely expressed in a Confucian-derived "natural" hierarchy of *shi-nō-kō-shō:* warrior, farmer, artisan, and merchant classes). These extraordinary conditions facilitated the resuscitation of extraordinary cultural forms such as *bakemono* in the signification of dis-ease and discontent. This reading is at least one way to interpret the conspicuousness of supernatural images in public places in *bakumatsu* Japan, whether they were overtly charged with a political meaning in a public protest or merely offered as exotic grotesqueries in a commercial spectacle. In either case, supernatural signifiers commonly associated with the beliefs of an unsophisticated rural populace (although equally produced and reproduced in the city) saturated both city and country in mid-nineteenth-century Japan to a surprising degree and were available for reuse in new texts and contexts. Through a sketch of some of the cultural and intellectual sites where *bakemono* figured prominently in late Tokugawa and early Meiji Japan, this chapter sets as its modest goal the mise-en-scène of the conditions for a new discourse on *fushigi* that arose with Japan's modernity.

Because Tokyo, as a progressive and bustling city, would become a symbol of the modern in Japan, the monsters and spirits abiding there from late Edo days command our attention in an investigation of the folk and the fantastic in Japanese modernity. Indeed, the city became the center for the production and organization of a modern discourse concerning items of *fushigi* gathered from peripheral regions, for which reason I focus the stage setting of this chapter primarily on the cultural scene of mid-nineteenth-century Edo/Tokyo. Whereas *bakemono* had persisted for centuries throughout the archipelago, they now appeared in Edo/Tokyo with alarming gusto and new social significance. Certainly not the only urban area that possessed the means of reproducing the supernatural in the forms of commodities and signifiers to be consumed, exchanged, and used (the Kansai area was also extremely vital in this respect), the Kantō region did possess the additional attribute of being the seat of the shōgunal (and then Meiji) government. If *bakemono* were to take on a political inflection as the shōgunate deteriorated, they would best conduct their hauntings among the *daimyō* (feudal lords) mansions concentrated in Edo. Still, because many supernatural motifs had been transplanted from rural origins owing to Edo's relative youth and distinctive demographic mélange, it is also useful to consider, if only briefly, how they were mobilized in demonstrations throughout the countryside during this same period. Finally, to underscore the *modern* aspect of the intellectual preoccupation with the folk and the fantastic that concerns the body of this study, I round off this chapter with a glimpse at prior intellectual engagements with the supernatural as represented in the late Tokugawa *kokugaku* (nativist) thought of Hirata Atsutane.

The *misemono* at Ryōgoku Bridge were one of the major cultural productions relevant to the circulation of forms of *fushigi* in the late Tokugawa period. The history of the bridge itself is fittingly framed by the spirits of the dead. The plaza on the Honjo side of the river, one of two that became sites for the Ryōgoku *misemono*, was adjunct to the Ekōin temple, a memorial situated on the mass grave of the victims of the Meireki fire that devastated the area in 1657, two years before the bridge's completion. More than two and a half centuries later, in the early Taishō period, Ryōgoku Bridge became known as a popular suicide spot.[4] Between those times, from as early as the 1730s to as late as the 1880s, *misemono* at the bridge's plazas displayed diverse oddities that often featured *bakemono* of one form or another. Despite the hideousness of some exhibits, the *misemono* during the Edo period were free from official censure and boomed in the nineteenth century, suggesting that authorities did not consider them particularly threatening. The attraction of *bakemono* exhibits in general is also demonstrated by the unexpected crowds that traveled eight miles outside of Edo to see the monster-filled "haunted teahouse" that theater set designer Izumiya Kichibei, specialist in supernatural scenes, built in 1830 in Omori. Due to its persistent draw of crowds to this suburban area, it became one of the few exhibits ordered to be closed by local authorities. The same Izumiya also designed in the 1830s a sideshow depicting grisly scenes such as "mutilated corpses bound to tree trunks, disembodied heads swinging by the hair, a wizened corpse peering from its coffin, etc."[5] Hashizume Shinya confirms that a "haunted house" (*obake yashiki*) boom began at Ryōgoku from about March 1838 and notes that one popular *misemono* of the time was an archery shooting gallery that had assorted monsters as the targets.[6]

Within five years after the Meiji Restoration, however, *misemono* themselves became the targets of a series of ordinances that initiated their demise. The new morality, the new technology, and the new economy of the Meiji establishment were the ostensible justifications for clearing out the open-air Ryōgoku carnivals. A law of 1870 banned fraudulent displays; an ordinance of 1872 prohibited, on humanitarian grounds, the display of human deformities; an 1872 government requisition of lands for the building of telegraph offices appropriated the western Ryōgoku plaza; and ordinances in 1873 banned the makeshift construction of temporary screen booths such as those used in *misemono,* which were not subject to property taxes. Soon after this legislation, items of entertainment appropriate to civilization and enlightenment were later introduced from the West: the gramophone, the Edison kinetoscope, and eventually cinema.[7] Many ex-*misemono* entertainers sought new life in the *yose* (variety halls) that housed vaudeville acts as well as *rakugo* raconteurs, but it is significant that popular performers and the crowds they attracted were effectively taken off the open streets (historically the space of revolutionary action) and contained within a controlled economy of structures.[8] It seems fitting that the word for the variety halls called *yose* signifies "a place that brings in the crowds."

The history of the *yose* and their principal attraction, the tellers of generally comical but often ghostly stories known as *rakugo,* roughly paralleled that of the *misemono* as a popular form of commoner culture in Edo. Offering a type of *hanashimono* (spoken thing), *rakugo* tellers were an auricular counterpart of the *misemono* spectacle. The first permanent *yose* in Edo was established in 1798 and, like the *misemono,* had boomed by the mid–nineteenth century; by 1855 there were 172 *yose* in Edo, a number that did not decline appreciably until the late Meiji period.[9] Among the stories told by *rakugo* performers a good number were ghost stories, especially during the eighth month, the traditional time for tales of spirits. Others dealt with supernatural or occult figures such as the *tengu* goblin, *yamabushi* (mountain ascetics), and mysterious *ijin* (strangers). Regardless of the specific type of character or setting involved, Sasaki and Morioka argue that "ultimately, dramatization in *rakugo* is achieved through the skillful coupling of the real with the unreal" (434).

From this juxtaposition of the real, everyday world as the audience knew it with an unreal, fantastic world that defied the laws of that everyday world, *rakugo* attained its grotesque (and usually humorous) effect and its power as a carnivalesque expression of social critique. Sasaki and Morioka have argued that the grotesque exaggeration and distortion used to elicit laughter in *rakugo* "exists between two worlds, our real world and, at the same, something that surpasses it" and thus serves to dramatize an alienated world to which the artist can respond with a positive attitude about the superiority of this world or with a negative attitude that criticizes it: "Objectively looked upon with detachment, grotesque is an unrealistic description of the real world. But from the subjective point of view of the expressing artist and what he is trying to express, grotesque can be a pointedly realistic denunciation of a sham reality, of a world that has become absurd and fake" (435). Much in the same vein as Komatsu's theory of monsters appearing in spades in times of crisis, Sasaki and Morioka point out that the critical attitude of grotesque art and literature is likewise especially evident in such times of social and political anxiety. They directly link the eruption of late Tokugawa *rakugo* with the increasing dissonance between the ideological representation of the strict class hierarchy of warrior-farmer-artisan-merchant and the social reality engendered largely by an aspiring merchant class and burgeoning commoner culture. However, because the satirical social criticism that *rakugo* could deliver was in the setting of a witty and playful entertainment, Sasaki and Morioka conclude that, like the practitioner of grotesque art in post-Romantic Europe, *rakugo* raconteurs of the late Tokugawa period did not intend disseminating "serious moral and social messages" (436). In this judgment Sasaki and Morioka take the playful aspect of *rakugo*'s social satire perhaps a bit too lightly. If organized and sustained beyond the moment of ritualized reversal and release, carnivalesque laughter could become a powerful catalyst for action that seriously upsets a reigning social order. Because the disorder of *bakumatsu* social reality, in contrast to its imagined conception, was the implied subject of parody in many *rakugo,* it is not unlikely that in the laughter of the *yose* serious social commentary existed. The question is how it became mediated to do otherwise.

One approach to this question is to consider official (or quasi-official) treatment of *rakugo* material after the Meiji Restoration. Such an analysis goes beyond the stage-setting purposes of this chapter, but there is one provocative case concerning *rakugo* that directly prefigures an important thematic that I discuss in some detail in chapter 3. It involves the literal redefinition of ghost tales told by the most prominent *rakugo* storyteller of the latter half of the nineteenth century, San'yūtei Enchō (1839–1900). In 1859 he created a ghost story called *Kasane ga fuchi gojitsu-kaidan* (The ghost story of Kasane Pool) that he later adapted and performed during the first half of the Meiji period under the changed title *Shinkei Kasane ga fuchi.* The neologism *shinkei* used in place of the word *kaidan* to designate the genre of the story was coined by Enchō's patron (a sinologist) and could be literally taken to mean "the true view" (of Kasane Pool), but at the same time it was also an intentional pun on the homonym *shinkei* (nerves), the word that had become fashionable by mid-Meiji to refer to forms of mental (nervous) disorder (*shinkeibyō*).[10] Thus the "true view" of the supposed supernatural events recounted in the tale about Kasane Pool is that they are the product of the protagonist's nervous disorder and not of an otherworldly visitation.

After one of his live performances of *Shinkei Kasane ga fuchi* was recorded by a recently devised Japanese shorthand writing system and published in book form in 1888, Enchō, who like much of his audience believed in the existence of spirits, commented on the Meiji transformation of *kaidan* into *shinkei(byō)* in the preface to the printed version of his story:

> What are called "ghost stories" [*kaidan-banashi*] have greatly declined in recent times; there is hardly anyone who does them at the variety halls [*yose*]. That is to say, since there are no such things as ghosts and they all have come to be called neurosis [*shinkeibyō*], ghost stories are unseemly things to the professors of civilization [*kaika senseikata*]. . . . By saying that it's a neurosis because there's no such thing as fox-possession and goblin [*tengu*]-abduction, they completely fob off any and all frightening things on neurosis. But, even if enlightened and eminent people of late have established that ghosts absolutely do not exist, shrieking and falling on your ass when something mysterious [*ayashii mono*] appears at the tip of your nose is after all probably because nerves [*shinkei*] are rather mysterious.[11]

Enchō's sarcastic tone in this excerpt works to undermine what was probably a forced "recantation" of supernatural beliefs by his patron and his publisher. His position seems to have been that, call them what you will, there are still mysterious spirits in the world that cause inexplicable events.

Analyzing this renaming of Enchō's ghost tales, Kawamura asserts that this incident is a clear sign of *rakugo* and other popular storytellers being "mobilized as instructors by the demands of the state for the purpose of preaching civilization and enlightenment and the ideology of the national body [*kokutai*]."[12] During the Tokugawa period, ghost stories and other fantastic tales in the repertoire of raconteurs were subjected to very little government censure; at the onset of the Meiji program of enlightenment they became not so much outlawed as recycled. Even though nerves themselves could produce frightening experiences, these were fears that could be explained and thus controlled with a newly coined language that represented a newly constructed knowledge. This technique of managing popular beliefs and spirits afforded the "professors of civilization" a source of power to redefine the psychic as well as the physical reality of the populace, a crucial step in the production of a modern nation-state.

As an avid collector of *bakemono* prints that must have inspired his oral tales, Enchō offers a segue to the final form of popular mid-nineteenth-century cultural productions that I would like to mention briefly as part of the primer for the discourse on *fushigi* that coats modern Japan. Surveys of the history of woodblock prints (*nishiki-e*) invariably characterize the aesthetics of those of the *bakumatsu* period as "decadent" or "grotesque," lacking in the subtlety, sensitivity, and beauty of "classic" prints. The overwhelmingly negative artistic evaluation of prints of this period by connoisseurs and art historians ranges from the apologetic to the acerbic. A taste of the latter extreme is provided by James Michener, novelist and self-styled connoisseur of *nishiki-e:* "Nevertheless, from 1850 on Japan seemed to prefer such junk for it constitutes the bulk of publishing. More than three dozen artists whose names begin either with Kuni- (borrowed from their teacher Toyokuni) or Yoshi- (from Kuniyoshi) filled new-born Tokyo with repellent prints of this nature. Moreover, pathetic as this Kuniyoshi print is, it looks quite acceptable when compared to what happened when vile German aniline dyes reached Japan. Then all restraint disappeared and some of the most grotesque prints ever issued flooded the shops."[13] The print (Yoshitsune fighting with Benkei) by Utagawa Kuniyoshi (1797–1861) offered here as proof of the "death" of *nishiki-e* is described by Michener in a telling and utterly accurate way: "The sovereign line is missing, spacing is barbarous and color is violent." As much could be said for the crisis and confusion that plagued *bakumatsu* and early Meiji Japan. The sovereign line *was* missing; social space *was* barbarous; the color of the age *was* violent. In this respect, the productions of "the Kuni's and the Yoshi's" (as Michener disdainfully refers to this generation of artists) were perhaps the most authentic depictions of the social reality of the times. For Michener and other highbrow commentators, however, such realizations in woodblock prints are "monstrosities" and "debasements" of true *nishiki-e*—which says more about the conservative co-optation and depoliticization of cultural productions than the character and use of the product itself.

But one man's decadence is another man's political and social critique. Recent lines of research into *nishiki-e* of *bakumatsu* Japan suggest that given their rapid reproduction and dissemination among a mass audience, they constituted a significant medium for political parody and social satire that covertly ridiculed the Tokugawa government.[14] Through time-honored techniques of *mitate* (parodic allusion; also, interestingly, the same word used to mean "diagnosis"), artists responded to the restrictions placed on the content of woodblock prints in 1842 under the Tenpō Reforms by concealing contemporary critical commentary within subject matter that government censors deemed acceptable (generally historical and mythical figures of Japan's heroic past).

The most famous and most heavily documented example of such a print is the triptych executed by Kuniyoshi in 1843 depicting an ill and bedridden Minamoto no Yorimitsu on the verge of being enveloped by the web of the monstrous Earth Spider while Yorimitsu's four henchmen variously mull over a game of *go* and cups of *sake*. In the background, as if emerging from the spread of the spider's curtainlike web (or from a nightmare behind Yorimitsu's closed eyes), two groups of diverse monsters charge angrily and chaotically toward each other. Two of the henchmen seem to sense a disruption in the air as they peer toward the parade of monsters, which by some counts number forty-seven, a clear allusion to the forty-seven *rōnin* (masterless samurai) of the famous Chūshingura vendetta.[15] Most commentators agree that the populace—through a network of rumor at the time—understood these monsters as representations of the various occupations and individuals that had most keenly felt the oppression of the Tenpō Reforms. Yorimitsu, on the other hand, represented the shōgun Tokugawa Ieyoshi, whose chief advisor and power broker, Mizuno Tadakuni, had instigated the reforms. Such an interpretation of this print's social and political significance provides a graphic example of the proliferation and symbolic use of supernatural figures in a popular medium to express discontent in periods of crisis and change. If, as Komatsu hypothesizes, the symbolic control of monsters was an important pillar of the shōgunate's ideological foundations, the symbolic unleashing of the same monsters could certainly serve to shake it.

And shake it they did with the Ansei earthquake in the tenth month of 1855. Immediately after this quake that devastated sections of Edo, a genre of prints now known as *namazu-e* (catfish pictures) began to circulate in great numbers. Based on the belief that the quake was generated by the activity of a prodigious catfish that lay at the base of the *kaname-ishi* (pivot stone) at Kashima shrine about sixty miles east of Edo, the prints typically depict a monstrous catfish in the role of a *yonaoshi* (world renewal) god destroying Edo so that it may be renewed.[16] Komatsu interprets these prints as an example of commoners in *bakumatsu* Edo resurrecting the demons that authority had confined and imbuing them with expressions of counterauthority. He also stresses the role of woodblock print artists in materializing the feelings of discontent and the desire for change among commoners in the form of such parodic depictions of otherworldly creatures.[17] Regardless of what such *bakemono* prints might have been intended to *mean*, what they *did* was threaten the authorities.

If the report can be believed, perhaps the most striking symbolic image of the resurrection of *bakemono* over and against the authority of Tokugawa officials is the daily appearance of dozens of big *bakemono* kites flying above the art district of Azabu in *bakumatsu* Edo. According to one anecdotal account, the flying of kites with pictures of ghosts, monsters, bloody heads, and skulls became a frequent means to draw business among the competing artists, further attesting to the extent to which the grotesque and supernatural figured in the economy of imagination and desire of consumers and producers alike. Also around the same time, a huge coil of excrement said to be that of a monster or demon was discovered on a path in the Azabu neighborhood.[18] Motives behind the hoax are unreported, but it could have been a simple practical joke done out of boredom, a sensationalistic advertisement of the supernatural artistic productions in the area, or a conscious gesture of civil disobedience done in a truly carnivalesque spirit. What is clear in these examples of cultural productions—from *misemono* and *rakugo* to *bakemono* prints, kites, and monstrous shit—is a preeminent appeal to creatures of another world, whether gods or demons, to instigate a change in the present one.

This appeal to *bakemono* was not restricted to productions of popular cultural media. Of the variety of riots and protests outside of Edo proper that were concentrated in the years just before and after the Meiji Restoration, a conspicuous number, involved supernatural creatures in one form or another. For example, in the great merchant metropolis of the time, Osaka, so-called monster riots (*yōkai sōdō*) broke out among the residents of the Tenmanchō district in the northern section of the city. As the north-northeast in Chinese-derived geomancy was traditionally believed to be the direction from which demons appeared from the world beyond the borders of human settlements, it was appropriate that the monster riots were organized from this section of the city.[19] The implication was that past methods of managing the threat of demon-enemies— whether monsters of traditional shapes or in the form of the foreign "barbarians" who had increasingly infiltrated Japan throughout the nineteenth century—had lost their efficacy.

The political inflection of *bakemono* is something that even Yanagita Kunio alluded to during a 1927 discussion with Akutagawa Ryūnosuke, Kikuchi Kan, and Osatake Takeki. In an exchange with Kikuchi about the prevalence of *kappa* and *tanuki* stories in Kikuchi's home region of Shikoku, Yanagita mentions that during a period of subjugation and unification of the inhabitants of the island, it was said that the *tanuki* of Awa (Tokushima prefecture) had extreme antipathy toward the *tanuki* of Yashima (an island in the Inland Sea just off the coast of Takamatsu in present-day Kagawa prefecture), leading Yanagita to comment that in the provinces "even *tanuki* have become political."[20] There is seemingly nothing very profound about reading the characteristics attributed to folkloric creatures as expressions of attitudes toward political events, but it did afford Yanagita one way to detrivialize material that he had been trying to organize for serious study within a new discipline of *minzokugaku* that set out to explicate the feelings and mentality behind folk beliefs and practices.

It appears more significant, however, when supernatural figures are employed not simply to reflect sentiments toward certain authoritative actions but to rally action against the authorities. Earlier in the same discussion, while speaking about the abundance of reports concerning the mountain goblin known as *tengu,* Yanagita notes that from late Tokugawa to early Meiji, looting and rioting known as *tengu sōdō* broke out in Mito and Shimōsa (present-day Ibaraki and Chiba prefectures). These disturbances, he makes clear, were distinct from the famous insurrection staged in Mito by the so-called *Tengu* faction (*Tengu-tō*) from 27 March

1864 through the summer of that year.[21] The scope and level of concerted organization was much higher in the Tengu Insurrection, which
was comprised of several hundred commoners led by a diverse group
of Mito samurai, Shintō priests, *shugendō* practitioners, and rural samurai. Yet, the use of the name *tengu* in these riots could of course have
been modeled on, or perhaps even models for, the appellation of the
Mito activists who instigated the pointedly political challenge against the
conservative domain and *bakufu* authorities. Interestingly, according to
sources that J. Victor Koschmann cites in his study of the Insurrection, the
name *tengu* was first given to the Mito reformists Fujita Tōko and Aizawa
Seishisai by their opponents, who aimed to imply that the reformists, like
tengu, were arrogant about the power they had achieved through study.
But later, the reformist Mito daimyō Tokugawa Nariaki, who supported
the radical Mito factionalists, applied it to them for its positive connotations of supernatural power and heroism.[22] It was this positive aspect
as superhuman avenger, I believe, that generally characterizes the attraction of the supernatural in the popular cultural media and the appeal
to images and to a grammar of the supernatural in protests and world-
renewal movements in crisis-ridden mid-nineteenth-century Japan.

There were other cunning ways in which supernatural signifiers were
manipulated to generate action among commoners in the countryside.
Protest organizers often played on common fears and folk beliefs to coa-
lesce the complaints and frustrations of commoners into riots against
the policies of both the authorities of the *bakumatsu* period and their
early Meiji successors. Since Perry's arrival in 1853, the increased news,
presence, and fear of foreigners in Japan—especially among xenopho-
bic commoners—created conditions that were ripe for the strategic use
of *bakemono* to exploit a general fear of strangers. One such example of
the exploitation of folk beliefs to counter new policies of the Restorers
involved connecting military conscription to folk tales concerning the
appearance and subsequent murder of a "stranger" (*ijin*) in the village
community: whereas Komatsu links the spread throughout the countryside of these so-called *ijingoroshi* (stranger-killing) stories to the outside
introduction of a capitalistic monied economy to the village community
during the mid-Tokugawa period, in Meiji the image of the *ijin* was put
to other uses.[23]

After being repeatedly tortured by government police, Fudeyasu Shigetarō, the ringleader of the 1873 Okayama "blood-tax riots" (*ketsu-zei ikki*), confessed to having exploited false rumors circulating around Okayama concerning the military conscription order that had been issued that year. In his account it was revealed that the people in the region had spread stories that those conscripted would be taken away by a "person in white" and have their blood drained. To avoid this fate, it was imperative to kill such a stranger if he or she appeared in the village. Just before the riot broke out, Fudeyasu purposely had a person dressed in white wander through the villages in the area to incite the uprising.[24] The government and newspapers attributed the riots to a misunderstanding of the word *ketsuzei* (blood-tax) in reference to military conscription. Kawamura, however, presents evidence that the Okayama blood-tax riot, as well as those in Tottori, Kagawa, and other areas, arose from a much more broadly based sentiment against government collaboration with foreigners in the program of civilization and enlightenment. *Ketsutori* (blood-taking) was not the only word commoners used to signify the object of fear associated with military conscription; *aburatori* (fat- or marrow-taking) and *kotori* (child-taking) were also used. According to one contemporary article critical of the official explanation for the riots, the idea of blood-taking (or fat-taking or child-taking) circulated among the populace well before the 1873 conscription order, usually in association with Western foreigners who, since the end of the Tokugawa period, had been believed to "take the lifeblood of children and refine medicines with it, mix the fresh blood of pregnant women and drink it in medicines, and also coat electrical wires with the blood of virgins."[25]

The blood-drinking Westerner was an old misconception among the Japanese dating back to their first encounter in the fifteenth century with Christian ritual that professed the drinking of wine transubstantiated into Christ's blood. Consequently, the drinking of any red wine, unfamiliar to the average Japanese, became associated with blood-drinking foreigners. Kawamura interprets the mention of medicines and electrical wires in early Meiji allusions to blood-sucking strangers as an emblem of *bunmei kaika,* a movement that entailed the introduction of foreigners, many of whom truly appeared as monsters to the common folk. The modern blood tests and inoculations given during the health examinations of new military conscripts could only intensify the unease already felt toward government officials, themselves strangers to local areas, who hobnobbed with strangers of an even higher order.

In all three of the blood-tax riots—in Okayama, Tottori, and Kagawa —that Kawamura documents, news that "the blood extractor" or a "suspicious-looking stranger" had been seen in the area circulated just before the riots avalanched. In the case of Okayama, the population seemed particularly primed for the ruse that Fudeyasu pulled to incite the riot. Within a year before the incident, a foreigner employed by the Ministry of Industry toured the mines in the area, and it was reported in a local newspaper that people "saw him drinking beer and red wine, and were suspicious of this."[26] In all other areas too, real foreigners figured in the events leading up to the riots, giving the protesters a concrete target. It was not simply a misunderstanding of the word "blood-tax" that motivated them.

The blood-sucking stranger and the civilization and enlightenment that he came to represent in the Meiji context was the real object of attack in these communities that had developed their own scapegoats to maintain the integrity of inner communal order against threats from the outer world. To many village folk, the new rulers of Meiji Japan, by associating with monsters, had themselves become monsters. In other words, at the same time the state began striving to cast folk knowledge as a demon-enemy to be avoided, the folk was striving to cast state knowledge as a demon-enemy to be expelled. This predicament marked the very real supernatural dimension within the conditions of conflict over the minds and bodies of a diverse Japanese folk as they were being turned into a modern Japanese citizenry.

Besides the forms of *fushigi* inundating late Edo commoner culture and surfacing in disturbances across the country in the period before and after the Meiji Restoration, a "premodern" intellectual engagement with the strange and mysterious should be given brief notice before exploring in depth the modern discourse concerning the folk and the fantastic. The Confucian ploy of explaining away the world of spirits (*kishin*) by naturalizing it within the workings of *inyō* (the cosmic forces of duality behind natural phenomena) was openly criticized by the most prominent nativist thinker of the time, Hirata Atsutane (1776–1843). In *Kishin shinron* (New thesis on spirits, written in 1805, published in 1820), Hirata sees through this explanation, identifying it as an administrative construct used to mediate and control common belief in the spirit world and to curb human passion associated with these beliefs.[27] As such it was a premonition of the modern control of Japanese Spirit via a control of spirits. For Hirata, the invisible yet present spirit world becomes central in his theory of the relationship among the gods (*kami*), the ancestors, and the living who worship them. But it is a spirit world cleansed of misguided beliefs about demons, ghosts, and goblins, the existence of which he attributed more often than not to the deceits and corrupting effects of Buddhism and syncretic, "vulgar" Shintō.[28]

Hirata's polemic against Buddhism and his aim to define in positive terms "the work of worship" of ancestral spirits and *kami* help explain the selective interest in various *bakemono* that he shows in texts that deal with them, such as *Kokon yōmikō* (On marvels past and present, 1822) and *Senkyō ibun* (Strange tales from fairyland, 1824). Haga Noboru, for example, characterizes the former as a study in evil spirits directed mainly against Buddhism.[29] Drawing from the material on *tengu* in these texts, Yanagita will come to critique Hirata on the same grounds, a topic touched on in chapter 4. For Yanagita and others who begin to take up the topic of *bakemono* seriously during the modern period, the real importance of Hirata's particular opening up and delving into the spirit world—whether it concerns *kami,* ancestors, foxes, or *tengu*—existed as a scholarly precedent for the recording and interpretation of reports of contemporary supernatural incidents. Of course, participants in the modern discourse on *fushigi* relied on many other pre-Meiji sources for information and raw material, but as a serious intellectual endeavor, Hirata's work provided an aura of legitimacy to the scholarly pursuit of monsters.

Every one of the writers and intellectuals whose texts are discussed in the pages that follow had occasion to read and draw on, in varying degrees for varying purposes, Hirata's texts concerning *bakemono*. Not all, however, necessarily agreed with Hirata's interpretation and use of such material. Rather than turning to his texts and other prior sources to enshrine a past meaning, they pillaged them for material that could be re-emplotted to address a new historical situation. What I pursue throughout this study are the differences of articulation, interpretation, and (re)use of the things described most frequently in the texts of these modern writers and intellectuals as *fushigi* and associated most intimately with "the folk." In doing so, I underscore not only the modernity of this phenomenon, but also its constituent role in the formation of Japanese modernity. At the very least I hope to coax from the shadows a figure too often obscured by the high road of modernization in Japanese history.

CHAPTER 2

Words and Changing Things:

Grasping *Fushigi* in Meiji Japan

I find it greatly displeasing to think about things that are as intangible as a cloud —
things such as ghosts, curses, and karma. But to Tsuda's mind they were rather astonishing. As this astonished teacher earnestly spoke of ghost stories, even I began
to feel obliged to revise my attitude toward this issue. To tell you the truth, I had
believed that ghosts and palanquin-bearers had long since closed up shop after
the Meiji Restoration. However, when I saw Tsuda's expression a moment ago, it
seemed as if somehow or other these ghostly things had unknowingly revived. I
remember that when I asked before what the book on his desk was he answered
that it was a book about ghosts.

—Natsume Sōseki, "Koto no sorane" (The empty sound of the *koto*)

Tsuda, the "psychologist" in Sōseki's 1905 short story "Koto no sorane,"
surprises his old school chum, now a practical-minded lawyer, with his
serious interest in folk tales and superstitions. The lawyer concedes that
such topics are better left to men of arts and letters, for they do not follow the laws of reason as he knows them. At first doubtful of the value
of his friend's research, the lawyer slowly becomes susceptible to the sug-
gestions of the contemporary *fushigi na hanashi* (fantastic tales) that Tsuda
relates to him, one of which concerns telepathic knowledge of the death
of a loved one. Returning home from Tsuda's place, the lawyer begins to
read the coincidence of unusual sights and sounds around him as supernatural signs of his sick fiancée's possible death. Racked by a night of
horrific hallucinations, he lies awake gripped by an irrational fear that
her illness has indeed taken a turn for the worse. He is finally compelled

to check on his fiancée's condition and learns that she is actually all right. In the end, after he relates his strange experience to Tsuda, Tsuda asks if he may include it in his latest book. As the lawyer reports in the final line of the story, "That which is recorded as the case of Mr. K on page 72 of *On Ghosts* by Tsuda Makata, Bachelor of Arts, is my incident."[1]

Sōseki's Mr. Tsuda, graduate in the humanities and dabbler in the marginal field of psychology (*shinrigaku*), researched his study of ghosts at his lodgings in the Hakusan neighborhood of Tokyo, site of the Tetsugaku-kan, the School of Philosophy that Inoue Enryō had founded in 1887 to counter popular beliefs in the supernatural by popularizing modern philosophy and psychology.[2] Given the description of Tsuda's interests and approach, it is entirely possible that Sōseki indeed had Inoue in mind when drawing the character of Tsuda Makata. Tsuda's collection and citation of contemporary "true life" mystery tales, his dedicated attitude toward their study, and his reliance on the explanatory framework provided by psychology for the rationalization of supernatural phenomena all point to a personage like Inoue as a model.

I leave the proof of this speculation to scholars inclined to seek the "real sources" of literary fictions, the things behind the words.[3] What I will take up in this chapter are the words that gave rise and order to things, specifically to the "changing things" (*bakemono*) that Inoue, graduate in the humanities and dabbler in the marginal field of psychology, researched in Meiji Japan. As a counterpoint to Inoue, I then turn to his younger contemporary Minakata Kumagusu, who offered an unorthodox conception of the fantastical qualities of causality and change in the human world that antagonized the enlightenment program behind Inoue's rationalist taxonomies. Their intersecting projects set in motion an earnest attempt to grasp and circumscribe *fushigi* for a changing world. In so doing, they introduced certain words, categories, concepts, and epistemologies derived from Buddhist metaphysics, rationalist philosophy, natural history and science, psychical research, and dreams. Applied in response to the demands for a modern knowledge of things—even "things that are as intangible as a cloud"—their efforts formed a tentative though divided basis for addressing the fantastic with a straight face.

Inoue Enryō and the Taxonomy of the Supernatural

Natural history is nothing more than the nomination of the visible.
— Michel Foucault, *Les Mots et les choses*

If Foucault is right, can one then analogously say that *super*natural history is nothing more than the nomination of the *in*visible? Insofar as one accepts the dyads natural/supernatural and visible/invisible as parallel, the twist on Foucault's assertion retains the ratio, but would it be reasonable? That is to say, could the naming and classification of supernatural creatures and events that usually escape the direct observation of the researcher, that exist most substantially in the mediation of fanciful pictorial and verbal representations and least substantially in the gossamer of belief, be executed according to the rule of scientific reason? Not without caveats that would pervert the application of the rule itself. The ideal of taxonomic knowledge, as Foucault emphasizes, lies in the "immediately perceptible variables of the visible" under the gaze of the scientist as the eye becomes the organ of knowledge in the discursive organization of the natural sciences.[4] Under these conditions, a science of the supernatural would be, strictly speaking, impossible. Without an empirical object at which to gaze, those who still desire to construct a taxonomy of the supernatural face a methodological fork in the road: Either make visible and naturalize the supernatural by attaching its representations to things visible in the natural world, or find an organ of knowledge other than the eye. On the former path, the object of knowledge sacrifices its original "supernature" (it gives up the ghost, so to speak), and on the latter, the subject of knowing risks the fate of Cassandra, possessed with a knowledge that no one will believe.

Inoue Enryō was no Cassandra. As an educator who crusaded for civilization and enlightenment in Meiji Japan, he could not afford to operate outside of credible and accredited forms of knowledge. The son of the chief priest of a Buddhist temple in Niigata prefecture, Inoue rejected the priesthood to preach as a layman a practical amalgamation of Western and Eastern idealism that sought to distinguish, in the context of modern scientific understanding, the realm of finite and relative phenomena from the realm of infinite and absolute mind. He relegated the explanation of natural phenomena to the sciences while establishing philosophy as a metadiscipline within which all disciplines were founded. As such, philosophy for Inoue, especially as he wedded it to Buddhist metaphysics, was a path toward an essentially religious awareness of the ultimate reality of the universe. An important first step in clearing away this path to enlightenment, he argued, was the eradication of what he designated "false" or "ephemeral mysteries"; in other words, superstitions. In concrete terms, this process meant providing natural (i.e., rational and scientific) explanations for phenomena that the "benighted folk" (*gūmin*) considered to be supernatural. To carry out systematically this "crushing of superstitions," as he frequently referred to his project, Inoue founded a companion discipline to philosophy which he named *yōkaigaku*—literally "monsterology," but in Inoue's usage it designated something closer to "superstition studies," "psychical research," or simply "folklore studies."[5] In addition to his appeal to science with the designation *-gaku*, (-ology, study of, science of), Inoue's choice of yōkai*gaku* also has a sensationalist ring about it, which certainly must have enhanced its popular appeal. "Monsterology" captures the nineteenth-century scientistic quaintness, sensationalism, and seriousness of the pursuit that would become Inoue's contribution to the management of spirits into Spirit in Meiji Japan. In light of its style and scope, I will characterize it as supernatural, as opposed to natural, history.

Biographers record that Inoue read a good deal of natural history and philosophy while in school, but even without this tip one can readily discern, sprouting from his texts on *yōkaigaku,* the branches of a classical taxonomy bisected by philosophical categories of mind and matter and delineated within institutionalized disciplines.[6] The result is a variation on a positivistic natural philosophy that simultaneously and contradictorily appeals to both a metaphysical realism (in which the laws of the mind are mere instances of universal laws of nature) and a metaphysical rationalism (in which the laws of the universe merely reflect the laws of the mind).[7] But before Inoue rigorously laid out his grand (two-thousand-page!) scheme of things supernatural, he had to specify what exactly his object of research would be.

As a preamble to his project of organizing the inexplicable, Inoue offered a redefinition of *yōkai* that in one stroke impugned popular notions of supernatural phenomena and paved the polemical pathway for the practice that he advertised as "the science of superstitions." In his articulation, Inoue collapsed the meaning of *yōkai* as "monsters" into a virtual synonym of *fushigi* as "mystery," rendering the former closer to the sense of "supernatural beings." Always ploddingly methodical and systematic in his argumentation, Inoue initiates his discussion of monsterology in a bluntly logical fashion: People commonly describe monsters (*yōkai*) as *fushigi* and *ijō* (unusual), as things that cannot be known by usual standards of knowledge and everyday reason. But, he asks, what is "usual knowledge" and "everyday reason"? Even more important, if one were to accept this common judgment that *yōkai* are *fukachiteki* (irrational or beyond reason), then it would be foolish to investigate the topic at all.[8] The first of many dualisms that form the infrastructure to Inoue's writing—an a priori division of the knowable and the unknowable—arises with this assertion. In Inoue's epistemology, human knowledge is positive, accumulative, and measurable up to the frontier of the unknowable and absolute True Mystery (*shinkai*) of the universe. It reflects a progressive revelation of the principles (*genri*) of nature as they are graspable by the proper application of reason (*dōri*) to observable phenomena of the natural world. In Inoue's view, the benighted folk are quick to call any phenomenon they cannot explain a *yōkai* and *fushigi* when, in fact, one who is educated in the sciences (*rigaku*) can offer explanations for the same phenomenon. Inoue therefore took the words *fushigi* and *fukachiteki* quite literally by reserving their use specifically for phenomena that are truly beyond any reasonable scientific explanation. This specification is the reason why Inoue did not accept the popular definition of *yōkai* and *fushigi;* the folk's *yōkai* are not at all mysteriously inexplicable and therefore are "false and ephemeral mysteries" (*kakai;* 1:4).

At the same time, Inoue berated the self-satisfied scholar who asserts that there are no such things as true supernatural beings or mystery in the universe. Using an example that appears repeatedly throughout his writings, Inoue enumerated the levels of knowledge that a scientist can have of a water drop, down to the existence of its constituent atomic particles. Scientists cannot, however, explain beyond atomic particles, which therefore appear as a kind of "mysterious thing" (*kaibutsu*). This same situation exists when studying the vastness of the universe: beyond a certain observable point, nothing can be said about celestial bodies. These limits of scientific observation mark the borders of the inexplicable, of "true supernatural beings" (*shinyōkai*). What lies between them is "the bridge

of human knowledge," but Inoue "cannot help but laugh at the narrowness of vision of scholars who, standing upon this bridge of knowledge,
proclaim to the pathless ignorant folk huddled and lost among the rocks
below that there are no supernatural beings [*yōkai*]" (1 : 4). His point here
is twofold: first, that while the folk might not have a scholarly knowledge
of natural phenomena, scholars do not know everything because their
knowledge too is relative within the absolute mystery of the universe;
and second, that the idea of "true supernatural being" is best associated
with the realm of wonder that fundamentally exists in all things in the
universe and in human nature.

To distinguish this conception of wonder from the vulgar notion of
yōkai, Inoue designates it True Mystery (*shinkai*). True Mystery demar-
cates a transcendent realm, the existence of which one can apprehend
or intuit through spiritual awareness, but not concretely comprehend
through ratiocination. It appears as Inoue's response to Herbert Spencer's
category of the Unknowable and Kant's noumenon, without being fully
identifiable with either. As the site of transcendental religious experience,
Inoue's True Mystery resembles Spencer's Unknowable; as the ground
of phenomenon, the contours of which are circumscribed by human
knowledge, it is akin to Kant's noumenon. Described as such, it can be
rationally approached but only irrationally entered.[9] For Inoue, then, the
question of monsters revolved around the boundaries of knowledge, in
sorting out what could be known within the sciences (viewed as the sum
and summit of positive human knowledge) and what could not. His appeal to science therefore served only to discredit popular folk beliefs, not
a religious practice (i.e., his form of neo-Buddhism) that aimed to glean
the wonder of True Mystery and from this experience bring a sense of
joy, well-being, and security into human life.[10]

Amid this rearrangement of the relationship between scientific reasoning and common beliefs, local practices are branded by the stigma of
superstition (*meishin,* literally "errant belief"). Representing to Inoue a
compendium of aberrant forms of knowledge in the world, they belong
neither to proper learning nor to proper religion. Consequently, they lose
all status as knowledge by which to understand phenomena and all status
as belief by which to apprehend noumena. By treating them as forms
of knowledge invalidated by modern science, Inoue trivializes quotidian
habits and ways of representing the mysterious that existed among com-

moners. Rather than considering them alternative and functional foundations of social existence, he submits these "false *yōkai*" to a rigorous taxonomy that works to eradicate their raison d'être, for they have, in his view, no legitimate reason for being. They become the darkness from which his enlightenment project could shine. Inoue accomplishes this legerdemain by first dividing alleged supernatural phenomena—ranging from classical apparitions and strange dreams to telepathy and madness— into categories of the material (*butsuri*) and the mental (*shinri*) and then assigning each to one or more appropriate academic disciplines (physical or psychological) with which he could elucidate them. The work of monsterology is then to recognize by "philosophical reasoning" the field of specialized knowledge under which a particular specimen of the supernatural belongs in order to reveal its "true form."[11] At this point, the would-be monster is nominated to the ranks of *meishin*.

Well before he formally began lecturing and publishing on the topic, Inoue indulged in this strategy for dealing with local practices and mysterious phenomena, parceling them out to various disciplines where specialists could rename them *meishin*. A friend of Inoue's and fellow student at Tokyo Imperial University, Minosaku Genpara, wrote in March 1885 of the need in Japan for a research group like Britain's Society for Psychical Research, which was founded in 1882 for the investigation of the supernatural, and mentions with approval "the plans of our university's Mr. Inoue Enryō for research in the strange and mysterious."[12] A year after graduating in philosophy, Inoue, along with Minosaku, realized this plan with the organization of the Fushigi Kenkyūkai (Mystery Research Society), which first met on 24 January 1886. The group's goal was to investigate rationally and comprehensively *fushigi na genshō* (fantastic phenomena) along the lines of the Society for Psychical Research. From the onset, then, Inoue's study of folklore was articulated within the blossoming field of *shinrigaku* (psychical science or psychology). The other founding members of the Fushigi Kenkyūkai included recent graduates from several of the university's departments: Miyake Yūjirō, philosophy; Tanakadate Aikitsu, physics; Yoshitake Einoshin, chemistry; Tsuboi Jirō, medicine; Tsuboi Shōgorō, zoology and anthropology; Sawai Ken, physics; Tanahashi Ichirō, Japanese and Chinese literature; Tsubouchi Yūzō (Shōyō), political science and economics, dramatic literature; Fukuya Umetarō, graduate of the Tokyo Forestry School; and Satō Yū-

tarō, graduate of the University Prep School science department (1:15).[13]
Among the first articles on mysterious phenomena that Inoue published
during 1887 in *Tetsugakkai zasshi* was one based on the results of investigations this group made concerning "the secret practice of drawing thin
threads from the tips of the hands" while worshiping in front of a Buddhist image. The Fushigi Kenkyūkai had discovered that the mysterious
threads that seem to grow naturally from one's hands when praying were
in fact filaments of particulate matter floating in the air.[14]

The disciplinary affiliations of the members of Inoue's Fushigi Kenkyūkai provide an introduction to the classes, orders, families, and genera
into which Inoue placed species of *yōkai*. Inoue structured the body of
his lectures on folklore and unusual phenomena around six basic disciplines that can be thought to correspond to the taxonomic level of family
after the Linnean system of classification in natural history.[15] These families are the physical sciences (*rigaku*), medicine (*igaku*), pure philosophy
(*junsei tetsugaku*), psychology (*shinrigaku*), religious studies (*shūkyōgaku*),
and pedagogy (*kyōikugaku*). Under each, on the level of genus, Inoue
typologized groups of individual species of *yōkai* according to general resemblance in content. For example, the eight genera under the physical
sciences are striking celestial phenomena (*tempen*), terrestrial calamities
(*chiyō*), flora (*sōmoku*), fauna (*chōjō*), strangers (*ijin*), strange lights (*kaika*),
foreign bodies (*ibutsu*), and strange incidents (*henji*). The species named
under the genus "strangers" include mountain men (*yamaotoko*), mountain women (*yamaonna*), mountain hags (*yamauba*), snow women (*yu-
kionna*), hermit wizards (*sennin*), and celestial beings (*tennin*), all of which
figure frequently in Japanese folk tales as marginal and fearful human-
oids who occasionally appear to unsuspecting villagers. From these families of disciplines one can follow Inoue's larger divisions of "supernatural
history" up to the level of order, which comprises mysteries of matter
(*mono*), mysteries of mind (*kokoro*), and mysteries of principle (*ri*). The
level of class breaks into his two broadest divisions of "false mysteries"
(those of matter and mind) and "true mysteries" (those of the essential
principle in all things). *Yōkai* (true and false) in general, then, wind up
on the level of phylum or simply kingdom.

In spite of this homology between classical natural history and Inoue's
project of *yōkaigaku*, there is a marked difference in their theoretical aims.
Whereas natural history as a descriptive science of forms and categories

abstains, in theory, from providing explanations of causes of living or nonliving natural phenomena, *yōkaigaku* is fundamentally organized to bring apparently inexplicable objects into the purview of rational explanation. Inoue's descriptive categories are in fact explanatory categories that subject to the rule of scientific reason "unreal" objects that already exist meaningfully within systems of folk knowledge. This process necessarily changes the constitution of the objects themselves. They are turned into real and natural objects that can fall into fields of rational meaning. The philosophical basis for this strategy of dealing with unreal objects can be found in the work of the nineteenth-century German philosopher Franz Brentano, whose essays on the distinction between mental and physical phenomena Inoue may very well have encountered in his study of German philosophy. Brentano argued against the possibility of nonexistent objects by stating that for every sentence about a nonexistent object "one can form an equivalent in which the subject and predicate are replaced by something referring to a real thing."[16] This strategy was later developed into what has become known as "elimination by paraphrase" in Bertrand Russell's theory of descriptions.[17] In his dismissal of unreal or fictional objects in the everyday discourse of the folk, Inoue too enacted a kind of elimination by paraphrase, rewriting the unreal in terms of the real. What is significant in this approach is that it assumes beforehand that commoner beliefs and practices are merely objects to be explained away bit by bit by a universal reason and never something to be respected and known in their own integrity and particular context. They become suddenly discovered in the light of modern scientific knowledge only to be covered in the ignominy of superstition. This attitude toward the folk later became one major point of difference between Inoue's conception of folklore studies as an enlightenment project and the aim of folklore studies as conceived by others after him.

But those folklorists who came after Inoue, most notably Yanagita Kunio, also had some important points in common with him on the levels of method and practice. The particular monsters that filled the branches of Inoue's supernatural history did not come from nowhere. Much like the information network that Yanagita was to cultivate throughout Japan years later, Inoue established the practice of collecting stories concerning unusual events and beliefs from regional informants and newspapers. As early as one month after the founding of his Fushigi Kenkyūkai in 1886,

Inoue began running public announcements in *Kyōju tsūshin—shinrigaku* (Teachers' correspondence: Psychology) for "facts concerning supernatural beings of each particular region [in Japan]."[18] By the time his lectures on folklore were published in their entirety ten years later, Inoue could boast of having collected 462 items concerning the supernatural, having read over five hundred texts from the past and present that dealt with the supernatural, as well as having participated in about ten on-site investigations of table turning, hypnotism, sorcery, magic foxes, and so on (1:15). One commentator has reported that in total Inoue personally visited 1,579 sites throughout Japan to record "observations and information of the actual place" and that his records often rank in detail and content with those of folklorists.[19] Yanagita himself, although deploring the aim of Inoue's work, found several occasions to cite as documentary evidence material from Inoue's books.[20]

Another substantial similarity between Inoue's monsterology and Yanagita's folk studies is that both appear as fledgling disciplines outside mainstream academics. As Oshima Tatehiko points out, both shared a dilettantism that was endemic in an age of newly arising disciplines and shifting, competing fields of anthropology, ethnology, folklore, and sociology.[21] Amid the fray of these sometimes cooperative, sometimes conflicting fields, Inoue and Yanagita were in general agreement about their distrust in the narrow-mindedness and elitism of the professional scholar (*gakusha*) who operated within the strict confines of institutionalized fields of knowledge.[22] They both were, in effect, arguing against ivory-towerism and seeking to provide the foundations for a human science with a practical, social application. But, when outlining exactly to what kind of practical application such a human science should aspire, these two academic dilettantes and pioneers of folk study parted company.

In Inoue's case, his characterization of monsterology's relationship alongside established disciplines and his pronouncements of its social value expose the polemics behind his seemingly innocent cataloguing of folk beliefs. At the root of his objections to the common definition of what constituted *yōkai* or *fushigi* was the recognition of quantitative changes in the supernatural as a function of qualitative and quantitative changes in a people's fund of knowledge and experience. What is unusual and unknown, Inoue argues, is variable according to the person, time and place: "So then, the question of the existence or non-existence of supernatural beings [*yōkai*] lies not in objective things [*mono*] but in the person; not in objectivity, but in subjectivity. There is in fact no set standard for supernatural beings themselves. In other words, the standard for supernatural beings is the knowledge and intellect of the person. The reasons for numerous supernatural beings among the lower classes are their shallow knowledge, limited experience, and the high number of unfamiliar places they observe or hear about" (1:7). Accordingly, an extraordinary and inexplicable thing, the nature of which does not change according to time, place, or person, is called *shinkai* (True Mystery; 1:8). As analyzed in the following chapter, this atemporal, atopic, and transpersonal characterization of *shinkai* became key when Inoue defined the social utility of his practice in relation to education, the state, and the emperor.

Monsterology, Inoue claims, bears a close relation to the disciplines of history and anthropology. In his view, because anthropology deals with differences among ethnicities, monsterology as the study of the development of knowledge among humans is a type of anthropology. Likewise, because history is the study of the development of humans as a single people (*kokumin*) forming a society, monsterology is a type of history. In particular, it belongs to the subdiscipline that Inoue refers to as "historical philosophy" (what today might fit somewhere between intellectual/cultural history and history of mentalities), which examines "the inner thought" of these developments. However, these disciplines ignore the study of the mutual relations between the mental and the material, the inner and the outer, the individual and the social (1:17). And, speaking more broadly, Inoue points out that the academic world is lacking a science that deals with the social phenomenon of monsters as the product of improper forms of knowledge (*henshikigaku*) which arise from individual misapplications of the principles of the variously established proper forms of knowledge (*seishikigaku*). In this respect, he argues, every discipline has its "normal" and "abnormal" sides (1:15–16). While recognizing that monsterology is not yet an established science because it still occasionally relies on speculative thought rather than solely on the certainty of demonstrable proof, Inoue offers it as the discipline to fill in these gaps in academia (1:9–10).

First, as the metadiscipline that sorts out and identifies improper (folk) forms of knowledge, monsterology has a complementary relationship with philosophy, which stands as an organizing metadiscipline for proper (modern, scientific, rational) forms of knowledge. The former is the flip side of the latter. Both also have analogous and complementary transcendental anchors; for Inoue's philosophy it is the Buddhist notion of *shin'nyo* (True Reality), and in monsterology it is *shinkai* (True Mystery). In effect, True Reality and True Mystery are the same thing reached from different approaches.[23] For Inoue, philosophy provides the pure logic and form of reasoning necessary for all of the other disciplines, and monsterology is "the applied science of the principles of all disciplines" (1:15).

The one science that Inoue showcased in particular as indispensable to monsterology is psychology. Inoue was in fact one important figure in the introduction into Japan of Western psychology, itself an incipient discipline of indeterminate status during the Meiji period. At about the same time that he began his lectures and writings on *yōkaigaku* Inoue also began lecturing and writing on *shinrigaku*.[24] He even became the director of a correspondence course in psychology from February to November 1886 and was the first director of applied psychology at the Tetsugakukan in 1887. Psychology not yet having been institutionalized as a separate discipline while he was in college, Inoue received his training in the subject from Toyama Masakazu (1848–1900), a specialist in sociology. Until Motora Yūjirō (1858–1912), the first specialist in psychology to become a professor at Tokyo Imperial University, returned from study in America in 1888, Inoue is said to have probably been the number one person among psychological circles in Japan.[25] The immediate relationship between psychology as Inoue understood it and his monsterology project is readily visible in the title and preface to his Tetsugakukan lectures in applied psychology. The preface of *Shinrigaku (ōyō narabini yōkai setsumei)* (Psychology: Application in the explanation of monsters) describes psychology as consisting of both theory and application, with Inoue desiring to present the explanation of *yōkai* under the latter because "80 to 90% of all monsters are born of the operations of the mind." As Itakura suggests, Inoue's applied psychology was another name for monsterology.[26]

This enlistment of psychology empowered monsterology to supplement the other lacuna in academic disciplines mentioned above, namely, their nonrecognition of the relationship between the mental and the material, the inner and the outer, the individual and the social. After arguing for the organization of a science to research abnormal phenomena — something that conventional science for the most part does not deign to do—Inoue admits that as a nonspecialist in science he must defer the details of science to specialists. At the same time, however, he effectively limits the authority of the conventional scientist by emphasizing the mutual relationship between the material object and the mind of the subject (1:164). Taking his cue from Kant, he privileges the importance of thought in the figuration of the thing through the medium of perception and cognition (1:171–72). Thus, although Inoue divides the universe into matter (*mono*) and mind (*kokoro*), he heavily weights the role of subjective mind in understanding or, rather, misunderstanding phenomena. Correspondingly, he offers in theory two general divisions of supernatural beings based on this matter/mind dualism, *butsuriteki yōkai* and *shinriteki yōkai,* but in practice he ultimately reduces all varieties to mishaps in the conceptual, emotional, or volitional operations of the mind. He recognizes a monster as material only when the source of illusion, hallucination, or insanity can be entirely attributed to an organic defect in some part of an individual's body (brain, eye, nerves, etc.; 1:153–56).

Likewise, the dualism of outer/inner parallels that of matter/mind. In his typology of psychological monsters he initially outlines three classes: those that are outside, such as ghosts, *tengu,* demons, and the like; those that occur via a medium, such as a shaman, a fortune-teller, or a diviner; and those coming from one's own mind, such as dreams, hallucinations, delusions, insanity. The first class he identifies as belonging apparently to "the outer world," which he defines as the "material world seen before our eyes"; the latter two classes belong to "the inner world," which he defines as "the mind within our own bodies." Immediately after making these distinctions, however, Inoue is quick to emphasize that "since all monsters are produced from inner mental operations, in the case of so-called outer-world monsters the outer thing is merely a subordinate catalyst" (1:26–27). Again, it is a question of mind over matter for Inoue. He can therefore privilege psychology, "the science of the principles of the mind," as the most important tool for understanding the psychological aberrations and inadequacies that condition the appearance of monsters. In the fortress of monsterology, "psychology is the castle-keep, the physical sciences the front gate, philosophy the back gate" (1:15, 171).

The final pair of relations that Inoue claims monsterology takes into account and other disciplines do not is that between the individual and society. Rather than analytical categories on the level of his two previous binarisms, the dyad individual/society is invoked by Inoue to make a case for the practical value of monsterology. Conceptualizing the whole of society as the sum of the individuals who live in it, Inoue simply reasons that the intellectual and cultural development of society is therefore dependent on the intellectual and cultural development of the individual. It is of absolute necessity, then, that the minds of individual Japanese be free of the obstacles that superstitions present to the modern learning and scientific knowledge that will transform Japan into a modern society.[27] Monsterology as the practical application of psychology to "abnormal forms" promises to provide a method by which to clear the path for this "correct" knowledge. It will, however, become apparent in the following chapter that this formulation was instrumental in the restrictive management, not the liberating enlightenment, of Japanese individuals in the ideologizing processes of the Meiji state.

Inoue's psychologization of phenomena was clearly not aimed at a critique of the objectivity of the physical sciences nor at the scientific method as a whole, for he relied on the discoveries the physical sciences provided to give natural explanations to supernatural phenomena when they could. Rather, psychology, insofar as it is accepted as a valid science, was offered as a supplementary heuristic to be applied in cases of abnormal phenomena that the folk ignorantly dubbed monsters. It enabled Inoue to proclaim that all so-called monsters were "subjective errors of the human mind" and consequently did not exist supernaturally in the outside material world of things. The supernatural thus became located within the human mind and with a science of the mind could be naturalized by identifying supernatural objects either as misrecognitions of natural objects or as natural products of organic defects in the brain. Inoue's taxonomy of the supernatural appears then as in fact a taxonomy of the natural pathologically displaced. Inoue's explanations of various supernatural phenomena involved the substitution of the abnormal with the normal, the irrational with the rational. The prefix super- in supernatural was detached from objects in the field of folk knowledge as they were nominated to categories dominated by the suffix -*gaku*. As a result, these objects were rediscovered, renamed, and reordered according to the rules of a new epistemological discourse. The beliefs (*shinkō*) in the supernatural that had furnished the theoretical foundations of folk knowledge were literally transcribed into errant beliefs (*meishin*) as the scientific demonstration of natural principles of cause and effect behind phenomena served to discredit any other explanatory mode. Inoue was quite pointed in his use of the tag *mei* (errant) in reference not only to folk belief but also to folk knowledge when he designated the understanding derived from folk belief as *meigo* (errant understanding; 1:8).

This systematization and normative practice of monsterology worked to transfix the "changing things," the monsters that beliefs in the supernatural had spawned, with words—many of them newly coined—that identified, arranged, and explained the fantastic under a new regime of modern reason. In remapping monsters with the guidance of the new, albeit marginal, science of psychology (in fact, its marginalism is what allowed Inoue the space to fashion his form of folklore as he did), Inoue interiorized what in the past the folk had described not only as an external physical thing but also as a radically outside other, an unknown to be feared and respected. This formerly outside other now resided inside one's head as the monster of unreason. With this interiorization, the source of supernatural fear and awe among the folk was to become susceptible to the subject-call of the state that would strive to institutionalize this dis-ease with the conjuration of new superstitions. This operation of "supernatural ideology" is the main topic of chapter 3. In the meantime, Inoue's enlightenment taxonomy of a natural supernatural history was not the only mid-Meiji attempt to conceptualize the fantastic that arose from the twilight of Japan's modernity.

Fact, Tact, and Phantasmagoria in Minakata's Theory of Culture

Of the transformations of dream we barely retain the intermediate stages. And yet it is this *transformation,* these *transformations* that make oneiric space the very seat of imagined movements.
 —Gaston Bachelard, "L'espace onirique"

Positive estimations of his breadth of knowledge have admiringly dubbed him "a walking encyclopedia," though the more critical might simply consider him a dilettantish knowledge parasite, jack of all trades and master of none. Both views point to the fantastic fluidity of the intellectual space that Minakata Kumagusu (1867–1941) shared with Inoue Enryō in

Meiji Japan. Caught in the riptide of new waves of scientific knowledge that carried away many a young Japanese student to foreign shores, Minakata found himself collecting specimens of knowledge—in person and in texts—throughout Asia, Europe, and the Americas. Although known principally as a naturalist and folklorist, his range of interests was truly encyclopedic: comparative religion and philosophy, classical and popular literature, bacteriology, anthropology, human and natural history, human sexuality (homo- and hetero-), zoology, ecology, politics, psychology, and occultism were all among the prominent topics in his writings.[28]

Like Inoue, Minakata felt an intellectual imperative to address the question of the supernatural within categories of *fushigi* comparable to yet ultimately different in orientation from those dealt with in Inoue's monsterology. Although similarly aligning categories of material and mental phenomena with various academic disciplines and fundamentally grounding his metaphysical conception of the universe within a paradigm derived from Mahayana Buddhism, Minakata cast his project differently from Inoue's in method, scope, and aim with the introduction of a theory of human culture lacking in monsterology. Whereas Inoue's idea of culture was synonymous with a notion of cultivation and education centered around an ideology of *bunmei kaika,* Minakata's theory of human culture had more in common with the cultures of slime molds that had fascinated him: both were sites of ceaseless phantasmagoric change—not unilinear progress—that spurred the unfixing and mixing of sharply cut taxonomic boundaries and consequently necessitated rethinking notions of causality and tactics of understanding in the human sciences.

One is hard-pressed to find explicit statements of theory and method in Minakata's books and articles.[29] For that one must turn to his voluminous correspondence. His most broadly theoretical musings on epistemology and the supernatural appear in his letters to Toki Hōryū (1854–1922), a top Shingon priest of the time who made Minakata's acquaintance in London on his way back from the World Parliament of Religions held in Chicago in 1893.[30] Part of Minakata's project in these letters written from London was to convince Toki of the compatibility of Mahayana Buddhism with modern science and to dissuade him from relying on the mystic and superstitious side of Buddhism to fuel its revival in Meiji Japan. He viewed Buddhism and modern science as mutually beneficial in the development of the people, not on the ethical level, as Inoue emphasized, but on the deepest level of providing a worldview and theoretical model of the causal relations among ceaselessly changing things in the world. In short, Minakata believed that science reveals the principles of cause and effect that Buddhism posits. He even went so far in these letters as to describe science as "one part of Shingon that can benefit society if managed properly."[31] Unfortunately, a large part of this correspondence with Toki is lost, but from what remains of this discussion of science and religion one can glean the specter of a theory of human culture that arises from an encounter with the fantastic.

Minakata's organization of types of mysteries in the world initially recalls that of Inoue in its reliance on a basic division of matter (*mono*) and mind (*kokoro*). In one of his earliest extant letters to Toki, dated 21 December 1893, Minakata laid out his scheme of the universe. For him as for Inoue, *mono* designates objective things apart from human mind or consciousness, and *kokoro* designates human consciousness. Also in the same pattern as Inoue, Minakata, no doubt recycling the Confucian philosophical term, calls the reason or principle that encompasses and governs matter and mind *ri*, but the *ri* of matter and the *ri* of mind are not necessarily one and the same for him. He further parts company with Inoue by adding a third term to the dyad *mono/kokoro*: *koto* (thing), which he defines as the intersection of *mono* and *kokoro* (9:15). He visualizes this intersection in a sketch depicting the relationship among the triptych *mono/kokoro/koto*, which he includes in the margin of this letter: two overlapping ovoid areas labeled *mono* and *kokoro*, the common portion of which is labeled *koto*. He further explains that "that which mind activates and gives rise to when working on matter is called *koto*" (9:18) and that the field of *koto* ranges "from the taking of a tissue in hand and blowing one's nose to the founding of religions to benefit people" (9:16). A single English equivalent for *koto* that gets across Minakata's meaning is difficult to find. "Thing" lacks the sense of the human participation necessary for its production and is too easily confused with objective, material thing (*mono*), whereas "affairs" suggests the human element but lacks the sense of materiality involved. "Cultural thing," I will submit, is closer to Minakata's usage. As the operation and product of mind interacting with the matter around it, *koto* emerges as the basis for a concept of human culture that is nonnormative and allows for heterogeneity. It is the pivot on which Minakata distinguished his approach to the folk and the fantastic in particular and the human sciences in general.

In a later and very long letter to Toki dated 18 September 1903, Minakata again brought up this conceptual scheme, this time in the context of the mysteries and wonders of the world. In contrast to Inoue's strategy of a comprehensive taxonomy of superstitions, Minakata simply offers the genres of *monofushigi* (mysteries of matter), *kokorofushigi* (mysteries of mind), *kotofushigi* (mysteries of cultural things), and *rifushigi* (mysteries of reason), which correspond to the above conceptual categories (9:271–73). The first two forms of *fushigi* are analogous to Inoue's *butsuriteki yō-kai* and *shinriteki yōkai,* whereas what Minakata calls *kotofushigi* can find a place only in the latter of Inoue's two basic categories. *Rifushigi,* being concerned with the mysteries behind the abstract operations of logic and reason itself, encompasses the other three categories and is also something that Inoue does not explicitly consider. It never occurred to Inoue to problematize reason in this way because it would be tantamount to admitting deficiencies in his master discipline, philosophy.

At the apex of both Minakata's and Inoue's models of the universe, however, is the same notion of a transcendental *Daifushigi* (Great Mystery), as Minakata called it. Minakata even arrived at the borders of this Great Mystery with an example uncannily similar to Inoue's example of the levels of knowledge science can provide about the composition of a water drop. Minakata points out that although the results of Mendeleyev's chemical research into the development of elements leads to the conclusion that all matter will eventually return to hydrogen, when one asks whence hydrogen comes the only answer is "the immortal soul of Dainichi Nyorai [the Cosmic Buddha]" (9:107). Whereas Inoue identified this Great Mystery (in his terminology, True Mystery) with the Buddhist notion of True Reality (*shin'nyo*), Minakata opted for the specifically Shingon Buddhist image of Dainichi Nyorai as his metaphor for that mystery of mysteries that lies completely outside human knowledge (9:273). This particular choice of a Shingon image might have been more out of deference to Toki Hōryū's sectarian affiliation than out of Minakata's own denominational preference.

Within the range of human knowledge, on the other hand, Minakata identifies the first four types of *fushigi* with the current academic disciplines that attempt to explicate them. In this act he again recalls Inoue's practice of defining families of sciences to which genera of supernatural beings are assigned, but the tone with which Minakata does this is noticeably different from Inoue's. Inoue is glowingly optimistic about the explanatory powers of science, whereas Minakata, although appreciating and indulging in scientific practice, is more skeptical of its ability to get at the true causes behind things.[32] For example, contemporary physical sciences (*kagaku*) "only put mysteries of matter [*monofushigi*] in order." Rather than actually analyzing the reasons or causes behind *monofushigi*, they "go only so far as to dissect mysteries [*fushigi*] and turn them into groups of phenomena." For *kokorofushigi*, Minakata continues, there is psychology, but because it cannot yet ultimately detach itself from the materiality of the brain and sense organs in its explanations of mental phenomena, "at the present time there still is not a science of the mysteries of the mind alone." Mathematics and logic attempt to get at the causes and effects behind *kotofushigi*, but not satisfactorily, and Minakata hesitates to name any discipline willing to tackle *rifushigi* (9:271–73).

What seems to motivate Minakata's intellectual activity are the gaps rather than, as in Inoue's case, the fullness of the sciences in their treatment of natural and human phenomena. He concedes a certain efficacy in the physical sciences' ability to bring order to the chaos of nature as he himself was deeply involved in the activity of naming and classifying specimens in botany and bacteriology. One type of protozoa that he discovered even bears his name: *Minakatella longifila Lister*.[33] Yet despite this success of the physical sciences, the question of cause and effect among things involving human activity is never answered to Minakata's satisfaction. In the physical sciences, certain laws of nature that describe the causal relationships among matter are discoverable and do fulfill the conditions of repeatability and predictability required by science. These laws are comparable to the laws of karmic transmigration (*rinne*) in Mahayana philosophy, but whether or not the world of mind—composed of human thoughts, desires, and feelings—and by association the world of human affairs (*koto*) follow these or any discernable principles of causality is, Minakata admits, difficult to say and perhaps impossible to know (9:15). For Minakata, this mystery is the central concern for any science that purports to investigate human action and it qualitatively distinguishes such a study from the physical sciences.

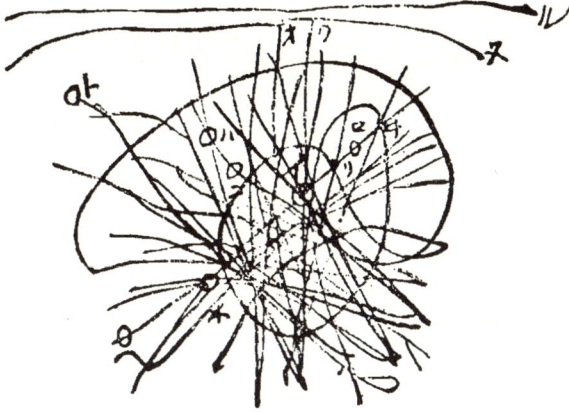

Figure 1 Minakata's Mandala (Source: *Minakata Kumagusu zenshū,* vol. 9)

In a letter to Toki dated 18 September 1903, Minakata diagrammed his approach to this mystery of discovering causal explanations for the operations of *koto* (figure 1). As he describes it, this diagram (which he asks Toki to imagine as being three-dimensional) represents the relations of reason or principle (*ri*) among various mysteries of matter, mind, and (cultural) things in the universe and indicates levels of human accessibility to the comprehension of this network of reason. The intertwined lines represent "the reason of things" (*jiri*) that trace causal relations between the various indicated points. The central point labeled with the Japanese *i* (イ) is what Minakata names the *suiten* or gathering point from which all reason of things emanate. The other labeled points symbolize phenomena and their possible relations with other phenomena within the field of human reason. With humans placed at the center of the diagram (it is unclear if Minakata means at the *suiten,* but it seems so), human ability to comprehend causal connections between things diminishes as they are located further outward from the center and human awareness of them becomes more tenuous. The lower of the two distinct outer lines, *nu* (ヌ), represents things on the outskirts of human reasoning that are barely gleaned through points *wo* (ヲ) and *wa* (ワ) touching *nu.* Outside the reaches of reasoning and inference "one can imagine something to the extent that it is thought that there seems to be a reason '*ru*' (ル) [the outermost line]" that is incomprehensible but nevertheless felt to exist. The vague and passive wording of this articulation accords with the fact that no direct lines of reason reach *ru* in his picture. Minakata associates this overarching line labeled *ru* with the mysteries of reason, as opposed to the mysteries of matter, mind, and thing that lie within it. Its existence is problematical for Minakata because he is skeptical about being able to investigate the principles of reason with reason itself. (This can also be seen as the source of his skepticism about the ability of psychology as a science of mind to understand truly and purely the principles of the mind.) Finally, that which is outside the diagram is the transcendental realm of "Dainichi, the Great Mystery of Being" (9:273–75).[34]

For Minakata, the most important aspect of this abstract model of the universe in any consideration of cause and effect in the human world is the relationship among these lines of causality as they mutually influence and distort each other. The Western model of the physical sciences is good at discovering independent lines of causality between material phenomena, but cannot successfully handle the intersection and mixing of these lines with human forces that lead to unpredictable results.[35] For this reason, Minakata introduces a Buddhist model of "[karmic] relations" (*en*) to supplement this theoretical shortcoming in science: "Contemporary science understands (or rather, expects that it should understand) causality [*inga*], but does not understand relations [*en*]. Our task is to research these relations. However, if relations are that which result from the imbrication of causalities, then it is our task to seek the causality above the whole of all causalities."[36] Minakata introduces *en* into science without the religious motivation associated with the popular understanding of this key Buddhist (and Hindu) concept of the ethical connection between human action and consequent rebirth in the transmigration of the soul. Rather, he limits it to a conceptual category that designates the relations among forces generated by human action. The ethical consequences of such actions for one's next existence is a problem he sets aside for religious thinkers, because what he is interested in studying are the consequences of human action during one's current existence.

After having specified the production of (cultural) things as the interaction of mind with matter, Minakata then attempts to lay out the principles for the investigation of this realm of human activity. Because the model of causality in the physical sciences, which requires predictability and repeatability, does not hold in the study of the human world of *koto* (i.e., human culture), Minakata insists that the investigator must oper-

甲　（ハ）　　　　甲　（ロ）　　　　甲　（イ）

八十（情）　八十（智）　　二百（情）　五十（智）　　五十（情）　二百（智）
八十（意）　　　　五十（意）　　　　五十（意）

乙　　　　　　　　乙　　　　　　　　乙

（情）百　百（智）　　五十（情）　五十（智）　　（情）百　百（智）
百（意）　　　　二百（意）　　　　百（意）

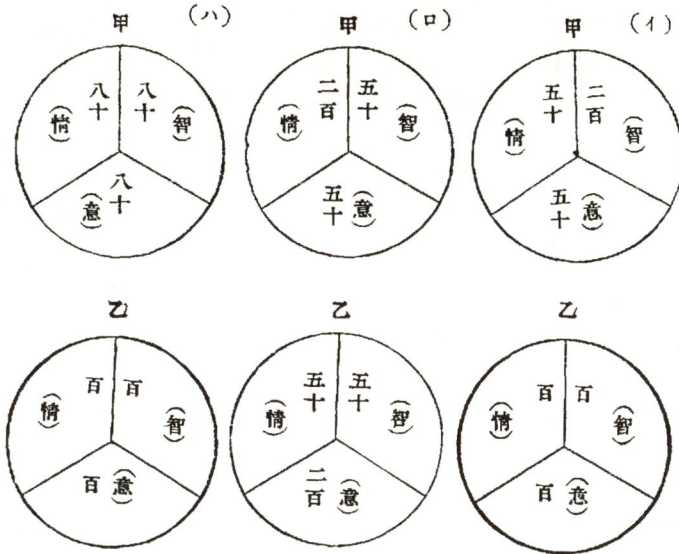

Figure 2 Inoue's tripartite economy of the mind (Source: *Yōkaigaku*, vol. 1)

ate in a different epistemological mode. Whereas prediction and repeat-ability, Minakata states, are based on the accumulation and measure of fixed objective facts, no such quantifiable fixity appears to exist in the thoughts, feelings, and desires of the human mind (*kokoro*) and by exten-sion in the realm of cultural things (*koto*) that the human mind produces through matter (*mono*; 9:15–18). This view of the creative human mind as nonquantifiable and therefore beyond the measure of applied reason is a radical departure from Inoue's picture of the mind (figure 2) existing as a tripartite economy of intellectual, volitional, and emotive activi-ties which as a whole always maintain a static equilibrium via the con-trolling faculty of "attention" (*chūi*). According to Inoue, an increase in emotion, for example, entails an inversely proportional decrease in intel-lectual and/or volitional abilities in a "normal human." If the calibrating control of attention is lost, the ratio is sent askew and one goes insane. For Inoue, the thought of the ordinary folk, too, suffers from this form of mental deficiency when they insist on believing in and acting on en-counters with the supernatural. Inoue's drawings schematizing examples of mental activity stand in stark contrast to "Minakata's Mandala."[37]

In contrast to Inoue's rewriting of human mental phenomena into terms manageable by the proper application of reason and scientific method, Minakata sets out to reassess reason and method as they apply to everyday human experience. In Minakata's view, when a human subject—with his or her thoughts, feelings, and desires—is inserted into the scheme of things, the strict laws, repeatable and predictable, governing natural objects are distorted so as to no longer be applicable to explain the processes of human creativity and discovery. The concept that he introduces at this point in his 1903 letter to Toki, immediately after explaining the intricacies of his "mandala" of causality in the human world, is that of "tact" (9:274–75). He uses the English word because, as he twice confesses, he does not know an appropriate Japanese translation, although some have suggested *jukuren* (trained skill). For Minakata *jukuren* does not quite capture the meaning he desires to express to Toki, so he proceeds to explain what he means by a series of glosses and examples. Even to the native English speaker, the nuance in Minakata's usage and the reason behind this choice of words in this context are not immediately apparent. It is therefore useful to follow in some detail the development of Minakata's definition as he presents it.

It is likely that Minakata encountered the word "tact" during his eight-year (1892–1900) stay in England, but in what context is unknown. He first introduced it to Toki as a way to understand the reason behind the mysteries of *kokoro* and *koto,* particularly the latter. Knowable reason, Minakata asserts, is not limited to that of measurable *monofushigi*: "Even with respect to its methods, reason [beyond the realm of *monofushigi*] is not necessarily incomprehensible just because it is presently not instrumental [*kikaiteki*] and quantitative [*sūryōteki*]. In actuality, there is also present among people something called 'tact' " (9:275). For his first example of tact in action, Minakata offers his own experience of preparing specimens for the microscope. Although another person would use the best chemicals and carefully mix them to precise measure but ultimately fail in the preparation, Minakata observes that he can haphazardly throw them together and achieve excellent results, even (perhaps especially) when drunk (9:275–76).[38] He can accomplish this feat, he says, "because I have been doing it for some time" (*hisashiku yatte iru yue*). He is careful to distinguish the meaning of this phrase, which for him indicates a level of unconsciousness in his actions, from "because I did it for some time" (*hisashiku yatta yue*), which would suggest that his success was the result of consciously setting his mind to what he was doing, adding adjustments and improvements as he went along for a certain duration until finally achieving success. This tact guides one through practical use, "as when a stone-cutter works a long time, he can correctly and practically cut blocks of stone while talking" (9:277).

Insisting on distinguishing this faculty from an idea of *jukuren* that implies spending years of concerted training and toil, Minakata associates tact with something he calls *yariate* ("the noun for '*yariateru*,'" as he parenthetically comments; it can be provisionally glossed as "hitting upon something through doing" or "chance hits through trial and error" or simply "experimentation"). *Yariate* generally designates for him a kind of open and unsystemizable method, or rather, attitude toward the materials and conditions that lie before one. As Minakata turns to specify what *yariate* means, he again relies on concrete examples. This time he points out that in chemistry one can mix two extremely flammable chemicals such as hydrogen and oxygen together and produce a new substance, water, with completely different and unexpected qualities. Likewise, though tapioca is very beneficial to the sick, the raw seeds of the plant from which it is produced can kill a person. No amount of mere measurement of their constituents can discover these results: "In the case of discovery, chance hits through trial and error [*yariate*] are more frequent than expected (generalizing frequent chance hits as a whole, one calls it 'fate')" (9:277). In other words, chance hits gained through free experimentation are ultimately more fruitful in human discovery than measurable, predictable quantities, and when one strings them together they seem to form some kind of pattern outside human control.

Minakata offers these simple examples of the unpredictable aspect of scientific discovery not so much to critique explicitly the systematicity and objectivity of the physical sciences—that is, the sciences that deal exclusively with the world of *mono*—but rather to suggest the intangible and unquantifiable complexities of human involvement with the natural world ("from blowing one's nose with tissue paper to founding religions"). There is an implicit critique of the supposed continuity of scientific progress in Minakata's emphasis on the vagaries of scientific discovery, but he does not develop it here. Later, in his pointed critique of evolutionary theory, appears a more sustained questioning of the validity of one important pillar of nineteenth-century natural and social science.

In the meantime, his examples of discovery through a process of trial and error that is not necessarily rationally guided serve to raise the question of the mysterious processes at work in the human mind as it meets matter to create cultural things (science itself would have to be considered one such cultural thing under Minakata's scheme).

Immediately following this characterization of scientific discovery, Minakata bluntly states why, in order to get at the heart of these mysterious processes of cultural production, one cannot rely on the methods of measurement used in the physical sciences to study *monofushigi*: "Now, because the world of physical mysteries [*monofushigikai*] has size and volume as well as discrete bodies, quantification serves its purpose and makes its authority felt. As for the world of the mysteries of mind [*kokorofushigi*] as well as of the mysteries of cultural things [*kotofushigi*] (excluding mathematics), there isn't size and volume" (9:277). The tangibility and specificity of physical objects is a condition for their quantification in the physical sciences. The usefulness of quantification in affairs of human mind and culture, Minakata goes on to say, is limited to making convenient biographical and historical periodizations, or, as in psychology, to gauge the level of acuity of one's sense perceptions. But "one cannot say how many times more intelligent someone is over another or, for example, that Hideyoshi's ambition was ten times that of Kenshin's. For this reason, in research of this kind I wonder if the aforementioned 'tact' is needed more than quantification" (9:277). Mathematics, being one discipline that deals with *kotofushigi* in Minakata's breakdown of academic fields, is "applied" along with tact when seeking new discoveries, but in Minakata's articulation here mathematics has the reduced role of providing statistical probabilities rather than quantifiable certainties. His idea of tact begins to take shape as a tactic by which to tackle the intangibles—of intent, volition, emotion—that must be taken into account in any model of causation in the human world. Its practical application, however, still remains quite undefined. The question, however, is whether this lack of formulaic specification is out of neglect or necessity. The next part of this letter, when read with part of an earlier one to Toki, provides some strong hints toward the latter.

This tactical tact is most dramatically exemplified in two intriguing stories that Minakata relates to Toki. The first concerns a dream he had about a type of duckweed; the second a dream about a slime mold. Mina-kata describes both as clear demonstrations of "tact" at work in his personal experience.

> In the 23rd year of Meiji [1890], I detected in Florida a duckweed called *pithophora*. Up until that time it was a type found only in the northern section of America. Well, I returned to Japan and during the end of September of the year before last [1901] I frequently dreamt that if I were to go to Seiten in Yoshida village in Waka-yama there would be without fail the abovementioned duckweed. Accordingly, on October 1 I went to Seiten, but when I walked the area there wasn't anything at all. However, they had dug a pond in the vicinity of the spinning company where my younger brother worked. (Since it wasn't there when I was in the country I couldn't be expected to know about it.) In this pond there floated a bit of black-green duckweed. A duckweed called *kuradophora* was also visible. The *pithophora* wasn't among them, so with a sigh I decided to return home. But since how could I spend half a day without gathering anything, I thought it would at least be fun to show something or another to my kid so I gathered a sample and went home. Then, upon looking at it with a microscope, not only was it the *pithophora* that I saw in the dream; it was the identical species that I myself had discovered in America. (9:278–79)

After this incredible story of dream and discovery Minakata assures Toki that he is "not one who believes in dreams" and that he had no reason to believe that this particular species of duckweed, the family of which was limited to the Western Hemisphere as far as he knew, could be found in Japan. Nevertheless, without the dream he never would have discovered it in Yoshida village.

As if to speak for the likes of Inoue Enryō who would insist upon a psychological rationalization for this uncanny experience, Minakata (mockingly) offers what "your typical psychologist would say": that even without having recently gone out to this area after returning to Japan, you knew the place called Yoshida from childhood and associated the waters there with those that gave birth to that particular duckweed in Florida. Given your passion for such things, you inherently wondered if that kind

of duckweed might not exist there. Et voilà! From these thoughts, rec-
ollections, and associations it manifested itself in your dream. End of
mystery.

Whether or not such an explanation is reasonable Minakata leaves up
to Toki's own judgment, but he then ups the ante with a second dream
experience that he believes defies any easy psychological reduction. This
instance concerns a recent dream that indicated that if he searched the
Nachi area in Wakayama he would find a certain slime mold (*kurateresu*)
that he had never before encountered live. Having the example of the
previous dream experience that turned up profitable, he decided to set
out in search of this slime mold. He combed the area indicated in the
dream but found nothing. With dusk approaching he turned home, but
experiencing some physical difficulties he was forced to take a roundabout path and finally lie down. Upon doing so he discovered the dreamt
slime mold in abundance before him: "This was a species I had never before witnessed. Also, I've seen only a picture of it but I had never even
read about what kind of soil it grows in nor what kind of trees it grows
under. Even now I haven't been able to read up on it." Because he knew
only the name and a picture of this slime mold, the kind of psychological
reasons possible in the previous case were, he claimed, nonexistent. "In
that case, as in the previous example, it was nothing other than 'tact'"
that led to this discovery (9:280).

The question of whether or not Minakata's dream-discovery stories
are true is not a question worth asking. Rather, it is more fruitful to consider how the deployment of dreams throughout Minakata's discourse
functions as a way to speak about the putative nonrationality of folk practices. Clearly dissatisfied with the psychologization (i.e., rationalization)
of dream experiences as well as the mystical explanations that his friend
Toki might offer, Minakata sees dreams as a possible model for creative
processes of cultural production that escape the logic of the rational. A
discussion of dreams that appears in his earlier, 21 December 1893 letter
to Toki is set in this context and prefigures his latter elaboration on the
relationship among tact, *yariate,* and *koto* as key concepts in the study of
human culture.

In response to Toki's desire to exploit the popularity of occultism in
Japan for the revival of Buddhism by identifying the "transcendental reason" (*rigai no ri;* literally, "reason outside of reason") assumed in both of

them as one and the same, Minakata declares that there is "nothing special" about occultism; rather, it is full of "chance hits" (*magureatari;* 9:6–7). The word *magureatari* used here in reference to the apparent successes of practitioners of the occult—such as shamans, diviners, and fortune-tellers—seems to be a precursor for the relatively more refined notion of *yariate* that Minakata later applied in his description of tact in human discovery. To seek scientifically the truth of these occult practices that do not possess normal logic and reason is, Minakata tells Toki, a foolish waste of time. But he does not dismiss these folk practices as meaningless. Their truth value and efficacy lie in believing the shaman's declaration that an occasional chance hit is indeed something wondrous. Given the limitations of human knowledge, even a nonbeliever, he points out, has a difficult time proving that such wonders do not exist as such: "On that account, you can see that logicians [*rikutsuka*] too merely laugh at such techniques [*jutsu*] of shamans and their ilk as not being in accord with the dictates of reason; they are not at all able to say with certainty that [such wonders] are nonexistent. One shouldn't say, however, that because of this what logicians can't declare to be nonexistent are necessarily things of proper reason [*seito no jōri*]" (9:9).

How should one read Minakata's qualification of these chance hits, these possibly true wonders, as not necessarily being of proper reason? One way is to recognize that Minakata wants to avoid an either/or dualism when it comes to logic and reason. In other words, shamanism and divination may not properly follow the logic of logicians, but that does not mean that these folk practices are absolutely illogical. Rather, they possess a certain logic of their own. To suggest the possibility of such alternative logics Minakata then turns to the common experience of dreams:

> I think that "transcendental reason" as you [Toki] call it is for the most part unworthy of investigation. Dreams on the other hand, which in psychology are taken to be akin to madness, are something I've investigated exceedingly. If there were a "transcendental reason," wouldn't dreams and the like be it? This is because somehow or another even things that are unreasonable [*fujōri*] in the waking world are not considered unreasonable in a dream; one thinks of them as having reason. That is to say, because it's a reason the reason

of which is out of place, it's a "reason outside of reason" [*Sunawachi, jōri hazureta ri yue, rigai no ri nari*]. (9:10)

Despite the seeming contradiction involved in applying the reason of the waking world to that of dreams, Minakata confesses, "Nevertheless, I have been studying dreams for many years. Since it's a study that requires neither money nor anything else, it's interesting" (9:10). He then shares with Toki three dreams that he had occasion to write down. Although the material and self-analysis of his dreams are fascinating, rather than recounting in detail their content I would emphasize how they enable Minakata to describe *koto* as a field of human study and tact as an episte-mological mode appropriate to it.

Immediately after offering a chain of associations (not unlike Freud's method) to explain the "reason" behind the last of these three unusual dreams, Minakata comments: "If one examines them with this method, even dreams and the like have more or less a source reason, albeit a dis-ordered one. As far as what I call the science of cultural things [*koto no gaku*] is concerned, the cultural things that manifest themselves daily in the meeting of the world of mind and the world of matter also, like the aforementioned dreams, call up extremely old things, join them with things from yesterday and result in disorder. But, I think that at least their general outlines ought to be comprehensible" (9:15). At this point Mina-kata describes for the first time his conception of the world composed of *mono, kokoro,* and *koto,* which I discussed earlier. His drawing depicting the interrelationship of these components also appears here.

Despite the meandering quality of Minakata's letters, the segue from the world of dreams to the world of *koto* in this instance is not unpre-meditated. The "illogical logic" commonly and undeniably experienced in dreams offers the closest and most convenient model for his concept of causative connections in human culture, which falls under the category of *koto.* It is a model that strives to make general sense out of an apparently disorderly complex of unquantifiable human factors without reducing the alterity and heterogeneity of the rules organizing this complex to the rule of a single Reason. As such, it is a difficult, perhaps impossible, project that requires a high degree of tact itself, for Minakata is constrained by the limits of expression within the regime of Reason in which he finds himself. After all, one cannot forget that he eagerly studied and practiced Western science although questioning some of its theoretical short-comings when applied to humans as objects of study. Yet, regardless of his own ultimate success or failure in this respect, the import of Minakata's approach to the question of human action is that it is openly willing to entertain the idea of a plurality of logics and a variety of reasons among people. With an artful tact, rather than with a precise measurement, one might glean an understanding of the tact that motivates the dynamics of different cultures. This attitude contrasts sharply with that of Inoue En-ryō, who casts his lot with a single universal Western reason, calculating and calculable, that measures all cultural practices by the same standard.

That Minakata had a critique of Inoue in mind when theorizing about cultural practices, especially those of the "unenlightened folk," is evident when reading the final pages of his 1903 letter to Toki.[39] After the discussion of the dreams about the duckweed and the slime mold, Minakata explicitly identifies tact as the operative concept in the human world. He implies that because tact governs human activity, the method of study of this activity should follow suit. This study, he says, is one of "various differences" and thus bears no relation to quantification, the arch principle of the physical sciences. It follows that there are doubtless many ways to apply tact to guide one's actions, including "curses, spells, and a variety of other presently nameless mental operations," so one cannot merely scoff at their seeming irrationality. Still struggling, however, to define the study of this human world of *koto* as a science of sorts, Minakata parenthetically notes that because the reason and application of such things as magic spells and incantations are known not to be completely outside science, they are not the kind of "reason outside of reason" for which Toki has argued. Rather, they belong to a reason outside that which governs matter as well as outside that which governs mind to the extent that it is presently understood.

Thus acknowledging a level of efficacy and purposefulness in unen-lightened practices, Minakata explicitly distinguishes his thought from that of Inoue: "For this reason I don't think, as does Enryō and others, that the incantations, prayers, occultism, curses, spells, and so forth prac-ticed in the past by Shingon Buddhism are all ineffective products of mere empty boasting" (9:282).[40] Minakata's view is that just because there are some instances of outright swindles and empty boasts, this does not mean that all are frauds. Some possess a genuinely effective social function in their respective contexts. What Minakata values and what he designates under the rubric of "tact" is any beneficial technique that stimulates thought, discovery, and cultural production. Many human activities in general and so-called folk ways in particular do indeed attain this function with a logic of their own. Thus, in spite of their shared interest in the powers of science, Minakata and Inoue differ profoundly on this point: whereas Inoue would banish all nonrational forms regardless of their practical functioning, Minakata will welcome them because of it. Such a position opens the way for a much more respectful, sympathetic, relativistic study of the rationale, no matter how irrational it may seem, for everyday folk practices. In short, it turns away from the kind of dissection and dissolution of local practices that Inoue's enlightenment program promoted and toward the foundation of the kind of folk studies that would emerge from the work of Yanagita Kunio and others.

I have, somewhat brazenly, been speaking about Minakata's concept of *koto* as if it were his way of speaking about culture, but I wonder if I am justified in doing so and what compelled me to do so in the first place. Certainly his description of the generation of *koto,* his few offhand examples of it, and his affiliation of its study with disciplines such as anthropology, sociology, and his own folklore studies together provide a reasonable basis for the jump from *koto* to culture. That may suffice as the justification, but what about the compulsion to designate *koto* as culture? I think perhaps it derives from a notable absence of the word that one might expect to designate "culture" in Minakata's texts; namely, *bunka.* Granted that this word, like so many others in Meiji Japan, was newly coined to correspond to a foreign term, but Minakata's not using it was not out of ignorance. Rather, I suggest it was out of defiance. Sensitive to the ideological baggage that the word *bunka* carried in the context of *bunmei kaika* in Meiji Japan, Minakata consciously chose not to use it. Still wanting, however, to study what one would nowadays commonly refer to as culture, Minakata was compelled to find another way of speaking about it. I am compelled to follow him.

Minakata's uneasiness about both the term and the common Meiji conception of *bunka* comes bundled with his critique of nineteenth-century evolutionism, especially in its Social Darwinistic form that was extremely popular in mainstream Meiji academia. In the middle of another letter to Toki, dated 3 March 1894, Minakata questions the appro-

priateness of interpreting Darwin's theory of natural selection as unilinear, progressive change and applying it to human civilization. After
enumerating some of the barbarisms of supposedly civilized peoples past
and present, he notes:

> Mr. [Alfred Russell] Wallace, who at the same time as Darwin pro-
> posed to the Academy the theory of natural selection, nowadays
> trumpets "civilization, civilization!" [*kaika kaika*], but insofar as this
> is the gradual accumulation and acquisition of things that prede-
> cessors have accomplished it amounts to nothing special at all; it's
> merely that with the passage of generations good fortune results. It
> seems to me that civilization from the standpoint of mind differs
> greatly from civilization from the standpoint of matter. It waxes
> and wanes, waxes and wanes, but it's hard to declare by any means
> that present things are better than those of the past. Rather, one can
> say that the past is better than the present. . . . It's difficult for me
> to accept Herbert Spencer and others who, declaring for all things
> "evolution, evolution!" [*shinka shinka*], would say that religion too
> is in a more advanced stage now than in the past. (9:110–11)

Minakata aimed his critique at both the ideological application of Darwin's theory of natural selection to human civilization, which was used to
bolster claims of Western cultural and intellectual superiority, and at the
ideological deployment of Western science in Japan, which was used to
disarm the folk by discrediting their forms of knowledge. Politics, Minakata rightly notes, had distorted Darwin's original notion of evolution as
transmutation. But change—even that which can be called progressive—
Minakata insists, is much more haphazard than Western thinkers think:
"For this reason, the world, with the progress and decline of its civilizations being utterly dream-like, retrogresses while you think it's pro-
gressing and progresses while you think it's retrogressing" (9:111). Again,
Minakata conjures the figure of the dream when considering causal relations and change in the human world. This time it is invoked to combat an ideologically twisted notion of social evolution that rationalizes
smooth, straight lines of ascent. *Bunka,* being bound with the ideology
of *bunmei kaika* informed by such a notion of social evolution in Meiji
Japan, becomes equally twisted. For Minakata, the odd logic of dreams
more accurately describes the observed reality of the random and often

nonrational nature of relations in human culture. The inability to accept this indeterminacy for what it is, Minakata observes, belies a weakness in a Western philosophy that insists on unilinear progress whereas Shaka-muni acknowledged these situations as chance hits (*magureatari*). Because such chance hits characterize the human world, a science of that world must be sensitive to them rather than gloss over them. Mahayana Buddhist thinking, Minakata believed, provided this supplement.

Minakata continued his critique of evolutionism in another letter, written about two weeks after the one just cited. In this instance, he directs his criticism not at arrogant English naturalists and philosophers but at those people in Japan who would translate the word "evolution" as *shin-karon*. Disliking the idea of a one-way process, whether it be progression (*shinka*) or retrogression (*taika*), Minakata insists that a more proper translation for evolution would be simply *henka* (change or transmutation; 9:154–55). With this suggestion Minakata is actually arguing for a return to Darwin's own idea of evolution as transmutation before it became washed over with Spencerian notions of general progressive change.[41] Evolution in this sense, Minakata implies, can then be talked about in a human science so long as one maintains a certain tension (and humility) when trying to explain lines of cause and effect in the human world.

Minakata's ruminations point toward the possibility of a human science. Yet he found inspiration for a theoretical model of causation in human culture not only in dreams but also in what amounted to their waking counterpart: slime mold cultures.[42] In them he observed the same kind of ongoing change—not necessarily progress—that he recognized in the human world. He excitedly details this phantasmagoria to his friend and fellow researcher of folklore, Iwada Junichi, in a discussion centering on the unclassifiability of slime molds as purely plants or purely animals.[43] Fascinated by the utter ambiguity of the slime mold and its lack of a true stable state, Minakata can only trace its circular and never-ending transmutations from amorphous blob to fingerlike filament to lollipop-shaped pollen bulb, never finally deciding whether in fact it is a plant or an animal. Neither is it certain which of these states actually represents a slime mold's true form. Despite a certain level of predictability in this cycle of growth once it begins, the conditions that set it off and determine its pace often result from the conjunction of unpredictable surroundings and events: the level of light and humidity, the temperature, winds and rain to carry spores to other places, and so on. Although Minakata himself does not explicitly call this process dreamlike, I believe that if the fantastical quality of dreams could be made manifest they would, for him, take the shape of slime molds. And in a way it did when he discovered slime molds in, and through, his dreams.

The ceaseless metamorphosis of slime molds and their transgressions of analytical categories represented to Minakata the closest thing in this world to true monsters or *bakemono*. In this respect, I believe there is some merit to Tsurumi Kazuko's suggestion that Minakata's most favored field of physical science, *nenkingaku* or mycetozoology (the study of slime molds) bears an analogous relationship with his favored form of human science, folk studies. As she describes it, what attracted Minakata to the study of slime molds was their intermediary and ambiguous status between plant and animal. They are marginal, frontier phenomena. Similarly, folklore, as the study of phenomena that belong to a category that Minakata defines as lying between the material and the mental, is also situated around the borders of established categories.[44] Both, in their own way, deal with fantastic phenomena that upset clear, rational categories. Tsurumi characterizes both of these interests as allowing a kind of "play" of Veblenian "idle curiosity" in Minakata's intellectual activity that she sees as playing an instrumental role in creativity and discovery.[45] Though I essentially agree with this characterization, I would rather stick with Minakata's term tact to refer to the faculty that the production and the study of cultures, both mold and human, put into play. In its operation this faculty of tact, I suggest, is allied with the fantastic imagination that Rosemary Jackson conceptualizes as a mode that breaches the boundaries of rational and unitary categories of the "real" in order to question the nature of the real and unreal while it "introduces confusion and alternatives" into dominant cultural formations.[46] The ramifications of this role of the fantastic among the folk and folklorists in Japanese modernity is a topic explored in the chapters that follow.

The object of Minakata's encyclopedic inquiries was certainly the nature of reality, but it was an object that he approached via its most fantastical manifestations in the complexities and contradictions of phenomena that are not either/or. In this sense he joined Kyōka in the twilight of the in-between: slime molds are between plants and animals; *koto* is between *mono* and *kokoro;* human activity happens between will and chance; culture arises between logic and illogic. For Minakata, the world is filled with fixed physical facts and floating phantasmagorias. To navigate among fact and phantasmagoria humans apply tact in addition to mere calculation not only to discover and create what become the products of human knowledge and culture but also to study in retrospect the processes of these cultural productions.

In summary, then, the connotations that emerge in Minakata's examples of tact can be grouped into two general spheres of meaning: the first refers to the role of experimentation in the process of discovery. Hunches, intuition, and a willingness to follow any leads no matter how illogical in the pursuit of a mystery come into play here. This instance of tact comes close to our dictionary definition of "a sensitive mental or aesthetic perception," which suggests a form of thought the basis of which is not restricted to formal logic.[47] The second meaning of tact revolves around the idea of knowledge gained through practical experience until it becomes an almost unconscious part of one's body. One develops a certain ingrained artistry or knack for things.[48] In this respect it bears a relationship to habit and custom and therefore becomes important in the defense of local folk practices, which Minakata explicitly directed at Inoue. At the heart of this defense was a theory of culture (*koto*) that recognized the limits of applying science to the study of humanity in all its wonder and mystery. Stressing the multivalent sources and unexpected aspects of human cultural productions, Minakata's idea of culture was directed against the centralizing power of scientific discourse, especially as science and rationality were enlisted to clear the way for the ideological construction of a modern national culture. As is readily apparent in his protest of the Shrine Merger Movement, a topic touched on in chapter 6, Minakata bemoaned more than anything else the obliteration of local cultures for the sake of national culture.

Finally, the boundary phenomena that attracted Minakata's interest found a physical embodiment in the conduct of his own everyday life as it related to mainstream academia in Meiji Japan. Living in the backwater of the Kii peninsula where he collected botanical and entomological specimens and wrote on local customs, Minakata seemed to mimic in his lifestyle the marginality that he found in his objects of study. He had despised institutionalized learning as a youngster and made concerted efforts to stay only on the outer boundaries of academic circles as an adult.

Upon returning from abroad in 1900 he maintained scholarly contacts, but remained physically removed from the center of learning that Tokyo represented. Such a self-positioning on the periphery of the Academy, it can be argued, allowed for a certain freedom, flexibility, and heterogeneity of thought that might otherwise never have sprouted in Tokyo. In an aside to Toki in a letter dated 2 March 1894, Minakata suggested as much in terms of the power and knowledge relationship between urban center and rural periphery. He writes that "not only are there libraries and museums only in Tokyo and none in the provinces; centralizing power in the center threatens things in the provinces. Seeing that this takes place even in the customs and learning that fertilizes the city and blights everything in the countryside, I greatly lament it." He continues by attributing the withering of provincial customs and schools of thought to the concentration of power in Edo during the Tokugawa period, and for this reason vows that upon his return to Japan he will live in the provinces and work as much as possible for their enrichment without "going out to big cities too much" (9:100–101). The cultures to which Minakata was dedicated evidently flourished much better in the darker corners of the countryside, away from the bright lights of the big city. Tokyo may have been a spectacle of intellectual activity for the wide variety of disciplines in which Minakata dabbled, but in it also lurked the specter of a discipline to which his heretical spirit could not submit.

PART II

DISCIPLINING DEMONS

CHAPTER 3

Modern Science and the Folk

The training of the mind under civilization has been directed toward the conquest
of fear in general, and—excepting that ethical quality of the feeling which belongs
to religion—of the supernatural in particular.

    —Lafcadio Hearn, "Vespertina Cognitio"

The formation of "disciplines," both in the sense of academic fields
of study and in the sense of methods designed to produce "subjected
and practiced bodies, 'docile' bodies,"[1] was a principal exploit during
the Meiji enlightenment. The institutionalization of scientific disciplines
after Western models in late-nineteenth-century Japan was dedicated primarily to the acquisition of utilitarian, technical know-how considered
necessary for the economic and military development of a modern state.
The knowledge gained by study in specialized disciplines was the province of an elite few, and the position of a would-be discipline such as
folk studies, conceived of by an urban intellectual elite as a knowledge
of and for the folk, is the topic of the next chapter. Converting scientific
(disciplined) knowledge into manifest wealth and power in the form of
industries, capital, commercial networks, and a large modern military required disciplines of the type that concern this chapter: the production
of a mass of "docile bodies," of a citizenry that could be easily taught,
managed, and mobilized for the good of the nation.

    As has often been noted in studies of Japan's modernization, the most
wide-ranging and highly visible state apparatus, outside military conscription, installed to achieve this end in Meiji Japan was the educational
system under the direction of the Education Ministry (Monbushō). These
same studies, however, rarely go beyond simply attributing the ideologi-

cal successes of the Meiji educational system to a repetitive inculcation or indoctrination of the masses with retooled Confucian platitudes concerning loyalty and filial piety to the emperor, as if inculcation were an uncomplicated political ploy uniformly and universally practiced. This kind of easy explanation of the ideological state apparatus that Meiji education represented never considers that the strategies and tactics of inculcation might actually vary according to the historical situation at hand.

This chapter presents one arena of ideological production, situated at the crossroads of folk knowledge and state knowledge in Meiji Japan, which, due to the fanciful nature of its content, has typically been either passed over or snickered at in polite discussions of modern Japanese intellectual history. Much of the ideological confrontation and competition between what I refer to as "folk knowledge" and "state knowledge" was waged over a supernatural terrain in late-nineteenth- and early-twentieth-century Japan. By this I mean that expressions of protest and methods of administrative control (disciplines) were often articulated through a network of signs—magical, grotesque, religious—indexed to a world beyond the visible realm of the ordinary. Of course, the idea of "the ordinary" is relative to time and place, but the very definition of what was to be considered ordinary and normal under the new time and space of Meiji Japan was a central point of contention. What might appear as meaningless meanderings into folk fancy had great stakes involved given the energy with which supernatural motifs were mobilized in popular protests and the equally energetic efforts that rulers throughout Japanese history had expended to exert control over and thereby extract authoritative power from real and imagined demonic enemies.

To wit: In 1860 *bakufu* officials posted a sign at Nikkō outside the mausolea of Tokugawa Ieyasu in preparation for a visit by one of his descendants, the fourteenth Tokugawa shōgun, Iemochi. The sign read: "To the *Tengu* and the other demons: Whereas our shōgun intends to visit the Nikkō mausolea next April, now therefore ye *Tengu* and other demons inhabiting these mountains must remove elsewhere until the shōgun's visit is concluded."[2] In contrast to this order that gives recognition to at least the hypothetical existence of *tengu* and other demons if only to display shōgunal power over them (shōgunal power at this time having actually hit an all-time low), another notice concerning *tengu* and other supernatural beings appeared a half-century later in an elementary school ethics textbook published under the auspices of the Education Ministry of the Meiji government. Among a list of items that the Ministry would like to see educators teach their students is the unambiguous declaration: "There is no such thing as *tengu*."[3]

What had happened from the end of the Tokugawa period to the end of Meiji to affect relationships of power as they are inscribed in these two statements? In the first statement, the power of the shōgun is represented in the mastery over "*tengu* and other demons," in the ability to utter the imperative "Get ye hence!" That no *tengu* appeared at Nikkō during the shōgun's visit to the memorial of the origin of Tokugawa rule is proof of the ruler's power, at least in the eyes of those who believe in and fear *tengu*. This articulation would seem to follow Komatsu's theory of power and authority being asserted by a symbolic display of control over "the other world" and "the darkside of the country," mentioned in chapter 1. But what does it mean, then, when the voice of official reason in Japan declares fifty years later that *tengu* do not exist? Have the supernatural and the power attached to its control vanished? I don't think so. Yet, the basis of power and its field of articulation have clearly changed. To foster a modern citizenry dedicated to a national body, the symbolic mastery over age-old demons—an art that too many nonofficial exorcists and political upstarts could claim local knowledge of—would not be sufficient. It is no surprise that the reign name Meiji, usually rendered in English as "Enlightened Rule," can also be read as "Enlightened Cure," suggesting not only a confrontation with a metaphoric illness in the national body, but also a competition with unenlightened cures— that is, folk cures and the beliefs that supported them. New demons, new knowledge, and new state-controlled institutions to effect the "enlightened cure" had to be formed. It is this reformation of relations of power and knowledge between the rulers and the ruled as played out in the arena of the supernatural that I consider in this chapter, with an examination of two important institutional sites in this period of flux called Meiji Japan: education and medicine.

Education and Monsters

The 1879 and 1880 revisions to the Education Act of 1872 introduced *shūshin* (ethics) into the Japanese school curriculum, marking an official turn away from the earlier ideals of liberal education epitomized in Fukuzawa Yūkichi's *Gakumon no susume* (An encouragement of learning, 1872–76) and toward an emphasis on the indoctrination of a Confucian-derived loyalty to the Emperor Meiji as embodiment of the Japanese polity. In the years that followed, *shūshin* became the top priority in Teachers' Schools in accordance with an imperial proclamation that stressed the secondary status to which the individual pursuit of knowledge and practical skills must be relegated in the education of commoners. Concurrently, Motoda Eifu (1818–1891), one of the emperor's tutors and one of the codrafters of the 1890 Imperial Rescript on Education, compiled the first morals textbooks that these newly trained teachers were to use. A state system of school textbook certification was adopted in 1883 and stricter guidelines were added to it in 1886 by Mori Arinori (1847–1889), who had been appointed the minister of education in the previous year. Finally, by 1903, the Education Ministry took full and direct control over the compilation and publication of school textbooks, and in the following year their use became mandatory for all public schools. After the recitation of the Imperial Rescript on Education, the lessons on *shūshin* showcased in these textbooks were the first topic of the day in all elementary school classrooms in late Meiji Japan.[4]

The trajectory from the Education Act to the Education Ministry's seizure of the school textbook industry was not in fact as smooth as my lightning summary of it would suggest. The relations among the Education Ministry, other organs of government, political parties, and private textbook publishers in the development of government textbook policy during the Meiji period was complicated and antagonistic, fraught with infighting, bribery, and corruption. Textbook publication arose as a new industry with few or no guidelines in early Meiji Japan. By the 1880s the high profitability of textbooks was recognized and many publishers competed for unregulated prefectural markets. And with this new source of wealth came new sources of vice. Larger publishers, seeking monopolies over the textbook industry, cut illegal deals with local educational authorities to secure the exclusive use of the textbooks put out by their companies. Little regard was paid to the contents and quality of the texts themselves. To curb these abuses and to stem prefectural school power in the adoption of textbooks, Education Minister Mori sought the installation of a prefectural textbook screening system that would better centralize and standardize the national education system.[5]

Textbook companies were outraged and proceeded to lobby and bribe members of the prefectural screening committees (which eventually led to the infamous "textbook scandal" of 1903 that saw many committee members brought to trial and convicted on charges of corruption). While abuse in the system steadily worsened, the government took the heat from opposition party members who openly accused the Education Ministry of graft and gross mismanagement. On 6 December 1892, during the fourth session of the Lower House and in the wake of numerous textbook scandals that had been reported in newspapers, Representative Kiyomizu Monjirō questioned the motives behind a recent government directive that suddenly called for the temporary suspension of use of ethics textbooks. Kiyomizu implied that the suspension involved more illegal dealings between the Education Ministry and textbook companies. Education Minister Kawano denied the accusation, saying that the reason for the directive was to review and select the best texts for future use. Nothing was resolved, but the question of textbook policy and Ministry corruption appeared again in the Lower House during the spring 1894 session. It became clear that by the mid-1890s the publication of textbooks, which had begun as a private entrepreneurial venture, had turned into a major issue of public political importance.[6]

The prominence of the textbook issue in national affairs is borne out by the discussions that took place throughout the late 1890s in the Upper House, the organ of government responsible for deciding the national budget. On 4 February 1896 a proposal was introduced in the Upper House for the compilation of elementary school ethics textbooks with national funds. The sponsor of the proposal, Umayahara Kage, reasoned that because moral education is vital to the welfare of the nation, the textbooks that teach it should be put into the hands of the state. This rationale opened a new dimension in Meiji textbook policy.[7] In the arguments that followed, the range of the proposed state purview over textbooks was widened to include not only ethics textbooks, but all books used in public schools.

Following the budget proposals in the Upper House, the Lower House began to consider plans for a revised national textbook system under the

auspices of the Education Ministry. As in the initial Upper House proposal, appeals centered on the necessity of ethics textbooks funded and
prepared by the central government. "A Motion Concerning Elementary School Ethics Textbooks" that was introduced to the Lower House
by Andō Kametarō and three others on 2 March 1899 called for the
establishment of the means for preparing and distributing national ethics
textbooks that "by cultivating the morality of school children throughout the country under a common principle and by developing the spirit
of loyalty and patriotism would promote the civilization of the nation
and achieve wealth and power."[8] Arguments concerning the need for a
publicly funded and centrally administered ethics textbook ensued, and
on March 6 the motion was adopted without objection. One of the first
means established to enact this new educational policy was the Education Ministry's appointment in April 1900 of an Ethics Textbook Survey Committee (Shūshin Kyōkasho Chōsa I-inkai) whose charge it was
to examine and select appropriate materials for morals instruction. The
committee met a total of 123 times from its inception until the first
edition of *Kokutei shūshin kyōkasho* [National ethics textbook] was published in 1903.[9] It was headed by the former imperial advisor and later
Tokyo University chancellor Katō Hiroyuki (1836–1916) and had among
its members conservative educator and ideologue Inoue Tetsujirō (1856–
1944). The Education Ministry also called on another prominent figure
in late Meiji Japan to join this committee: Inoue Enryō.[10]

Inoue's research into folk beliefs was clearly articulated within the
Meiji discourse on state-sponsored education, so it is really no surprise
that he was appointed to the Ethics Textbook Survey Committee. In the
introduction to his 1916 publication *Meishin to shūkyō* [Superstition and
religion], Inoue enumerates all eight points in the Education Ministry's
directive against superstitions and implies that his earlier investigations
into folk beliefs during the 1880s and 1890s had already been executing
this educational policy even before it had become officially stated. The
first three editions of *Kokutei shūshin kyōkasho*, published from 1903 to
1910, all had sections specifically dedicated to the dangers of believing in
superstitions. Superstitions being Inoue's area of expertise, it is probable
that he had a hand in editing these sections. Having gone on extensive
survey and lecture tours all over Japan, collecting and explaining material
concerning supernatural phenomena, Inoue had gained the reputation

of being the foremost Japanese authority on monsters and soon became known as *obake hakase:* "professor of monsters." In fact, it is likely that it was his notoriety that had brought the question of superstitions to the Education Ministry's serious attention. At a lecture he gave in 1897 at the Tetsugakukan, Inoue mentions that not only had he been honored with "unmerited praise" for his work from the Education Minister but also that he was "deeply touched" by a recent invitation he had received from the minister of the Imperial Household for an audience before the Meiji Emperor himself.[11] Whereas the emperors of old might call upon an exorcist to control demons, the modern emperor in this instance summoned a different kind of specialist in the supernatural, one who had a different set of rituals by which to discipline threatening beings. By what incantations did this modern-day exorcist effect his magic? How would it come to be that by the turning of the twentieth century the rulers of Japan could emphatically declare, via a nationalized moral instruction, "There is no such thing as *tengu*"?

Both Yanagita Kunio and Inoue singled out *tengu,* a goblin greatly popular in Japanese folk belief, as a uniquely indigenous creation within the Japanese menagerie of monsters, most of which actually had continental roots. As far as their appearance is concerned, *tengu* too can be shown to have Chinese and Indian ancestors, but for Yanagita and Inoue the unique character of *tengu* in Japan predated and far exceeded in importance any superficial resemblance they may have shared with foreign counterparts. This point will become crucial for Yanagita, who in his earliest investigations of the folk will key on *tengu* stories as a rich source for the study of folk mentality and feeling. Yanagita will come to write several essays concerning *tengu,* which is the focus of discussion in the next chapter, and Inoue dedicated an entire book to the study of *tengu.* First published in 1903, the same year that the Education Ministry took direct control over the publication of school textbooks, *Tenguron* (figure 3) was an expanded version of Inoue's lectures on *tengu* in the early 1890s. All of his lectures on folk beliefs were published together in a six-volume set under the title *Yōkaigaku kōgi* in 1896. His lectures on *tengu* appeared in volumes 2 and 4, in sections dedicated respectively to explanations of supernatural phenomena according to the physical sciences (*rigaku*) and explanations according to psychology (*shinrigaku*).

This division of the world into the material and the mental is, as was seen in the preceding chapter, the first and most basic within Inoue's approach to all items of folklore. Although he initially recognized this division for practical purposes, Inoue, under a heavy dose of Buddhist Kantianism, was quick to point out that ultimately all phenomena are mental because it is only through subjective apperception that the world is experienced. As a science of mental phenomena, then, psychology was for Inoue the proper discipline with which to approach monsters. His leaning toward the preeminence of psychology as an explanatory mode was clear as he defined monsterology as "the practical application of psychology" to explain "errant and abnormal forms." Not only was Inoue's brand of folklore the complementary dark side of philosophy, it was also abnormal psychology.

It was this psychological component that distinguished Inoue's research on *tengu* from that of previous scholars, at least according to Inoue himself. Inoue spends the first half of *Tenguron* reviewing all available previous studies of *tengu*, most notably those of the early-nineteenth-century writer Takizawa Bakin (1767–1848) and nativist scholar Hirata Atsutane (1776–1843). In an 1811 article on *tengu*, for example, Bakin divided past explanations of *tengu* into five categories: shooting stars, flying demons, a type of animal, a mountain spirit, and a vengeful spirit of a wrongly executed person. Bakin himself emphasized the popular association of *tengu* with occult Buddhist mountain asceticism (*shugendō*) and suggested that *tengu* were evil Buddhist priests who, out of personal desire for knowledge and supernatural power, followed "the Way of the *Tengu*," or *tengudō*.

Hirata's conclusions about *tengu* on the whole concurred with those of Bakin. Perhaps out of his personal hatred of Buddhism, Hirata too stated that among the transformed entities that are called *tengu*, many are the spirits of evil priests and mountain ascetics. Both Bakin's and Hirata's explanations provided a kind of folk etymology to the idiomatic expression *tengu ni naru*, or "to become a *tengu*," which designates a braggart or boastful person, not unlike the greedy priest hungry for occult powers. On the other hand, what they did not provide in their explanations, according to Inoue, was the mental dimension of *tengu*. Approaching the problem of *tengu* only from the point of view of an outer physical phenomenon, even when considering them as spirits, all past scholars missed the psychology of *tengu*.

Inoue is harsh in his criticism of academics, saying that he "will ex-

Figure 3 The original cover of *Tenguron* (Source: *Tenguron*, 1916 edition in *Yōkai sōsho*, vol. 3)

plain what *tengu* really are since no educated person would believe the previous explanations offered by other scholars and writers." [12] After admitting that some cases of *tengu* are the result of intentional trickery by swindlers and fraudulent priests or else simple errors in perception (e.g., seeing a large man in the mountains and imagining him to be a *tengu*), Inoue places the cases that are left into the category of "actual mysteries" (*jitsukai*). This does not mean, however, that they are "true mysteries" (*shinkai*) that will forever be beyond human intellect—that is the realm of religious experience. Rather, they are "ephemeral mysteries" (*kakai*). That is to say, these *tengu* only seem inexplicably mysterious (*fushigi*) until the proper application of investigative reasoning and scientific method reveal them to fall within the realm of human understanding. What is inexplicable within today's knowledge of things, Inoue adds, might become explicable in the future as human knowledge advances. In the case of *tengu*, however, they all become explicable if one considers both the outer material conditions and the inner mental conditions that give rise to them.

Inoue treats the material conditions behind *tengu* stories in a very matter-of-fact way. *Tengu* are said to live in mountains. The climate and geographical conditions of the mountains are different from those of the plains, where most ("normal") Japanese people live. Many species of plants and animals in the mountains are also different. Therefore, this general state of unfamiliar sights and sounds, along with a glimpse of a monkey, or the shadow of a cloud, or a hermit, or Ainu aborigine naturally causes a sense of fear and apprehension in people who do venture into the mountains. At this point, Inoue argues, the explanation of *tengu* must turn to the subjective mental conditions of the individual. Besides fear of the unfamiliar, hearing *tengu* stories and seeing *tengu* pictures from childhood leave a deep impression on one's psyche and heighten one's expectations to the point where one's imagination can produce illusions based on the unfamiliar sights and sounds of the mountains or even generate visual and auditory hallucinations based on no physical presence at all. [13]

In the same way that he subsumes physical reality under the subjectivity of the individual, Inoue, after setting up the material conditions that might induce the appearance of *tengu*, focuses on the "abnormal state of mind" of the individual who claims to have seen a *tengu*. Abnormal psychology, he proudly announces, is the surest way to explain *tengu* stories. So-called *tengu*-possession, the term used to refer to the state of those who, after being lost in the mountains for days, return transformed in some way, also displays the same symptoms of "temporary insanity" that fox-possession and divine raptures do.[14] Finally, the acquisition of skills (writing, military arts, etc.) usually associated with *tengu*-possession are, Inoue stresses, due to the workings of the mind, not *tengu*. This way of explaining *tengu* follows the general interiorization of the supernatural analyzed in chapter 2. This interiorization of *tengu* was one major condition of possibility for an effective declaration that *tengu* do not exist (in "reality"): they are only in your head.

Inoue was only one participant in the Meiji discourse on education concerned with putting certain things inside the heads of the unenlightened masses. Although ostensibly sharing a common goal of advancing knowledge with education, Inoue chided his fellow educators and scholars for not dirtying their hands in the study of such base topics as folk beliefs: "Scholars nowadays," he said in an address to his students in 1897, "caught in the habit of looking high and ignoring the low, of throwing out what is near and grasping for what is far, think that they disgrace a scholar's dignity by engaging their attention on base things such as monsters and superstitions, although such things are actually of great interest."[15] Viewing superstitions as fundamental "disabilities in knowledge and will" needing to be "treated as a disease to be cured by the twin methods of education and religion," Inoue blamed both the educators and men of religion of his time for not getting at the root of the folk beliefs that presented an obstacle to the goals of both education and religion. "Not only is this situation unfortunate for the state [*kokka*]," he bemoaned, "but also for pedagogy" (15).

Inoue claimed that his monsterology was a discipline that did attack obstinate folk beliefs at their roots and that this eradication of superstition (*meishin-taiji*) was instrumental for the constitution of a healthy, modern Japanese state. Continuing with a remarkable string of medical metaphors, Inoue likens ivory tower academics to practitioners of internal medicine (*naika*) whose diagnoses and treatments of illnesses inside the body—without actually opening up the body—might gradually produce results but in a roundabout way. In contrast, monsterology is like a surgery (*geka*) that provides a prompt and direct treatment of the problem even if it means bloodying one's hands. Identifying the popular belief in fate or "the Will of Heaven" (i.e., a disability or lack of will in the human individual) as "the bacteria of superstitions" and "the biggest demon in the universe and the most difficult to exorcise," Inoue enlists monsterology as "the disinfectant to kill the bacteria of superstitions" and fashions himself as "the druggist who sells this medicine" (16). He even goes so far as to mimic the advertisements for medicines popular during the Meiji period, offering his own pledge that, "To cure fevers, 'Kiniiko' medicine is nonpareil; To cure superstitions, 'monsterology' is nonpareil" (17). The "professor of monsters" is the physician who cures the sick national body.

In an emphatic justification for the practice of monsterology, Inoue went to great lengths to demonstrate the relevance of his project to "the health of the nation." In a three-part series of articles entitled "Kokkagaku to yōkaigaku to no kankei" (The relation between nation studies and monsterology) appearing from August 1894 to February 1895 in *Kokkagakkai zasshi* (Journal of the Nation Studies Association), a publication he cofounded, Inoue explicitly outlined the value of his discipline for the development of the nation. The first essay of this series summarizes the general outlay of the definitions and categories that make up monsterology, offering little that has not already been covered in chapter 2. It does, however, introduce a shift of emphasis that will allow Inoue to link the scientific study of superstitions with the strengthening of the nation-state. Rather than focusing on *kakai* (ephemeral mysteries), which exist in nature and are the usual objects of study for monsterology, Inoue highlights another of his divisions of *yōkai*: *gikai* (artificial or man-made mysteries). The reason for this emphasis on man-made mysteries is that this type of monster designates superstitions that are purposefully conjured by humans in social and political affairs in order to play upon people's feelings, (lack of) will, or ignorance. The goal of man-made mysteries is to deceive others for one's own selfish advantage: monetary, political, or otherwise. "By studying man-made mysteries," Inoue announces, "one can know the ingenious and wonderful effects of society and human feelings."[16] Because it is this type of monster that is directly related to a science of the state (*kokkagaku*), he continues, the study of it produces a beneficial "reference for disciplines that concern the political state [*seiji kokka ni kansuru gakumon no sankō*]" (600).

Inoue begins the second installment of his essay specifying the social nature of man-made mysteries. Although admitting that they can manifest themselves on either a social or individual level, they, like all monsters, ultimately arise from the individual into a social form.[17] Inoue insists on this relationship between the social and the individual so that he may claim a social utility for monsterology while at the same time maintaining psychology (necessarily of the individual mind) as the explanatory science supporting monsterology. In other words, the health of the nation-state, as he would explain elsewhere, begins with the mental health of the individuals that compose it.[18] But the standard of individual, normal health is always defined by and for the state. In this context, Inoue asserts that most social, man-made monsters are political or military tricks, schemes, and strategies: in normal, peaceful times they appear as a political strategy; in abnormal times of war they appear as a military strategy. Even within the "deviant path in human affairs" that war represents, Inoue adds, there are proper and deviant strategies or ways of conduct. The latter might secure minor, temporary victories, but will ultimately lose to "the proper way." As an example of a deviant (and morally reprehensible) path of conduct in warfare Inoue offers, not surprisingly, the "methods of deception found in Confucian military tactics" used by the Chinese against whom Japan was currently fighting a war.[19] An examination of the political aspect of *gikai*—that is, their use in times of peace—is reserved for the third part of his essay. The rest of part 2 deals with the military use of man-made *yōkai*.

Inoue concentrates on what he calls "the three major intangibles" of war: intellect (*chiryoku*), emotion (*kanjō*), and will (*ishi*). These three components are what respectively form strategy (*gunryaku*), unity (*danketsu*), and preparedness for death (*kesshi*). While preparedness for death relates to the spirit (*seishin*) of the individual and unity relates to the spirit of the group, strategy is what organizes and deploys individuals as groups (820–21). In this respect it is the province of the state. A state deploys strategy toward its allies to gather up morale, unity, and spirit and contrariwise toward its enemies to disperse morale, unity, and spirit. It is therefore the most important of these intangible elements, and its connection to monsterology, Inoue asserts, is crucial: "When it comes to strategy as a whole, one must mention the relation between war and monsterology" (824). In particular, monsterology is valuable in understanding the operation of "deviant strategies" (*henryaku*), those that rely on the deviancies (i.e., superstitions) that plague the minds of commoners. In effect, Inoue is talking about the dynamics of war propaganda.

The same operations are at work, continues Inoue in part 3 of this essay, in the form of politically expedient ruses employed domestically and internationally during times of peace, but there is no discipline that studies their dynamics: "In the West, there is one branch of science called 'political science' [*seijigaku*], but I've yet to hear of a discipline that scientifically investigates so-called political expediencies [*seijijō no kendō*]." In China, he states, such a science deals only with the methods and circumstances of political expedients from an outward and objective point of view. Monsterology, on the other hand, attempts to get at the "subjective, inner causes" behind the successful deployment of such ruses among the people in whose *kokoro* (heart, mind) the susceptibility to conniving political persuasion flourishes. As Inoue might have put it, it is as if the immune system of the individual against the infection of political quacks is weakened by the bacteria of superstitions. Again, this formulation of the problem turns the solution over to "the principles of psychology."[20] Likewise, because expediency has already been defined as a deviant strategy,[21] only a science of deviant forms (*henshikigaku*) such as monsterology ("the practical application of the principles of psychology") can properly investigate it.

In promoting a scientific study of popular beliefs and superstitions that reveals and then eradicates the sources of vulnerability that the folk possess toward corrupt political manipulation, Inoue is, in a crude fashion, skirting the boundaries of a critique of ideology. But it is a critique that is completely one-sided and blind to its own ideological operations. In no way does he see the program of "civilization and enlightenment" and the government policies that went with it as possibly falling under the designation *henryaku*. They are given a priori as *seiryaku* (right/proper/moral strategies). Similarly, monsterology, positioned beneficently above the general populace and armed with right reason, is immune to charges of ideological manipulation, for its goal is merely to educate the masses, "to get rid of man-made mystifications [*gikai*], to wipe out ephemeral mysteries [*kakai*], and open up [the path to] True Mysteries [*shinkai*]."[22]

The closest Inoue comes to spelling out in practical terms what this path to *shinkai* is and why it is so important occurs toward the end of his preface to *Yōkaigaku*. Monsterology, he claims, is an application of his personal guiding principle "Defend the Nation, Love the Truth" (*gokoku-airi*): "Researching the principles of *yōkai* and expelling false mysteries is based on the spirit of loving the truth. By applying this in actuality one heals the errors of the masses. Standardizing reforms in public education is based on the spirit of defending the nation. Sure enough then, the single practice of monsterology can handily accomplish these two important goals." [23] Inoue then continues by stating that he believes in the actual existence of the Ideal (*risō*), a term he uses throughout his discourse to gloss both *shinkai* and *shin'nyo*. Considered from the viewpoint of the material world, he explains, this belief corresponds to believing in the "crystal-core of the Ideal" (*risō no kesshō-gyōkai*) that exists fundamentally in all matter. This description recalls the explanation of *shinkai* that he offers with the example of the limit of knowledge one can have of a water drop. Beyond a certain measurable point there exists, in belief, an impenetrable, crystallized core of True Mystery.

So far there is nothing too astonishing with this recasting of *shinkai* as the Ideal within all things, but, in the very next sentence, the ideological function behind this Ideal is astonishingly exposed: "Considering this [Ideal] with respect to the human world, it is believing that the Imperial nation-body [*kōshitsu-kokutai*] is also the brilliant light of the Ideal. For this reason . . . above the state [*kokka*] we see the pure spirit of the Imperial sacredness [*kōshitsu-shinsei*] and the energy of we loyal subjects mutually reflecting and glittering in the completely spiritual divine light of the national body" (1:27). Inoue's "path to True Mystery" seems nothing more than the channeling of religious truth and moral obligation, derived from the application of monsterology, into a nation-building ideology based on the myth of imperial divinity. In this articulation, the divinity of the imperial line itself appears as the true True Mystery, the ultimate unchanging Ideal in the individual subject's relation to the state Subject. In addition to its atemporality, the atopic nature of *shinkai* also fits this ideological role well; it is crystallized in the Imperial Household but exists everywhere, interpellating all persons with the call "Defend the Nation, Love the Truth, Follow Us on the Path to True Mystery." And who can resist a good mystery?

Inoue concludes his preface by announcing that in response to the loss of divinity in the national body in recent years due to "frivolity and incompetence in world affairs," he is offering monsterology as the panacea for the public spirit. Yet Inoue's folklore research aimed not so much, as he advertised it, at the surgical "eradication of superstitions" like *tengu,* but at the reinscription of folk knowledge into a form that could fall under the surveillance of state-controlled institutions. This process of transformation is where the significance of Inoue's medical metaphors lies. In fact, they are not metaphors at all, but rather are "naturalized" as direct descriptions of factual reality as defined by the state. The co-optation of folk knowledge for the regulation of Japanese bodies within a single national body (*kokutai*) involved in this instance the attachment of this folk knowledge to sites of knowledge, such as schools, that were becoming institutionalized under state control. This attachment relied first on this metaphor of nation as an organic body that has health and then on the metonymic identification of the individual body to the national body.[24] At the same time, as seen in the case of *tengu,* the source of the threatening object of fear and awe was brought from outside the body to inside the mind, thus connecting the sentiments and consciousness of the subject to the call of the state. When Inoue spoke of a lack of will in those who relied on the "Will of Heaven" he was encouraging not the development of free individual wills among the masses, but rather the formation of a collective will incorporated within the national body. The Will of the State, not the will of individuals, was the modern replacement for the Will of Heaven. In this light, Inoue's use of medical metaphors was not idiosyncratic. It was very much a part of a discourse that enfigured the relationship between the health of individual bodies and that of a national body in a narrative that displaced local folk purveyance over everyday life. Folk beliefs were thus brought into the sphere of Meiji education, and from that institutional site, Inoue's folk studies passed into another: medicine.

Medicine, Meishin, *and Madness*

The alliance of a state-operated educational system and a national medicine based on Western medicine during the Meiji period had a two-part ideological aim: first, to shift the fear of monsters among the folk to a fear of folk belief itself; and second, to transfer a blind belief in folk medicine to a blind belief in state medicine. Kawamura Kunimitsu, in his study of the fate of folk remedies in the Meiji period, emphasizes that the fear of monsters and illness residing within the dark recesses of the "folk heart," particularly that of the children who were to be molded into modern subjects, was not to be eliminated by enlightenment education and medicine; rather, this fear persisted despite natural explanations of the supernatural and became the object of edification and resystemization in an overall reorganization of folk sentiment. The practical result of this program was the divestment of local and private authority over the care of the body and the transfer of it to a public sphere administered by government authorities who then would guarantee the well-being of the individual. In other words, one couldn't care for one's own health by oneself or by the enlistment of local practitioners of folk medicine; one had to go to the Clinic.

One case of this reinvestment of folk fears—what Kawamura, playing off Flaubert's 1869 work, calls "The Sentimental Education"—revolved around the eye disease trachoma, a contagious conjunctivitis that could lead to blindness if untreated. Not formally acknowledged in Japan as a sickness until made known as such by German medicine toward the end of the nineteenth century, trachoma first appeared as a medical problem among military personnel. This is not to say that the infliction did not exist among the general populace; it most certainly did. Rather, it was first recognized by the state as a medical problem from within a state institution where the health of bodies for the defense of the nation was at a premium and then later spread as a general concern. The subsequent popularization of this newly named ailment, *torahoomu,* is attested to by the abundance of common eye medicines, such as *torahoomu mizu* (trachoma water), that soon hit the market.[25]

The stigmatization of folk remedies that had been practiced for the treatment of eye diseases took place primarily within a series the Education Ministry published in ethics textbooks under the titles "Meishin o sakeyo" (Avoid superstitions!) and "Meishin ni ochiruna" (Don't fall into superstitions!). In Kawamura's analysis, there was originally no connection between superstitions and eye disease, but the connection was established in these school texts through a moralistic tale that played on a basic fear of blindness and attached the source of blindness to the use of folk cures. In the 1910 edition of the elementary school ethics textbook, there appeared the trachoma story that Japanese educators would use, with some variations, until 1936 to delegitimate folk medicine. The plot of the story was simple, as it focused on the simple-mindedness of the superstitious and the consequences of their errant beliefs. First, to treat her ailment an old woman inflicted with trachoma uses, without success, "holy water" (*shinsui*) associated with faith healers and shamans. Next, the old woman, clearly a symbol of old-fashioned and benighted ways, is brought by her grandson to an eye doctor trained in Western medicine and is examined. However, her case is beyond hope and she is soon to go blind (in other versions, surgery, the doctor says, might save one of the eyes); finally, the story ends with the old woman's declaration of repentance for having regrettably followed the ways of faith healers and shamans. The simple moral of the story: Superstitions are poison to be avoided at all costs; they are the source of both literal and figurative blindness.[26] The use of an eye disease that was prevalent during the Meiji period thus dovetails nicely with the ideology of enlightenment articulated in this tale. Figure 4 is the scene, looking very much as it did in late Meiji, of the enlightened cure illustrated in a 1927 edition of the ethics textbooks. An important component in this process of resystematizing the fear of blindness in particular and fear of the unknown in general was the introduction of the official/scientific word for the eye disease in question. *Torahoomu,* the Japanese pronunciation for the German word for trachoma, was, like many new words introduced into the Japanese lexicon during the Meiji period, utterly alien to everyday speech and thus had no place within the indices of folk knowledge. As Kawamura describes it, "The disease-name '*torahoomu*' not only gave rise to a crack in the interpretive framework of the folk; it also produced a crack in the everyday life-world and worldview of the populace. It was a concept sufficient to bring about a dissolution and reformation."[27]

What it dissolved was the basis of practical knowledge that had previously guided everyday life. What it reformed, under the auspices of the state, was technical knowledge of the world (tantamount to a redefinition of reality) and the rules of conduct for survival in that world. When set against Western medicine, which was promoted in a system of national (public) medical treatment and as a system of truth and knowledge, folk remedies were turned into poisonous *meishin*. In the case of trachoma, "as the fear of blindness by 'superstitions' is aroused, the expectation or fantasy of recovery by Western medicine increases."[28] By this binary opposition, the feeling of fear is controlled and systemized while institutional knowledge is respected. Therefore, instead of the elimination of folk knowledge, it was this very maintenance of folk knowledge as *mei-*

もらはせましたおい
しやはしんさつをし
て「これははげしいト
ラホームです右の目
は手おくれになつて
ゐるので、なほすこと
は出來ません左の目
はまだ見こみがあり
ますから、手術をして

Figure 4 Granny at the eye doctor's (Source: *Dai-san ki kokutei Shūshin Kyōkasho: jinjō shōgaku shūshinsho*, vol. 4)

shin and "enemy" that was vital for the formation and administration (as a medicine is administered) of institutional knowledge, or of what I would call institutionalized irrationality, in the Meiji state. In other words, the foreign word *torahoomu* becomes one sign of a new demon, a new *tengu* as it were, to be symbolically quelled by the rulers of modern Japan.

Casting the cause of illness as a modern demon-enemy threatening the homeland of the body turns the body into a public battlefield in which the state, as guarantor of public security and well-being, wages war with the new weapon that Western medical technology represented. The metonymic identification of part to whole that Inoue articulated when he spoke of the health of the individual as crucial to the health of the nation was but one way the state justified entrance into the bodies of the people. The metaphor of war implicit in Western medicine (the eradication of an intruder that has invaded the body) also contributed to making public the care of the body because combating foreign invaders is a national task in postfeudal times. The private practices of local caretakers of the folk's health—faith healers, shamans, exorcists, medicine peddlers—could no longer be allowed the knowledge to cure the ailments of the individuals who relied on them because they constituted a "feudalistic" obstacle and threat to the formation of a national body. To strip them of their authority, the ailment—its look, its cause, its name—was discursively reorganized at sites of ideological deployment (the military, schools, medical clinics) so as to forge a state-sponsored monopoly over the knowledge used to combat it. In this sense, the introduction of Western medicine into Japan probably possessed as much value to the Meiji state in ideologically managing bodies as it did in medically curing them.[29]

At any rate, the threat of knowledges outside of direct state control needed to be neutralized to ensure the kind of unified national apparatus that the Meiji oligarchy desired. Turning folk belief upon itself, turning it into the object of fear for the folk, in an easily popularized binarism of ally/enemy (human/monster, enlightened present/benighted past) proved to be a relatively effective and painless strategy when not obstructed by others who could tap the sentiments of the folk in ways not necessarily in accord with state interests. What I have in mind here is not something as grandiose as oppositional political parties or even popular peoples' rights movements. Rather, I am thinking of examples of what might be called microtechniques or arts that organized the libidinal economy of the folk heart in everyday life. One of the more prevalent and persistent of such local arts that presented an obstacle to state control over the folk heart was practiced by a folk figure who ranged amorphously over and among the fields of education, medicine, and religion: the village shaman.

The majority of practicing village shamans in Meiji Japan were blind women.[30] This is not to suggest that they all had been inflicted with trachoma; they probably had not. It does, however, offer one signifier by which to link these caretakers of the local folk's physical and spiritual health to the chain of superstition that the Meiji establishment was forging. The description of the false healer whose cures had induced the blindness of the old woman in the "Tales of Superstitions" that the Education Ministry circulated was general enough to include village shamans. Such a healer and spiritual counselor, if not literally blind, was cast as intellectually and morally blind (and deaf and mute) to the truth of the Meiji civilization and enlightenment.

One way to undermine the authority of the shaman was to take away the need for her services. Another was to reinscribe her power to cure behavioral disorders as a disorder in itself needing special treatment. In his discussion of *tengu*-possession in *Tenguron,* Inoue suggested that it displayed the same symptoms of "temporary insanity" as did fox-possession and possession by *kami* (deities). Elsewhere he compared *tengu*-possession with the practices of shamans, describing the so-called deity-possession of the latter as an acute concentration of mental powers, developed in a fashion not unlike the abilities of *go* masters or fine musicians, which allowed them to feel and apperceive things that ordinary people could not.[31] Though admitting that shamans displayed highly unusual states of mind, Inoue nevertheless held back from condemning them to the mental ward. He merely rationalized their behavior as an art that resulted from a highly trained mental discipline; it was neither a divine possession nor a mental disorder.

The abnormal behavior known as fox-possession (*kohyō*), on the other hand, was in Inoue's opinion a clear example of mental illness (*seishinbyō*).[32] Typically manifesting itself in nonsensical rambling and strange activity, it was also one of the afflictions of the spirit that shamans traditionally treated. As Kawamura points out, among the common folk the term fox-possession was used to designate a condition that was inexplicable and incomprehensible. It was *fushigi*. As such, it was a problem that belonged to a supernatural discourse that only those qualified in supernatural communication could treat. Shamans and faith healers (*kitōshi*) were the ones usually called upon.[33] With the Meiji scientifization of the phenomenon, however, this supernatural discourse would be naturalized and ultimately placed in the hands of state police, as would many shamanistic religious visionaries.

As in the case of trachoma, the reinscription of fox-possession began with German medicine. The first "scientific" study of fox-possession was conducted by the German doctor Erwin O. E. Von Bealz, who had lectured on psychiatry at Tokyo Imperial University in 1879. His 1885 paper, "Theories on Fox-Possession Illness," inspired similar studies by Japanese counterparts throughout the 1890s and early 1900s. A notable trait of these new studies from the point of view of methodological approach was the abstraction of the concrete, experiential conditions of fox-possession by the use of new analytical terms with which to refer to the disorder. The term *kohyōbyo* (fox-possession illness) had been in use since early Meiji, and *aropekantoropii* (alopecanthropy, or the delusion that one has become a fox), coined on the model of lycanthropy (the delusion that one has become a wolf), was introduced by one of the first Japanese professors of psychiatry at Tokyo University in 1892. Two years later, Kuni Hidemitsu, in an outline to psychiatry, coined the generic term *hyōimōsō* (possessional delusions) from the German word *Besessenheitswahm*.[34] A shaman could deal with fox-possession, but alopecanthropy was an entirely different matter requiring entirely different treatment. In effect, the disorder actually changed in nature in the process of renaming it.

Much in the same vein as Inoue, Kuni argued that mental illness of individuals would ruin the economy and productivity of the nation, so it should be dealt with as a national concern within national institutions. With the health of the nation thus in mind, he became interested in fox-possession, and his approach to it had a particular slant toward women as (re)producers of Japanese citizens. His 1902 paper "On Fox-Possession" was first published in *Fujin eisei zasshi* [Women's hygiene journal] and then delivered as a lecture at the Women's Hygiene Association in Tokyo. In it he identified fox-possession as a type of depressive persecution complex related to hysteria. Kawamura reads Kuni's emphasis on fox-possession qua hysteria as an example of what Foucault has described in the Western context as "the hysterization of women," whose health and mental and sexual hygiene were increasingly handled by a psychiatry that surveilled and administered female minds and sexual desire.[35] Because psychiatry would be a male-dominated profession in the increasingly patriarchal legal and social order of late Meiji Japan, debunking female shamans' powers to cure fox-possession also worked to masculinize the cure of mental afflictions.

The treatment of fox-possession illness that village shamans practiced and the treatment that early Japanese psychiatry administered differed not only in theory but also in the assumptions concerning its cure. Under folk practice, fox-possession was assumed to be curable. The policies of Meiji psychiatry, on the other hand, acted as if it were not. Rather than being treated until they returned to a "normal" state, those diagnosed as afflicted by the illness were shut away in *yashikirō* or asylums, essentially privately run prisons for deviants and undesirables, to protect the health of the nation. The first official public law for the detention of people diagnosed as mental patients went into effect in 1900, making the police the custodians of the Health Bureau and mental wards.[36] With the technological aid of psychiatry, shamanistic jurisdiction over the supernatural discourse of fox-possession had been legally transferred to government police at the same time that the preparation of school textbooks admonishing superstitious beliefs was placed in the hands of government education administrators.

The scientific abstraction and generalization of fox-possession into possessional delusions also served to dissolve the distinction between patient and healer in the shamanistic context by the very fact that it did not consider the local social context of the shaman's art, which Inoue unexpectedly still took into account. To Meiji psychiatrists, shamans and their clients were mentally deranged. Yet, it is not as if shamanism ceased to exist in the countryside; communities of *miko* (shamans) thrive in the far reaches of Tōhoku to this day. Although pesky obstacles for the organization of nationalized networks of power and knowledge, village shamans were not an active threat against the Meiji government because their authority, like those of other faith healers, fortune-tellers, and folk physicians, was local and dispersed. Far more threatening was the poor peasant who, knowing the hardships and the hearts of the folk, drew upon shamanistic sources of authority to lead nationwide messianic movements that directly challenged the sovereignty of the state. Such actions made possessional delusions far too political.

For thirteen days in the middle of January 1892, at the age of 57, Deguchi Nao, the daughter of a poor carpenter in the town of Fukuchiyama, was possessed by a deity and had the following dialogue with the "invisible being" that she believed had lodged in her abdomen:

> *Invisible Being:* "I am a deity named Ushitora-no-Konjin."
> *Nao:* "I do not believe what you say; you deceive me, don't you?"
> *Invisible Being:* "I never lie, for I am a deity."
> *Nao:* "Oh! Such a great deity you are! But, aren't you a fox or badger deceiving me?"
> *Invisible Being:* "I am neither a fox nor a badger. I am a deity who wants to re-create and rebuild this Three-Thousand-World to become the world of Konjin at once, just as plum flowers open suddenly. Without me this world would not be rebuilt. . . . Though it may be a high ambition, I will endeavor to make the eternal divine world, and roll this Three-Thousand-World into one."
> *Nao:* "Is it true what you are saying?"
> *Invisible Being:* "I, a deity, could not do so if I told a lie." [37]

Within two years previous to this occurrence, Deguchi's first and third daughters experienced similar possessions after giving birth and were subsequently incarcerated in a *yashikirō*. After her own possession experience, Deguchi gained a following by performing faith cures for fellow commoners in the area. She became associated with the Konkōkyō sect, a so-called new religion of shamanistic origin that had been founded in 1859 by Kawate Bunjirō (1814–1883), a poor peasant who also had been possessed by Konjin.[38] In 1893 Deguchi herself was imprisoned in a *yashikirō* on suspicion of arson, possibly while possessed. During her imprisonment she spoke with the deity in her stomach, attempted suicide, and although illiterate scratched words on a pillar in her cell. She was finally released on the fortieth day after being arrested, precisely as the deity in her stomach had foretold.[39] Her attempts in 1896 to form a new sect separate from Konkōkyō met with repression from government police as well as Konkōkyō itself.

It was for the likes of Deguchi Nao that the words *mōsō* (delusion) and *kohyōbyō* (fox-possession illness) became stigma. In general, these and other words were applied to those who transcended ordinary life and imagined other worlds. For the believers in the other worlds that such religious visionaries hallucinated, the hallucinations were reality and therefore necessarily set another "empire" against that of the emperor. Many such other worlds were established with shamanism at their base before the Meiji empire was formed, but it was those imagined after the 1868 Meiji Restoration that suffered the most government suppression.[40] Basically accepting Kawamura's analysis, I would also point out the analogy with the problem that Christian mysticism posed for the Roman Catholic Church. The Church had always felt uneasy about mystics who claimed direct communication with God, for it bypassed the institutional control of the Church and therefore could be construed as superseding the Church's authority. If they could not be co-opted as saints or executed as heretics or witches, mystics at least had to be neutralized and placed on a powerless periphery of political affairs. Visionaries, it seems, could be a very dangerous bunch if they could mobilize enough souls.

Deguchi Nao's attempt to establish a messianic sect for the realization of the world of Konjin, the god who, according to Nao's transcription, wanted "to recreate and rebuild this Three-Thousand-World," could be seen as both stepping outside the bounds of government-approved sects such as Konkōkyō and as stepping too far inside the bounds of politics. As is clear in her criticism of the contemporary Japanese lifestyles, politics, and culture and in her warnings of the foreign threat to the creation of "the Land of Gods" (*Kamiguni*), Nao was not a mountain guru unconnected with the modern Meiji world. The political critique that her vision presented was so much connected with the Meiji world that it had to be forcibly disconnected by branding her extraordinary experience not as the deity-possession she had come to believe it was but as the fox-possession—that is, madness—that she initially feared it might be. Anyone who criticized the policies of the state had to be crazy.

The job of organizing Ōmotokyō, the new religion that she would be considered the founder of, was left to her son-in-law and fellow visionary, Ueda Kisaburō, who later changed his name to Deguchi Onisaburō. Although Onisaburō got much farther in establishing Ōmotokyō and a formidable following, attracting several intellectuals as well as a traditional peasant base in the early years of Taishō, he ultimately met with even harsher repression. He had gone beyond even Nao's claims of divine possession and proclaimed that he was the incarnation of Miroku, the future Buddha of human salvation who had often been the rallying point for agrarian revolts in the past.[41] Government police attacked his messianic movement in 1921. Fourteen years later, all Ōmotokyō buildings were destroyed and the religion persecuted under the pretext of disruption of the public peace and crimes against the sovereignty of the state. Onisaburō too had stepped beyond the bounds of religion.

The enlightenment of the benighted folk was certainly not designed to produce knowledgeable, free-thinking, willful individuals in Meiji Japan. Rather, it strove to rationalize individual bodies into a national body that functioned as an organic unit (i.e., a modern wage-labor system) under the direction of a state will. It was characterized by the establishment of new disciplines, of new routines of knowledge that rerouted the affects of the folk—their libidinal investments—to apparatuses of state power. Public education and medicine (physical and psychiatric) were key formations in this realignment of sentiment because they could directly work on the minds and bodies of the masses, offering new and improved cures against what was most feared in daily life, whether it be a mischievous goblin, spirit possession, or a dreaded physical affliction such as blindness. But there was a price for these enlightened cures: nothing less than renouncing the "evils" of the ways of life conducted under regimes of local folk knowledge. It was as ways of life needing changing that popular beliefs and practices were stigmatized as immoral, "errant ways" (*meishin*) under a modern regime that sought to organize national resources, natural and human, into fixed rationalized modes of production for capitalist modernity. Superstitions as such, themselves a creation of an enlightenment discourse, guided ways of life that were seen as unproductive for the national accumulation of wealth and power.

A survey of *yashikirō* conducted between 1910 and 1916 revealed that "Goes into the mountains" (*Yamanaka ni hairu*) was one of the reasons given for incarceration in an asylum.[42] Mountains had long denoted sites of wonder and fantasy that could produce magical effects on those who passed through them, but now such activity was redefined as a mark of madness. Why? Perhaps because leaving one's domicile, the legally fixed residence of docile bodies, literally unfixed bodies from a bureaucratic grid of management and taxation. In extreme instances, occult ascetic practices as exemplified by Kōno Yukimichi's 1887 fast-induced death (or "corporeal dissolution" into the invisible other world of spirits, as his disciples called it) literally wasted bodies away.[43] The ascetic might gain immortality, but too much corporeal dissolution among the labor force could only hurt the state. As Kristin Ross has observed of the prohibitions against vagabondage in nineteenth-century France, moralizing against "unproductive" ways of life was aimed at stemming "forces that perturb bourgeois society's reasoned march of progress. For that progress is disrupted by two phenomena: it can be slowed down by the superstitious and the lazy, and it can be thrown off-track by the impatient, violent rush of insurrection."[44] The same rationale can be discerned in the policies of the Meiji government toward folk beliefs, policies best exemplified by Inoue's monsterology that promoted national Spirit to the detriment of local spirits.

The folk practices, many of them enfigured around the supernatural, that had autonomously maintained the integrity of "local bodies" (*kyō-dotai*) when they were healthy and cured them when they were ill, were rewritten by modern education and medicine as the source of evil itself. The "ignorant folk" were subsequently made doubly ignorant: not only was the knowledge by which they conducted all aspects of their lives wrong, the new, "correct" knowledge was far too specialized for them to possess directly and comprehensively. In this very important sense, public education for the benighted masses effectively kept the masses in the dark, in fear not of *bakemono* but of their own belief in *bakemono;* in awe not of the power of the ancient gods but of the powers of modern science. Monsters could do without civilization, but civilization could not do without monsters.

Only those trained in specialized disciplines at state-sanctioned institutions were licensed to practice the new arcana called modern science, and then only for the health of the nation, not of individuals as such. An initiate to this new knowledge was thus a de facto servant of the state. Consequently, the bulk of the intellectual elite who passed through the normal channels of higher learning, themselves disciplined within disciplines, could develop little critical perspective on the form Japanese modernity was taking. On the other hand, some intellectuals deviated in varying degrees from the path of mainstream scholarship when it came to questions of Japanese folk life. They sought alternative ways of thinking about the folk and the fantastic in Japanese modernity. Minakata Kuma-gusu's unorthodox theories of *fushigi* opened some possibilities for a consideration of local cultures; Yanagita Kunio's investigations of folk belief in the supernatural, the topic of the following chapter, opened others.

CHAPTER 4

Modern "Science" of the Folk

When I finished reading this book [The Tales of Tōno] I had a kind of marvelous feeling. Indeed, just as I had said before, although I had begun reading in the spirit of listening to fairy tales, when I was through reading it the life of a certain village in the mountain depths was still lingering in my head. At the moment I realized this, I recalled again the words Mr. Yanagita had said: "They [the tales of Tōno] are valid firsthand materials for the subject matter that I'm researching."

—Mizuno Yōshū, "*Tōno monogatari* o yomite" (Reading *The Tales of Tōno*)

Thus far, this exploration of the figure of *fushigi* in a modernizing Japan has been concerned with locating the points where the question of the supernatural, invariably in concert with folk beliefs and knowledge, bubbled to the surface of intellectual discourse in late Meiji Japan. The networks and trajectories of these points have been sketched out to some degree, especially in the case of Inoue Enryō's affiliation with ideological state apparatuses. Minakata Kumagusu's entry into the discursive field of *fushigi*—and this is both its strength and its weakness—came unattached to such circuits of institutionalized power, as he maintained a critical eccentricity on the periphery of institutionalized disciplines. This positioning undoubtedly afforded him a certain freedom of thought, but at the same time made it difficult to realize his vision into a widespread practice. Nevertheless, his disapproval of Inoue's treatment of folklore in particular and his calling into question scientific orthodoxy in general opened a valuable break in thinking about the place of the folk and the fantastic in the constitution of Japan's prewar modernity. With his concept of *koto* and its *fushigi*, Minakata also offered an outline to a theoretical approach to the study of human cultural phenomena. Although his most profound theorizing relevant to the study of folk beliefs remained in private correspondence, it did not preclude his participation in the formation of folk studies in Japan, especially as one of his most frequent correspondents in late Meiji and early Taishō was the now popularly recognized "founder" of the modern "science" of the Japanese folk: Yanagita Kunio.[1] Setting aside for the time being the contents of Minakata's collaboration with and subsequent critique of Yanagita's early attempts at researching rural Japanese commoners, I open this chapter by looking at an intersection of texts and bodies that described the space from which the incipient discipline of Japanese folk studies (*minzokugaku*) was written.

Discussions of the founding of folk studies invariably turn on a trio of texts that Yanagita produced around 1909–1910: *Nochi no karikotoba no ki* (a record of hunting terms and practices gathered from the mountain areas of Kyūshū, 1909), *Ishigami mondō* (a compilation of correspondences dated from August 1909 to April 1910 concerning the origin and meaning of roadside stone deities), and *Tōno monogatari* (the tales from the village of Tōno told by Tōno native Sasaki Kizen, alias Kyōseki, and recorded by Yanagita from February 1909, published in 1910). The last of these has far and away captured the most attention among the genealogists of Japanese folk studies and is relatively well-known among the general populace of Japan. No doubt this phenomenon is due as much to the tourist industry and present-day Tōno's self-promotion as *minwa no furusato* (the native home of folktales) as it is to the text's grotesque and uncanny literary charm. The strange inversion of text and topos brought about by *Tōno monogatari*'s commercialization (Tōno and the surrounding area have been remapped, and to a significant degree the town's central space has been reorganized according to Yanagita's text and his travels through the area) can be lamented as being a vulgar commodification or lauded as being a significant civic accomplishment in scholarship and historical preservation.[2] Whatever one's opinion of this might be, certainly one positive aspect of Tōno's capitalization on Yanagita's text, as far as I see it, is the lionization of the local boy, Sasaki Kizen (1886–1933), as the true author of *Tōno monogatari*.

The reason I consider the lionization of Sasaki in Tōno a positive by-product of the town's opportunistic regeneration is not out of a concern for the settling of authorial claims (the tales represent, after all, a multivocal production gathered from many individuals and mouthed through Sasaki, whose role in this narration is more like that of a spiritual medium). Rather, it is simply because it has stimulated research into Sasaki's sentence, so to speak, within the discursive universe of Japanese folk studies. Against the sheer weight, figurative and literal, of Yanagita's writings and the commentaries they have provoked, Sasaki's utterance indeed amounts to little more than a sentence.[3] But it is an interesting sentence that opens a byway through some of the intertextual underbrush that grew around a newly blossoming "science" of the folk.

"Kyōseki is not good at storytelling but he is a reliable person . . ."

This characterization of Sasaki by Yanagita in the preface to *Tōno monogatari* inscribes one of the conditions of possibility for the writing of folk studies: a reliable, firsthand informant who provides raw material but does not know how to present it well (and the success of Yanagita's mode of folk studies, as I later detail, depends heavily on presentation). In this statement, Yanagita is implying that he, on the contrary, is a good storyteller; indeed, many have admired the simple literary elegance of his retelling of the tales heard from Sasaki. But there is more going on here than an innocent storytelling contest between the city mouse and the country mouse. Relations of knowledge and power that became crucial for creating a disciplinary practice out of the collection of expressions of rural folk life are already emerging. At this early date (1909–1910) it appeared as an aesthetic statement: The native informant Sasaki (despite his past five years of education in Tokyo, his association with literary circles, and his publication of several short stories) cannot tell a good story; I, Yanagita, can. However, the art of telling stories later revealed itself in Yanagita's project as the art of reading—that is, interpreting—stories. And the art of interpretation in this case implied a will to knowledge and entailed sources of authority, legitimization, and validation within Yanagita's intellectual community. Sasaki's "reliability" (*seijitsu,* which Ronald Morse translates as "honest and sincere"), had little to do with telling the truth, for even lies reliably conveyed provide, Yanagita recognized, grist for the hermeneutical mill.[4] It is a reliability akin to that of a mail pony, strong but dumb, delivering messages intact from person to person over vast distances.

Before delving into the theoretical foundations of folk studies' message, I would like to reflect on the figure, textual and corporeal, of Sasaki Kizen and his role as relay in a circuit of relations that sparked the first glimmers of Yanagita's project in the first decades of the twentieth century. My aim in doing this is not so much to tell Sasaki's life story and to give him his due as to make allegorical use of the coincidence of discursive paths that crossed his body, or that his body crossed. It is Sasaki as embodied intertext in the story of the formation of folk studies that concerns me here. For my purposes he serves in this chapter as an entrance into and an emblem of the cross-relations that made up the field of *fushigi* that informed folk studies at the turn of the twentieth century. Or perhaps he can be envisaged as a floating signifier that passed among various signifying systems that had the folk as their signified. His passage from Tōno to Tokyo and back to Tōno literally and figuratively ties together along the way many of the threads involved in the text of folk studies as Yanagita would come to fashion it: folk feeling and mentality as an object of study, the problem of the fantastic, imaginative literature, disciplined science, a critique of naturalist literature, and a response to Inoue Enryō's monsterology.

Born and raised among "superstitious ignorant folk" of rural Japan, Sasaki is a concrete example of the target Inoue had in mind for his monsterology. Inoue had always stressed that his newly formed discipline was intended for the practical education of the unenlightened masses, which is why he lectured and wrote in a simple, easily accessible form. It was with this aim in mind that he toured the countryside giving lectures and publicizing the opening of his Tetsugakukan in Tokyo.[5] One mind his message apparently reached was that of a young Sasaki Kizen of the Yamaguchi neighborhood of Tsuchibuchi village in the administrative town district of Tōno, Iwate prefecture. Although I have not been able to confirm the precise circumstances of Sasaki's first knowledge of the Tetsugakukan, it is probable that he either attended in Morioka, or caught wind of, one of Inoue's provincial lectures. Regardless of how he learned about the Tetsugakukan, it was for the purpose of enrolling in Inoue's school that Sasaki, against his family's wishes, left Tōno for Tokyo in September 1905.

This move came after two years of disillusionment at the Iwate Medical School in Morioka. Having become dissatisfied with medicine, he ac-

quired an interest in literature and history and decided to develop these
new interests in the humanities division of Inoue's Tetsugakukan. The
nature of his attraction to history and literature, however, does not seem
to have been very orthodox and undoubtedly dictated (along with financial concerns) his choice of school. In his later years Sasaki is reported
to have explained to his son that the reason he selected the Tetsugakukan was "to research ghosts."[6] But, one wonders, what was his reason for
such research? Was it out of a crusading desire to join Inoue's program of
"crushing superstitions"? Probably not. There are indications that Sasaki
was as out of place at the Tetsugakukan as he was at medical school, at
least as a student there. Steeped in ghost stories from an early age and witness to a variety of apparitions himself, he fit the bill as research subject
better than that of researcher at Inoue's institution. Rather than eradicate
fictions based on folk beliefs, he disseminated them. Several months after
arriving in Tokyo he began to associate with literary circles and to write
fantastic tales under the pen name Kyōseki, which he chose in homage to
a contemporary master of the genre, Izumi Kyōka.[7] Having heard enough
sermonizing against the "superstitions" that had filled his life in Tōno and
stimulated his creative writing, Sasaki transferred in September 1907 to
the literature department at Waseda University, where his formal studies
foundered but his fiction writing flourished. He had made the switch
from *yōkaigaku*, the *shōtai* (true form) of which revealed itself to be the
eradication — not study — of *yōkai*, to *bungaku* (literature), where the true
shape of his own interests began to manifest itself.[8]

A catalyst in the transportation of Sasaki away from the *yōkaigaku* of
the Tetsugakukan to the literary world of Waseda was Mizuno Yōshū
(1883–1947), a fellow student at Waseda and an up-and-coming writer
with a shared taste for ghost stories and fantastic tales. At a publishing
anniversary party for Mizuno in February 1938, folklorist, writer, and literary critic Orikuchi Shinobu actually credited Mizuno as having been
a major "hidden" contributor to the development of folk studies.[9] Sasaki
had learned of Mizuno's interests in supernatural themes and arranged to
visit him on 17 October 1906. Sasaki's diary entry for that day records:
"In the evening, I visited Mr. Mizuno and talked until 11:30. Although
it was our first meeting, we both spoke open-heartedly to each other and
the ghost stories began. Rain fell incessantly."[10] Fifteen months after this
first of many meetings, Sasaki appeared as the title character of Mizuno's

novella *Kitaguni no hito* (The person from the North Country), published in the magazine *Shinshōsetsu* (New fiction) in January 1908. Basically a fictionalized account of Mizuno and Sasaki's acquaintance, the story includes some of the legends from Tōno that Sasaki had related to Mizuno during their meetings. The most notable is the myth of the installation of the three sister goddesses on the three peaks—Hayachine, Rokkoushi, and Ishigami—that surround the Tōno plain. This myth, re-emplotted as a kind of foundation myth for the Tōno area, figured prominently two years later as the second tale of Yanagita's *Tōno monogatari*.

In fact, several of the tales appearing in Yanagita's book first made their way into print not only in Mizuno's *Kitaguni no hito*, but also in a series of retold tales simply entitled "Kaidan" (Ghost stories) that Mizuno published in *Shumi* magazine in September 1908 and June 1909. Seven of the ten recounted in the June 1909 "Kaidan" reappeared in *Tōno monogatari* the following year.[11] It is thought that Yanagita first became interested in meeting Sasaki after reading Mizuno's *Kitaguni no hito* and his first collection of ghost stories. Having known Mizuno since their joint participation in a literary society gathering in February 1902, Yanagita asked him if he could arrange an introduction with the storyteller from Tōno.[12] On 4 November 1908 Mizuno took Sasaki with him to Yanagita's house in Ushigome, Kaga-chō, and introductions were made. Three weeks later Yanagita sent Sasaki a postcard requesting to meet with him privately in order to listen to and record the strange tales of Tōno that Sasaki had brought with him from his native home. Their tales of Tōno sessions began in February 1909. According to one commentator, Yanagita considered Sasaki to be "a reliquary of stories" that contained "the deep spirit of heart-felt beliefs that Japanese of former antiquity had possessed."[13]

Both Mizuno and Yanagita had great interest in Sasaki's tales of supernatural phenomena and sought to put them to use, but in differently nuanced ways. Mizuno, loosely affiliated with the *Shizenshugi-ha* (Naturalist School) of writers popular at that time, recast Sasaki's tales as a kind of "supernatural naturalism" (to invert M. H. Abrams's phrase) while maintaining the pretenses of a literary genre. Yanagita too, in *Tōno monogatari*, emphatically presented the tales as "strange but true" and entertained similar literary pretensions, but wanted more from these tales than mere literary material. As Mizuno later recalled Yanagita's comments about Sasaki's stories: "They are valid firsthand materials for the subject matter that I'm researching." But what exactly was that subject matter, and why was it situated in the fantastic tales that permeated rural folk life? We will address these questions after the last leg of Sasaki's journey is told.

In the year that *Tōno monogatari* was published Sasaki fell seriously ill from what was diagnosed as a lung and kidney disease, accompanied by a probable hallucination-inducing nervous disorder, and was hospitalized in Tokyo. Physically, spiritually, and financially spent from his six-year sojourn in Tokyo, he returned to the North Country in 1911, first as a convalescing patient in a Morioka hospital and then as a prodigal son in Tōno. A cynical reading of his Tokyo adventure, a reading I am inclined to make, would see him as the victim of a dissolute lifestyle and a hawkish exploitation by his literary and academic acquaintances: he ignored course work at Waseda and sought tutors in foreign languages instead; with his unusual looks and a personal character that exuded the bizarre atmosphere of the ghost stories he told (he was very tall and spoke with a thick Tōhoku accent), he attracted writers seeking exotic topics;[14] and, of course, he had willingly shared his stories of Tōno with Yanagita only to have his storytelling abilities belittled. The "deep spirit of heart-felt beliefs," of which he was a vessel, had been extracted; in a word, he was used and then discarded. It seems only fitting then that the appearance of Sasaki's physical ailments and mental exhaustion coincided with the appearance of *Tōno monogatari*: his significance had been exhausted from his body and transplanted into a text.

Soon after returning to Tōno, Sasaki set about replenishing that significance with the collection of more folklore. With this new material, he wrote, in the late 1910s, *Tōno monogatari II,* the manuscript of which he sent to Yanagita for critical commentary. Again, Yanagita criticized Sasaki's work on aesthetic grounds, but this time he explicitly judged the style of presentation of the tales in comparison to what he believed was the proper practice and method of the folk study fieldworker. He wrote back to Sasaki advising that he moderate his literary prolixity: "To write as curtly as possible—this is an ironclad rule in the collection of old stories."[15] Similarly, in a 1919 letter to Sasaki, Yanagita explained that "one should not add excessive imagination beyond one's observations; that is something for future scholars. The duty of the collector lies completely elsewhere."[16] Without revising his manuscript according to Yanagita's specifications, Sasaki abandoned his *Tōno monogatari II* project (and, significantly, artistic writing in general) and committed himself to the collection of tales in Tōhoku throughout the 1920s.[17]

Although his actions appear to have been motivated by Yanagita's dictates, Sasaki also drifted from their restrictive pressure by associating, during the last six years of his life in Sendai (where he compiled his collected materials), with a renegade from Yanagita's group of folklorists, Motoyama Keisen. Sasaki published articles in Motoyama's journal *Tsuchi no suzu* and even dabbled in folk studies theory. Yanagita regretted Sasaki's association with Motoyama, but he regretted even more that one of his best local informants had left his locale. His value to Yanagita was as a reliable collector and transcriber, not as an interpreter or theorizer of folk tales, and certainly not as a competitor.[18] After all, Sasaki was not good at storytelling . . .

But his story has been worth telling here in order to evoke the agglomeration of texts and bodies that shaped the critical mass of folk studies in its incipient stages. Sasaki's journey from Tōno to Tokyo and back again to Tōno marked the passage of the "benighted folk" body through Inoue's discipline of enlightenment and on to a fictional, Kyōkaesque world of folkic marvels that in turn drew the attention of folk studies' principal—but not sole—organizer, Yanagita. In the end, Yanagita's younger colleague Orikuchi Shinobu paid tribute to Sasaki's spirit by doing the calligraphy for his tombstone that still stands in a decrepit graveyard on a lonely hillside overlooking his home village. Dispensing his tales and thus fulfilling his function as interface between the rural folk and those who would study them, Sasaki returned to the countryside physically, mentally, and, I would say, discursively exhausted. Yet Sasaki's bit part, his sentence in the prologue of mainstream folk studies, introduces the confluence of forces—flowing from folk narratives, from monsterology, from fantastic literature, from a scientific ideal of objective collection and transcription—that brought the scene of folk studies' writing to the surface of modern Japan.

Minzokugaku *as the Study of an Economy of Affects*

There are many indications during the first decades of the 1900s that the subject matter Yanagita was researching and working to center a field of study on was the affects, the feelings, of ordinary Japanese. For example, Yanagita opened his 1908 essay "Jijitsu no kyōmi" by flatly stating, "I've been thinking recently that I'd like to research the feelings of ordinary people of the past [*mukashi no bonjin no kokoromochi*]."[19] Similarly, during a 1927 discussion on the supernatural with the writer Akutagawa Ryūnosuke, Yanagita asserted that although Japanese academic knowledge may lose out to its foreign counterparts, the imaginative powers of Japanese common folk are unsurpassed throughout the world. He glossed this power as "the workings of the heart" (*kokoro no hataraki*) of the commoners and it is clear that his focus of study was this marvelous faculty.[20] Finally, in the preface to one of his few essays concerning folk studies methodology, Yanagita outlined three parts in the "collection" (*shūshū*) of knowledge about the folk: (1) collection of the external forms of daily life (*seikatsu gaikei*), which is done by the eye of the traveler; (2) collection of explanations of daily life (*seikatsu kaisetsu*), which is done by the eye and ear of the sojourner; and (3) collection of the gist (*kosshi*), namely daily life-consciousness (*seikatsu ishiki*) of the folk, which is done only by the heart of those from the same local area.[21] Okaya Kōji has rightly noted that this enumeration of three parts of the folk conceived of as an object of study was not value-free. In distinguishing his folk studies, *minzokugaku* (民俗学), from ethnology, *minzokugaku* (民族学), Yanagita made clear that the latter was limited to the first two levels of observation of the tangible aspects of a people, whereas his field of study aimed at reaching beyond the visible and audible surface to the world of invisible things, namely, the "daily life-consciousness" and "heart" of the folk. Yanagita's folk studies was to be the collection of feelings, not objects.[22]

Many commentators have properly identified Yanagita's area of interest as "the psychic realm" of the Japanese, but have stated so as if this object of study were unproblematically given.[23] Besides assuming a uniformly homogeneous group of people, such characterizations have failed to consider the implications of the intangible and *unreal* qualities of such an object of inquiry. By emphasizing the supposed scientificity of Yanagita's method of folk study (reduced to travel, observation, and collection), previous studies have downplayed or outright excised its imaginative—and I would say in some instances fantastic—moment. Nothing other than the unreal nature of folk studies' object required this imaginative opening, and nothing other than folk studies' disciplinary aspirations required its simultaneous closure.

This situation sustained a fundamental tension throughout the practice of folk studies that is visible in Yanagita's justification for researching *tengu* in particular and *bakemono* in general.[24] His sensitivity to the ridicule he might receive for giving such fanciful topics serious consideration appeared in his early essays. He opens his 1909 essay, "Tengu no hanashi" (which translate as "About our *tengu*" to be consistent with Fanny Hagin Mayer's rendering of the title *Senzo no hanashi* as *About Our Ancestors*), in a defensive tone: "My researching *tengu* is, of course, of spurious repute. But in order to know the life of past people it's natural that I also take into account to some small extent such items in considering [their life] from various angles. Accordingly, I don't hold any conclusions concerning *tengu*. People nowadays attempt to investigate things, all things, with ordinary logic, but since there is no logic in monsters (*obake*) they will be discovered even by illogic."[25] The movement of this short passage betrays Yanagita's dilemma in attempting to fashion his focus of study. He acknowledges the reproach he will receive from mainstream academia for studying something as incredible and fictional as *tengu,* yet insists on the necessity to include an investigation of this fabulous being in order to gain knowledge of the life of past Japanese folk. Even more amazing is Yanagita's defense for the apparent absurdity of such monsters: they seem inexplicable to moderns because monsters do not follow the rules of normal "logic" (he uses the japanized English word, *rojikku*). Yet the alternative logic of monsters did not dissuade Yanagita from carrying out his investigation. In fact, it propelled him.

In "Yūmeidan" (1905), his earliest published essay dealing directly with common beliefs in the supernatural, Yanagita associates the popular traits of *tengu* with spiritual sensibilities "unique" to the Japanese: "It seems, then, in any case that they [*tengu*] take on various appearances, and that they are by no means limited to having wings and long noses. Yet, as for their personality, they often possess special characteristics the origins of which, to exaggerate a bit, are in common with that of *Bushidō* and do not exist in other countries."[26] The exemplary traits Yanagita enumerates echo several of those that appeared six years before in Nitobe Inazo's *Bushidō* (1899): rectitude, correct action, purity, single-mindedness, and revengefulness. Sharing a concern for the investigation of rural communities and culture, Nitobe and Yanagita actually joined forces with others in 1910 to found the Kyōdokai (Native Place Association).[27]

The above traits are also alluded to in "Tengu no hanashi." In this piece, written while he was preparing the manuscript of *Tōno monogatari,* Yanagita associates what was known as *tengudō* with *bushidō*.[28] Explaining that *tengu* were originally the militia (*bujin*) among the gods, he points out that by the Middle Ages they had nearly completely acquired the traits of warriors (*bushi*) in response to the changing ethos of the times. This presupposed correspondence of Zeitgeist with the changing depiction of *tengu* qualifies them as narrative traces of the psyche of the Japanese people, past and, in theory, present. Yanagita further justifies this position when, after pointing out the reflection of Celtic character and sense of geography in the stories of fairies, he similarly relates Japanese character and the predominantly mountainous geography of Japan to the gloomy mood in *tengu* stories.[29] Yanagita's knowledge of Celtic legends likely came from his recent reading of Yeats's *The Celtic Twilight* (1893, 1902), the probable model for *Tōno monogatari.* Whether or not these "Japanese" traits that Yanagita notes are actually expressed in tales of *tengu* is not of prime concern here. Instead, what is important is Yanagita's move to read tales of *tengu* and other monsters as narrative embodiments of a collective Japanese psyche.

In this respect it becomes clear that marvelous stories about *tengu* and his own writing about them were not idle amusements for Yanagita. They were in fact crucial in the textualization of an essential knowledge of the "folk heart" in spite of—and, I will argue, because of—their fantastic nature. The more incredible and inexplicable an item of folklore was, the deeper the understanding of the folk mind would be once that item was interpreted; the toughest nut to crack was the tastiest for Yanagita. When dealing with *fushigi na hanashi* (fantastic tales) Yanagita frequently begins by highlighting, even exaggerating, the apparently absurd, illogical, and opaque nature of the tale before unraveling its meaning. One of many examples of this rhetorical strategy occurs in his setup of the problem of the meaning of widespread *hashi-hime* (bridge princess) tales, which I take up in detail in chapter 5. In the midst of recounting several versions of the tale, Yanagita states his topic of interest: "What I think I'd like to talk about here is the point that even in stories as foolish and absurd as these there is nevertheless a tradition from former medieval times."[30] By then relating certain motifs of this cycle of folk tales with motifs from earlier recorded stories from sources such as the *Konjaku monogatari,* regional *fūdoki* (gazetteers), and even *Genji monogatari,* he proceeds to crack the nut and extract a kernel of meaning.

This privileging of the fantastic as the deepest material for an investigation of folk sentiment appears as early as 1905, when Yanagita justified his unorthodox research in "Yūmeidan": "Among the people [*kokumin*] of whatever country, all have their own special wonders [*tokubetsu no fukashigi*]" and "special characteristics [*tokushoku*]" by which "one can probably research the history of the people . . . in particular, one can likely study something called the nature of the people [*kokumin no seishitsu*]."[31] For this reason an increased interest in, rather than government proscriptions against, *yūmeikyō,* or belief in the hidden world, "would be extremely welcome" (244). Yanagita acknowledges that because *yūmeikyō* was officially proscribed as being "harmful to the public good," his "way of viewing" this popular religious belief differs from that of others (242). "Others" in this case likely referred to fellow officials in the Ministry of Agriculture and Commerce, for whom he was conducting regional agricultural surveys at the time. Yanagita is thus directly confronting government opinion concerning the treatment of popular beliefs in the supernatural. Another "other" with whom he specifically disagreed on the question of folk beliefs is the ubiquitous Inoue Enryō. Toward the end of the essay, which was published the same month (September 1905) that Sasaki enrolled at the Tetsugakukan "to research ghosts," Yanagita launches a polemic against Inoue's monsterology:

> I cannot help but express absolute and utter opposition toward Mr. Inoue Enryō, among others. Presently, he conducts what he calls lectures on monsterology [*yōkaigaku*], but explanations of monsters and the like did not begin with Mr. Inoue Enryō. Among scholar-priests in the Tokugawa period there were impertinent types who concocted such things as "monster discussions" [*kai-i bendan*] and "rebuttals" [*benmō*] in which they stated that monsters were things produced from errors in our minds and therefore should not at all be thought of and feared as something mysterious [*fushigi*]. . . . Mr. Inoue Enryō and others have offered various reasons [to explain away inexplicable things], but they are theories [*gakusetsu*] that will

likely have to be revised in the future. I think that reports of the inexplicable [*fukashigisetsu*], on the other hand, will probably remain hundreds of years hereafter. (255)

In this passage Yanagita not only questions Inoue's claims to academic precedent; he also belittles Inoue (a neo-Buddhist philosopher-scholar) by implicitly comparing him to the "impertinent types" (*namaiki na yatsu*) among Tokugawa scholar-priests (*gakusō*). It is clear that Inoue's project provided the negative impetus for Yanagita's own writing on the folk and the fantastic.

To counter Inoue's much-publicized monsterology, Yanagita reformulated the approach to the question of monsters among the Japanese populace. In the scheme articulated in "Yūmeidan," in which each nation possesses its own "special marvels" and "special characteristics" through which the history of that country's people unfolds, Yanagita qualified the study of the hidden world of *tengu*—a goblin that he views as one manifestation of a generic *bakemono* that he defines in turn as an unexpected chance encounter with something inexplicable (248)—as a pragmatic part of the discourse on *kokutai* (national body) that was at a high pitch following the Russo-Japanese war.[32] He even privileged belief in the hidden world as the locus of a changeless national spirit, as "something that has continued [from ancient times to the present] and should also exist from the present to eternity" despite the historical fluctuations of its expression.[33] Thus, by accepting accounts of *tengu* and the like as source material, Yanagita established a means by which to investigate the motivating psyche, or what I call the economy of affects, hidden within the national body of the Japanese. Consequently, although Yanagita, like Inoue, situated his *gaku* around the mysterious workings of *kokoro* in a *kokutai,* the path that his folk studies would take led not to an "elimination [of unreal objects] by paraphrase" via an ideological application of Western scientific and medical knowledge, but rather toward the construction of an alternative type of knowledge of "the Japanese" via a passage through the poetic.

Desiring the Other (World): Yanagita's Turn Around Literature

To speak of madness one must have the talent of a poet.
     —Foucault, during his thesis defense

The assertion of a poetic knowledge founded on a privileging of the affects was one pursuit of Tokugawa nativism. Yanagita too followed this
pursuit in his early nativist studies under his tutor Matsuura Shūhei, and
it is in this context that I believe one should consider his early affec-
tion for poetry, his attraction to a "linguistics of speech," and his interest in the supernatural entities of the hidden world. On the other hand,
in the interest of founding a credible, modern academic discipline (science) to investigate Japanese passions, Yanagita was compelled to locate
folk studies at least ostensibly within the discursive parameters of institutionalized forms of contemporary academic knowledge. That academics
both then and now have questioned the "scientific" validity of Yanagita's
writing is not surprising. That he has not been fully accepted (by either
himself or the majority of his commentators) as a writer of fiction is also
not surprising.

At this juncture Yanagita shares the dilemma that Freud too faced,
which Certeau has analyzed as a problem of the "redistribution of epistemological terrain" over the boundaries between the "objective" and the
"imaginary" in the establishment of the positive sciences in nineteenth-
century Europe. The Meiji academic institution, to the extent that it
engaged in this scientific discourse, also accepted these same distinctions
concerning what constituted positive knowledge and its "remainder."[34]
As intellectual adventurers, both Yanagita and Freud had in common a
willingness to hazard the attempt to reclaim that "remainder" and reevaluate the foundations of the institution that determined the boundaries of knowledge. I emphasize, however, that this remainder was a remainder of positive knowledge, not of modernity itself; the two should
not be equated even though they are related. The act of reclaiming what
positive knowledge excises or passes over is a modern one; indeed, it is
part of what defines modernity as it emerges.

Drawing on the major phases of Certeau's examination of the question of discursive boundaries in "the Freudian novel," I now explore how
a similar analysis might be played out in relation to Yanagita's writing

on a fantastic hidden world in particular and his writing of folk studies in general. Certeau turns to Freud's development of psychoanalytic discourse in order to demonstrate how its relationship to literature and history brings out the determinate configuration between literary and historical discourse. His thesis is straightforward: "I will state my argument without delay: literature is the theoretic discourse of the historical process. It creates the non-topos where the effective operations of a society attain a formalization. Far from envisioning literature as the expression of a referential, it would be necessary to recognize here the analogue of that which for a long time mathematics has been for the exact sciences: a 'logical' discourse of history, the 'fiction' which allows it to be thought" (18). Freud's science of the mind, as Certeau then demonstrates, is displaced toward literature for its conception. This displacement gives analytic discourse the form of a "theoretic fiction," a term Freud himself used to define the psychic apparatus of the unconscious in *Interpretation of Dreams*. "Indeed, the Freudian discourse is the fiction which comes back to the realm of scientificity, not only insofar as it is the object of analysis, but insofar as it is the form. The novelistic mode becomes theoretic writing" (19–20). Malcolm Bowie further specifies Freud's use of the term *theoretische Fiktion* "to describe a state of affairs that a given theory seemed to require or predict but for which no supporting evidence could be found."[35] Given Yanagita's similar pull toward literature and push toward scientificity in his attempt at an alternative history of Japanese life, I suggest that the writing of folk studies falls within a similar problematic and that consequently the "hidden world," like Freud's unconscious, was born of a poetic gesture and functioned as the theoretic fiction that allowed the discourse on the affects of the folk to be thought.

In an effort to link Yanagita's early poetry with his later research of the folk, Okaya turns to the discussion of the hidden world appearing in "Yūmeidan." The leitmotif, Okaya explains, of nearly all of Yanagita's poetry is a dissatisfaction with this world and a subsequent longing for the other world that Yanagita refers to in one poem as "the beautiful world of dreams."[36] Likewise, in "Yūmeidan" Yanagita expresses the desire to return to a belief in the hidden world to research how such a strange belief relates to the characteristics and the history of the Japanese over the ages: "Recently I too have become a non-believer [in *yūmeikyō*] so my research won't progress, but some day—and I kid you not—I think I would like very much to try researching [this belief]."[37] As Okaya indicates, if one takes this statement literally it would imply that Yanagita too was formerly a believer in the hidden world during his young poetic years under the tutelage of Matsuura. He then goes on to conclude that this early belief in or at least the longing and concern for the hidden world that Yanagita displayed in his younger years was directly related to his much later researches into Japanese views of a distant other world, such as that which appears in *Kaijō no michi* (The journey overseas, 1952). In short, Yanagita's poetic desire for belief in another world—hidden and near at hand or distant beyond the horizon—becomes displaced and transferred into a desire for a "scientific" knowledge of such beliefs among other Japanese. This otherness is temporally other in the case of past Japanese, spatially other in the case of those Japanese apart from centers of civilization and enlightenment. Yanagita developed a view, discussed in the following chapter, in which relative temporal distance (i.e., the historical past) could be read from concentric diffusions of folk tale motifs and language usage mapped across the space of Japan, the most distant premodern (rural) past being located on the furthest periphery from modern (urban) centers.

I do not disagree with Okaya's interpretation as such, but I extend and recast it a bit differently. I would point out that in the above statement Yanagita curiously and tautologically establishes belief itself as the basis for knowledge of belief in the hidden world, and thus if one takes his declaration literally it would imply that he, through his eventual writing of folk studies, had become a "believer." The same logic is at work in Yanagita's characterization of the deepest level of collecting knowledge of the folk, which he reserved for his conception of folk studies. Assuming that only people native to a local region could glean the kernel of its *kokoro,* its "daily life-consciousness," one would, in order to legitimate one's claims to knowledge of this "folk heart," literally have to become one of these folk—or at least fantasize being one of them—before returning to the body of the scientific observer. This movement in the formation of a discourse on the folk is precisely where theory, belief, and poetic fantasy enfold to engender the conditions for a hermeneutical knowledge of an "object" (the affects of the folk) that by definition lies beyond the ken of positive science.

Certeau's examination of the "Freudian novel" reveals that what ultimately authorized Freud's assertions were not rational proofs but the poetic citations that formed his thought. In addition, the "stylistic" in Freud's writing is a "stylistic of affects" in which he "takes care to 'confess,' as he says, his affective reaction to the person or document he analyses. . . . With this golden rule, every psychoanalytic treatment directly contradicts a first norm, a constituent part of scientific discourse, which argues that the truth of the utterance be independent of the speaking subject."[38] In the case of folk studies, the affective reaction of the speaking subject to his object is also all-important in accessing the uninscribed material that will become the inscribed knowledge about the motivations of the folk. This affective "nonscientific" relationship between observer and observed, although rhetorically repressed in most of Yanagita's advanced writings, is foregrounded in at least one of his early major experiments at reporting the psychic reality of the Japanese countryside, *Tōno monogatari*.

In the famous preface of this work that many commentators narrowly view as the founding text of Japanese folk studies, Yanagita "confesses" his affective reaction to his material on at least two crucial points. The first is when he introduces the source of the tales of Tōno, his informant and Tōno's native son, Sasaki Kizen (alias Kyōseki): "All of these stories I heard from Mr. Sasaki Kyōseki, a person from Tōno. I have been writing the stories down as they were told to me during his many visits since February 1909. Kyōseki is not good at storytelling but he is a reliable person. I have written the stories as I felt them [*kanjitaru mama*] without adding a word or phrase."[39] Ronald Morse's translation of *kanjitaru mama* in the last sentence as "as they were related to me" completely glosses over and neutralizes the radical aspect of Yanagita's theory and practice of folk studies: access to knowledge about the psychic life of an effectively unseen and unheard rural folk—that is, the capture of their feelings and motivations—is gained by the impression that their speech makes upon one's own affectivity. The collector's task is then to find the best means by which to transmit this affective charge in writing to the reader.

Mizuno Yōshū, the writer who introduced Sasaki to Yanagita, seems to have felt that Yanagita had found an effective means of transmission of emotion in the style of writing employed in both Yanagita's poetry and in *Tōno monogatari*. Of Yanagita's poetry he said that "it is like the attenuated voice of a song sung softly and solitarily. It is neither a wind trumpeting brute force nor a storm of oratory, but this voice goes from a person's ear and penetrates into the heart."[40] Of *Tōno monogatari* he emphasized the stirring evocative force of the text in its re-creation of the spirit of life (and spirit life) in the village: "If there were anyone who, viewing this text, would consider it the work of a dilettante, I think I would flatly say 'That is an error.' The reason why is that from this text I could feel the life of the people of this village in the mountains. I feel it as if the people living there are speaking about the things they have seen with their eyes and have heard with their ears."[41]

By Yanagita's own account at this time, the best means of transmitting folk feeling in writing was some kind of adaptation to scholarly writing of so-called *shaseibun* (sketch-from-life writing) that was first popularized by the poet Masaoka Shiki around 1900 and then advocated shortly afterward by Yanagita's friend Tayama Katai, the self-fashioned leader of the *Shizenshugi-ha* (Naturalists) among Japanese literary circles. In an essay entitled "Shasei to ronbun" written two years after "Yūmeidan" and two years before he began *Tōno monogatari*, Yanagita discusses the possible application of *shaseibun* beyond the objective descriptions of empirical reality, which the Naturalists were in theory seeking. He is interested in extending *shaseibun* to speculative essay writing. To make this move, Yanagita asserts the distinction outer (tangible) world/inner (intangible) world and invokes Tayama's own formulaic characterization of *heimen byōsha* (flat description), the key to his technique of *shaseibun*. Tayama's manifesto, "I describe [my own experiences in reality] only as I saw, heard, and touched them,"[42] becomes in Yanagita's reformulation:

> Moreover, it is better if one can solely write about the things one saw, heard, thought, and felt only as they existed. . . . Heretofore, if one employed "sketch-from-life writing" [*shaseibun*] it was limited to descriptive writing, but I think that, in addition, essay writing too can be done by the same method. That is to say, just as descriptive writing sketches the outer world as it is, essay-writing sketches the thoughts inside one's head as they are. Even though there is a distinction between the inner mind and the outer world, I think there is no difference in the meaning of *shasei*.[43]

In Yanagita's reworking of Tayama's motto, "thought" and "felt" [*kanjita*] infiltrate the paradigm to displace the tangible and to allow entrance into the mind and feelings of the writer. This movement, Yanagita maintains, is the true foundation of writing: "Writing is achieved by the spirit [*ki*];

that is to say, it produces texts through the author's feelings [*kibun*]" (31). A field of feeling is thus fabricated among the writer, his or her object, and the reader.

It was exactly this kind of insertion of the writer's thoughts and feelings that Tayama's theory of description sought to avoid when he stressed that any kind of explanation or narration distorted and falsified the writer's objective sensory experience of the empirical reality around him.[44] For Tayama, a truthful writing inscribed the responses of the five senses to the surrounding empirical reality. It was therefore preoccupied with surfaces, externals (hence, *"heimen" byōsha*). To introduce the thoughts and feelings—that is, the imagination—of the writer would be to broach the "naturally" sensed surface of things and permit the possibility of a falsifying fabrication. Fictionality was thus banished from the scene of writing in favor of a realism that was identified with truth. The overdetermination of this identification in a hypermimetic theory of writing ultimately committed and confined the Naturalists to writing only their own immediate experiences in the form that became known as the *shishōsetsu,* or "I-novel" (which ironically becomes centered on the subjectivity of the writer). Truth for them would always be found in the familiarity of an "I" in this world and never in the unfamiliarity of a "thou" in another world. Yanagita's apparently innocent attempt to apply *shaseibun* to his own speculative writing is in fact the beginning of the subversion of the naturalist writing project through the reinstallation of imagination and fictionality. Rejecting the mimetic equation of empirical reality with truth, Yanagita assumes a truth that is not identified with empirical reality.

A year later in a much more direct critique of the Naturalist School, Yanagita follows through with the implications of his notions of writing in "Dokusha yori mitaru Shizenha-shōsetsu" (Naturalist novels from a reader's viewpoint, April 1908). Yanagita's complaint in this essay is the naturalist obsession with material realism and objective "scientific" description. In the same way that the Naturalists turned to Western literature for models of reform, Yanagita too invokes Western literature in this essay. But in his case, the purpose is to point out the limitations and fallacies of Tayama's theory of writing and to advance an alternative form of writing. One example is a short play by the Belgian dramatist and critic Maurice Maeterlinck called *The Intruder* (1890). Yanagita's stated purpose for citing this play is to demonstrate the possibility of a writing technique that conveys realistic emotions without the detailed specification of time and place: "It is merely described as a story of a certain time and place ('An old gloomy house in modern times') yet in spite of this it is seriously and acutely realistic. Isn't this a truly marvelous [*fushigi na*] way of writing?"[45] Indeed, the physical description of the scene is minimal because it is a play that achieves its "marvelous" emotional effect through dialogue and otherworldly intimations. What Yanagita is suggesting in this instance is, so to speak, a mimesis of the intangible and the invisible by which a "realism" of feeling can be portrayed. Using Tayama's highly valued term *genjitsu* (reality) to characterize what Tayama devalued, Yanagita sunders the naturalist identification of truth with a tangible empirical reality by placing the truth value of writing in what is intangible, in what is "thought and felt" regardless of its surface description.

This affirmation of a truth that is not identified with an empirical reality is additionally borne out in Yanagita's unspecified yet apparent reason for his selection of Maeterlinck's *The Intruder*. The play, of which Yanagita provides an outline, revolves around an old blind man who senses the presence of an invisible spirit ("the intruder") entering the house while the other characters, who can see, sense nothing. The intruding spirit, the old man fears, has come to take the life of his daughter, who lies sick in an adjoining room. Like the Cassandra of Greek legend, no one believes his supernatural knowledge, and sure enough the daughter dies. Those who could clearly see the empirical reality before their eyes were blind to the truth of the invisible presence that the old man, blind to that same empirical reality, felt. The implied allegorical critique of Japanese Naturalists is self-evident.

Through this division of the identification of truth and reality that Yanagita stages against the Naturalists in Tayama's own literary journal (*Bunshō sekai*), Yanagita qualifies fiction—particularly the fantastic—to be read and written for a superior truth. This type of move, Derrida points out in response to Lacan, is the orthodox Platonic distinction that the Western philosophical tradition makes: "Lacan insists much on the opposition truth/reality, which he advances as a paradox. This opposition, as orthodox as can be, facilitates the passage of truth through fiction: common sense will always have made the distinction between reality and truth."[46] In other words, "Once the assumption is made that truth and reality differ, there can be no other structure for truth than the structure of fiction."[47] Yanagita's valorization of a "marvelous way of writing" as well as of the marvelous itself is entirely dependent on this assumption. It will later become the sanction by which to present his rendition of the tales of Tōno as "present-day facts" expressing the true feelings of the ordinary rural Japanese. It is also no coincidence that he compared the twenty-second tale of *Tōno monogatari* to *The Intruder*.[48]

Taking Tayama's theory of writing to its logical end, Yanagita states that in making truth-in-realism their goal, "it must be said that the Naturalist authors fell into a very difficult predicament. If it were fiction [*kūsō*] from the start, people would accept it as fiction. Seeing that they depict truth-in-reality [*shinjitsu*] and not fiction, it turns out that they must, in short, compete with factual reality [*jijitsu*]."[49] And it is a competition that, Yanagita implies, the Naturalists must necessarily lose because the reader will always possess the priority of personal experience in reality as the standard of truth that is identified with reality: "In my own experience, my feelings are much more deeply touched when, during my travels, I am viewing a certain living reality than when I am reading a good novel" (14). Geoffrey Hartman makes the same observation concerning an ode by Wordsworth: "By seeking to overcome priority, art fights nature on nature's own ground, and is bound to lose."[50]

In his critique of the Naturalists, Yanagita embraced unabashed fictionality as a way to avoid what he describes as the Naturalists' "self-made trap" (*jijō-jibaku*). In so doing he abandons the exclusive preoccupation with empirical reality, but not the preoccupation with truth. It is the logic of this division that leads Yanagita to a fantastic "other world" as the site of truth, a truth of essential beliefs and feelings which lie outside (but must pass through) the reality that the positive sciences administer. Incredible stories about *tengu,* and folk tales in general, can now legitimately be read (or more ideally, listened to) for truth, but how can their truths be legitimately conveyed in writing to incredulous readers who value "scientific" descriptions even in their novels? To make visible and credible in words the invisible presence of "the intruder" in the "old gloomy house in modern times" without destroying its essential truth is the problematic structure that set in motion the production of Yanagita's writing. Moreover, it is a problematic structure that Yanagita sought to maintain, not resolve; that is, it became the condition for his textual productivity, and this condition had to be ceaselessly reproduced to ensure his writing life. In this respect it was crucial that not all of the Other be reduced to the Same, or all of the spoken to the written.

Whereas the Naturalists espoused a theory of "flat description" of a physical reality perceived by the five senses when they spoke of *shaseibun,* Yanagita seems to have been groping for a kind of writing that would facilitate a mimesis of psychic, not physical, reality, the kind of object that he had already begun to explore as a topic of research in "Yūmeidan" and would continue to explore in *Tōno monogatari.* For the same reason, Yanagita joined in the ongoing literary and linguistic debate over the notion of *genbun-itchi* or "the unification of the spoken and written." He admitted the appeal of a *genbun-itchi* style that is closer to the colloquial spoken language, which in turn is more efficient than a written literary style in transmitting one's thoughts and feelings.[51] In another essay concerning the possibilities of *genbun-itchi,* "Genbun no kyori," Yanagita seems to turn back his previous position on the efficiency of the spoken over the written in expressing one's thoughts when he argues that there is a certain compact economy of expression and capacity for affective impact in writing that a verbatim transcription of speech lacks.[52] But rather than a reversal back to a form of pure literary writing, Yanagita's new articulation attempts to amalgamate the best qualities of both speech and writing: the former's fluidity in expressing thoughts and feelings stemming from its putative proximity to one's *kokoro* and *kibun,* and the latter's precision and rhetorical capabilities.[53] In other words, the colloquial best externalized one's *kokoro* and a modified *genbun-itchi* style could theoretically transfer traces of that *kokoro* best. Considering the claims to objectivity that naturalist theories of *shaseibun* had originally made, Yanagita's move to include the writing of the thoughts and feelings of the "inner mind" within this theory of writing—to rehabilitate and reassert without reserve both subjectivity and the passions into an increasingly "scientificized" (but not scientific) form of writing—circumscribed the conditions for the tense relations between the scientific and literary that would be witnessed throughout Yanagita's writing of folk studies.

The second crucial instance in the preface to *Tōno monogatari* of Yanagita's confessing to being affected by his object of inquiry occurs in the account of his "impressions" of Tōno. After a vivid description of the unfamiliar geography surrounding the approach to Tōno, complete with a bird of a type unknown to him, Yanagita recounts the scene of an equally exotic (to both the visitor Yanagita and to the reader) event, the *Shishi Odori* or Lion Dance. Mingled with flutes and singing, the sounds of the villagers participating in the festival—the shouts, the cries, the laughter—have registered themselves in Yanagita's memory so that years later they still evoke in him "the lonely sadness of a traveler." The combination of this description of unfamiliar territory and the emotional impression that the festive communality of Tōno leaves on the outsider Yanagita further points up the counterpull of his epistemological positioning: he conjures up the image of the nineteenth-century ethnographer who in theory sees and hears in detail his subject from a detached, objective distance (which corresponds to Yanagita's first two levels of collecting folk material) but then superimposes on that image a film of what can only be called a romantic longing to be a part of the community that he is observing (which corresponds to his third and privileged level of folk studies). This configuration is distinguishable, I believe, from notions in early-twentieth-century ethnography of the participant-observer because it openly suggests a more radically subjective and emotional involvement of the observer with the observed. For Yanagita, the subjective experience—in particular, the affective impressions—of the researcher would become indispensable to the practice of folk studies. Nevertheless, the rhetorical effect of this scene in the preface of *Tōno monogatari* has many things in common with rhetorical strategies that in conventional ethnographies aim to achieve an aura of authenticity and scientificity that convinces the reader of the truth of the strange, exotic, and unfamiliar subject being related.

One trope commonly used in ethnographies to convince the reader of the text's authenticity is a personalized "arrival scene" that works to place the subjectivity of the writer. Often the solitary nature of the writing subject in the unfamiliar surroundings is highlighted to enhance the otherness of the object of study and the supposedly detached viewpoint of a scientific observer, much like Yanagita's narration of his arrival in Tōno. This kind of personal narrative, deployed in and around an impersonal description of what was observed, "mediates this contradiction between the engagement called for in fieldwork and the self-effacement called for in formal ethnographic description, or at least mitigates some of its anguish, by inserting into the ethnographic text the authority of the personal experience out of which the ethnography is made."[54] In this manner, Yanagita can encode both a poetic, personal engagement and a scientific, formal distance into his text. Rhetorical techniques such as these in ethnography have derived from a long history of travel writing in Western literature. Although distancing itself from the "unscientific" narratives of "mere travelers" and "casual observers," ethnography "blinds itself to the fact that its own discursive practices were often inherited from these other genres and are still shared with them today."[55]

Yanagita similarly learned his rhetorical ploys from the literature of Japanese travel writers such as Saigyō and Bashō, whose works he knew well and admired. Although he had actually heard the tales of Tōno from Sasaki in Tokyo, the personalized journey to Tōno that Yanagita fore-grounded in the preface was crucial in legitimating his account of the feelings of the Tōno villagers as a true representation that might even flirt with claims of being a scientific ethnography. Within Yanagita's conception of the representation of truth in writing, the establishment of place and presence that this preface effects is mandatory before the first-person viewpoint diminishes in the retelling of the tales that follow. Yanagita makes it a point to write that he *did* travel to Tōno in August 1909. But he did not go there to obtain firsthand accounts of the local legends he had already heard in Tokyo; he journeyed there so that he could write, in effect, I traveled to Tōno, I saw it with my own eyes, and this is what it's like, therefore what I present to you now is true.

This privileging of knowledge gained through travel and personal experience had already appeared in Yanagita's claims that his knowledge of the countryside was more authentic than that of the naturalist writers and that of his bureaucratic colleagues. By the same criteria he had even judged Shimazaki Tōson's landmark novel *Hakai* (Broken commandment, 1906) as being a misrepresentation of Japan's outcast class (*eta*): "As a novel, [*Hakai*'s] composition, without fully penetrating the heart, cannot be convincing. The *eta*'s conflicts are [depicted as] much too violent. By my own observations throughout the countryside I can say that it is not like that."[56] Reciprocally, Yanagita was inscribed in the writings of his contemporaries as the perennial itinerant. In Tayama's diaries, for example, there are repeated mentions of Yanagita's travels.[57] In his review of *Tōno monogatari*, Tōson, citing a large portion of the preface, further textualized Yanagita as "a traveler full of observations" rather than as "a researcher

of ethnic psychology." Tōson justifiably placed Yanagita in the long tradition of travel literature in Japan: "To the best of my knowledge, there
are few travelers to match you, Mr. Yanagita. Moreover, there are also
few travelers who are as rich in observational powers as you. Your foot-
prints have left their impressions from the depths of Tōhoku to the edge
of Kyūshū."[58]

Even without the standardized literary style that Yanagita adopted in
Tōno monogatari, which operates in part to modulate the reader's response
to an often harsh and vulgar content, the credibility of his representation
of the incredible is informed by the same tropes common to literature.
Uchida usefully describes Yanagita's writing style in *Tōno monogatari* as a
kind of "translation" into standard Japanese.[59] As such, it familiarizes the
unfamiliar speech of the countryside while defamiliarizing the content of
daily life in Japan for its urban audience through its rhetorical practices.
In this crucial sense, the foundation of Yanagita's writing on the fantastical beliefs of the rural folk was always set in literature. Another such
genre besides travel literature that is relevant here is the pastoral, which
functions in what James Clifford has defined as "ethnographic allegory."
Clifford's argument is that ethnography's "disappearing object" is,

> in significant degree, a rhetorical construct legitimating a repre-
> sentational practice: "salvage" ethnography in its widest sense. The
> other is lost, in disintegrating time and space, but saved in the text.
> . . . Every description or interpretation that conceives of itself
> as "bringing a culture into writing" . . . is enacting the structure
> of "salvage." To the extent that the ethnographic process is seen as
> inscription (rather than, for example, as transcription, or dialogue)
> the representation will continue to enact a potent, and question-
> able, allegorical structure.[60]

Clifford stresses that this allegorical structure not only arises out of a
simple nostalgia for the past, but "frequently involves a *critical nostalgia,*
a way to break with the hegemonic, corrupt present by asserting the
reality of a radical alternative." The positing of an uninscribed other
(such as unlettered *bonjin,* or "ordinary folk") as an object of inscription
(and therefore knowledge) enables a writing that is more a critique of
the center than a transcription of the periphery. The use of this kind of
rhetorical strategy in *Tōno monogatari* to critique the mainstream of Japa-

nese naturalism is well-known.[61] I have indicated that it is also present in "Yūmeidan" to critique the official treatment of beliefs in *yūmei* (the hidden world). In fact, an argument can be made that Yanagita's writings in general are a pastoral-allegorical assertion of "the reality of a radical alternative" which in the end has little to do with the Japanese rural population as it really existed. Rather, Yanagita could be seen as having been involved in the fabrication of a rural folk as he wanted to believe it existed. Indeed, at least among those of his writings examined in this chapter, Yanagita was working toward the construction of a social imaginary from which he could assume a critical posture against political, literary, and academic orthodoxies of the late Meiji period. Situated in this manner and context, Yanagita's writing appears very ideological in spite of his and his followers' denials of politically and ideologically motivated engagement in the practice of folk studies.

Hard to catalogue as a scientific ethnology or literary text, travelogue, or modern collection of myths and legends, *Tōno monogatari* can surely be called fantastic in the same sense that the nineteenth-century European fantasy novel "plays with/undoes the boundary positive sciences established between the real and the imaginary."[62] A primary reason that *Tōno monogatari* has been difficult to pin down within traditional disciplinary classifications is that it attempts to chart little-known epistemological territory (the psychic reality of the people of Tōno) and consequently forges by plan or by necessity a style of presentation from a mix of narrative modes. The text that likely served as Yanagita's closest model, Yeats's *The Celtic Twilight,* which he had read just prior to writing *Tōno monogatari,* shares many of the same ambiguities: it is travel essay, story collection, ethnographic description, poetry, history, and fantasy novel all in one. Both are hybrid, monstrous texts. In light of Yanagita's frequent complaints about contemporary literature and historiography during this time, the disrespect for the conventional boundaries of "scientific" and "literary" discourse that Yanagita's text displays becomes understandable; it openly plays with and challenges these established boundaries.[63]

On several occasions throughout his oeuvre Yanagita extends this disrespect to established academics in general. One pertinent example of his disdain for conventional methods of study occurs in his 1931 essay, "Obake no koe" (The voice of monsters). In this short piece Yanagita explores the basis of the use throughout the countryside of the sound *mōko* and variations of it to signify *obake*. Similar to his rejection of Hirata's Chinese-character-based analysis of *tengu*, he criticizes the idea that *mōko* derives from the homonym of this word which refers to the Mongols, who were "monsterlike" in their attempted invasions of Japan in the thirteenth century. He disparagingly labels this form of interpretation as "reeking of the academic" (*gakusha kusai*) in its failure to consider a survey of this verbal enunciation in the context of everyday spoken language throughout Japan.[64] Yanagita further specifies the importance of such a linguistics of speech in the investigation of the folk psyche in the more fleshed-out sequel to "Obake no koe" that he wrote two years later, "Yōkai ko-i: gengo to minzoku no kankei" (The original meaning of monsters: The relation between speech and the folk).[65]

In this essay he presents a complex case for relating the meaning of the sound *mō* or *mōko* to a peculiar lunar New Year custom of northern Japan called *namahagi,* which involves a child donning a frightening mask and making door-to-door inquiries around the village. Without going into the details of his argument, I would underline that it relies first and foremost on a widespread survey of the various regional vocalizations of everyday words used to signify this custom and the idea of *obake*. From this rough comparison, Yanagita then makes linkages among these words and the practices to which they refer. This process of linking he admits is the result of "hypotheses" and "imagination," suggesting that it is highly interpretive, but the truth produced he never doubts because it is his belief/theory that such an analysis of the spoken linguistic material he has collected offers access to true meaning and intent. Common academic explanations miss this level of truth because they are steeped in "the historical knowledge of the second Mongol invasion and the like."[66] That Yanagita's type of historical concern is angled differently is made clear in the opening paragraph: taking the word *namahagi* as a starting point, he would like to "consider to what extent . . . words leave traces of the movements of the human heart (mind) [*ningen no kokoro no ugoki*] on the world long after." The new field of human science that Yanagita envisions, one that turns around a literary and linguistic poetics, takes a strongly hermeneutical shape, a "hermeneutics of the heart," if you will. And this kind of science, Yanagita implies, does not belong to the work of conventional *gakusha*.

Hermeneutics of the Heart

The things a man has heard and seen are threads of life, and if he pull them carefully
from the confused distaff of memory, any who will can weave them into whatever
garments of belief please them best.

— William Butler Yeats, *The Celtic Twilight*

But what is Yanagita if not a *gakusha* himself?[67] Yanagita's answer would
be — and the distinction must be taken seriously — a *minzokugakusha,* a *ga-*
kusha for the folk. The "for" here is purposefully multivalent to suggest
the tension of being a scholar of the folk (implying an outside position
of observation of the object of study) while at the same time writing on
behalf of (for), with respect to (for), and even in honor of (for) the folk
(implying an inside position of identification with the object of study).
If the *gakusha* aligns himself with the enlightened mind that responds
to the phenomenal world (*gense*), the *minzokugakusha* aligns himself with
the folk heart that responds to the hidden world (*yūmei*). But if, according to Yanagita's description of the levels of folk collecting, the local folk
themselves possess "by heart" the gist of their psychic motivations, why
is the *minzokugakusha* needed? Because, as Yanagita often found out when
he asked locals about the origin of a particular word, even they did not
know it. They might possess it by heart (i.e., unconsciously), but they do
not know it consciously. In other words, they cannot fully articulate it
in a discourse of rational, scientific knowledge.

In his 1945 work *Senzo no hanashi* Yanagita actually names his object
of research the unwritten "traces" and "unconscious (habitual, involun-
tary) tradition" (*muishiki no denshō*) of the folk.[68] The resemblance of this
vocabulary to Freud's notion of the operation of an individual's psychic
apparatus may be entirely coincidental — I do not mean to compare their
ideas — but there is a real resonance between their respective positions as
purveyors of knowledge. As analyst, Freud listens to his patient's stories
and offers hermeneutical hints, often involving a play on linguistic material as well as an affective transference between analyst and analysand,
to bring to light the subconscious meanings hidden in them. It is never
doubted that the patient possesses "the answer." It simply requires the interpretive tact of the analyst to facilitate its articulation as fantasies are
turned into facts about the patient's psyche. Similarly, the *minzokugaku-*

sha, self-positioned between the *minzoku* and the *gakusha,* takes as his task the bringing to light of meanings hidden in the speech and acts of its subject. In effect, he too attempts to process what strikes the *gakusha* as formless fantasies (supernatural tales, strange beliefs, unfamiliar rituals) until they acquire the shape of facts that are narratively acceptable within institutionalized knowledge. The illogicities of the other—of *bakemono,* of the folk—are translated into a form that is meaningful within the logic of the same, of the enlightened modern.

In the case of the formation of folk studies, there are thus two related "hidden" areas: the "workings of the folk's heart," which are identified with unadorned local speech and are hidden from the writerly mind of the scholar; and the believed-in and heartfelt world of apparitions, gods, and ancestral spirits, which is hidden from the folk themselves. The duplicitous (doubled, shifty, and deceptive) subject position of the *minzokugakusha* forcefully works to defy both levels of hiddenness so that his epistemological position may in theory reign over both the benighted (but sincere and passionate) folk and the enlightened (but blinded) academic. But reigning in theory and reigning in practice are two different things. How does this upstart, the *minzokugakusha,* legitimate his rule of knowledge about the folk?

Although the *minzokugakusha* works in the name of the other, which in this instance is the hidden world and folk sentiment toward it, the other has no power to authorize his knowledge as belonging to an accepted discipline because the other itself exists only at the axis of belief, emotion, fantasy, and theory. Yanagita metaphorically recognizes this dilemma when he explains in "Yūmeidan" that there is a "law of silence" in the other world that prohibits even those people "pure of heart" who have managed to enter into "the way of the hidden world" from speaking or writing anything about it upon their return. Because of the lack of fully reliable oral or written accounts of the hidden world (and of daily folk beliefs and practices), he continues, "it has become such that we must skillfully employ our powers of imagination."[69] But this reluctant reliance on imagination is not in itself a firm enough foundation on which to form a discipline. Yanagita does end up, after all, advising Sasaki, a fiction writer turned folklorist, against the excesses of imagination because they do not suit the collector of folk tales. Likewise, Yanagita must make appeals to the tribunal of the institution for the acceptance of folk studies. It is the institution, Certeau reminds us, that legitimate claims at stake in the field of knowledge by designating what is real (and therefore knowable) and what is not. "Real" knowledge so defined can only be of the disciplined variety. Yanagita's discursive struggle in the early formation of folk studies, similar to Freud's in the founding of psychoanalysis, thus lies precisely in the redefinition of what is real. This is how I believe the defiant yet defensive and almost pleading tone of Yanagita's assertion in the preface to *Tōno monogatari*—that "this book contains present-day facts"—should be read. Despite their frightening, fanciful, and unfamiliar content, the speech acts (which are themselves the "present-day facts") of Tōno's inhabitants must be accepted within an institutional redefinition of the real. Contrary to taking as the referent of the phrase "present-day facts" the otherworldly content of the tales of Tōno (as Ivy seems to), Uchida rightly points out that Yanagita is referring to the speech acts through which this content is carried; in other words, it is a "present-day fact" that people still tell stories such as these.[70]

This question of the reality of folk tales and their consequent value as sources for historical research was a topic that Yanagita later debated with the cultural historian Nishimura Shinji in the journal *Minzoku* from November 1926 to March 1927. Whereas Nishimura dismissed them as valueless to a disciplined, scientific study of history, Yanagita insisted that although the content of tales and legends were not historical facts (*shi-jitsu*), the very telling of and belief in such stories among people were historical facts that could and should be dealt with in a cultural history of the Japanese. Again, Yanagita's thrust is toward the establishment of source material and methods for the historical study of the beliefs that guided the everyday life of the common folk. This point was lost on historians who were habituated to the use of concrete written sources that were conceived of as directly reflecting the facts of a concrete historical reality.

In a move parallel to that of reading beyond the meaning of words derived from their written representation in (Chinese) characters in order to get at their "substance" in everyday speech, Yanagita developed a method of reading beyond the surface of incredible stories like those of Tōno and rewriting (interpreting) them in such a way as to assert a credible truth located in the intangibility of the affects, a truth not identified with a measurable, empirical reality. Only then could he acknowledge years later the literary nature of *Tōno monogatari* and still insist that it was written from a scientific standpoint.[71] Based on a multilayered dichotomy in which one of the terms is always "invisible," Yanagita's implicit structure of signification is hermeneutic in a strong sense. His repeated insistence on personal experience and presence, rhetorically deployed in a kind of critical ethnographic allegory, served to mask the profoundly interpretive nature of his writing and the large role it assigned to the "power of imagination" to fill in the invisible silences. To reinvoke the Derridean insight, it is not at all a paradox that truth must reside in a structure of fiction once the distinction between truth and reality is made, as it was in Yanagita's case. This is not to brand Yanagita a willful falsifier; rather, in recognizing the necessity of imagination and fictionality he was perhaps a more honest writer than many of his contemporaries. But when it came to the legitimization of his texts as the production of a knowledge of the ordinary Japanese and their "spirit," he had to do so in a way acceptable to an audience that valued an objective, "scientific" description regardless of the incredulity of the content of his source materials. Some discursive boundaries he could not openly transgress despite the transgressive potential of his material.

The difficult work of doing folk studies becomes, then, not the collection of material or even the skilled interpretation of that material, but rather the presentation of it in a written form that respects both the integrity of its source and the bylaws of its destination. In short, the *minzokugakusha* must be a masterful writer, using all of the rhetorical tricks at his disposal to persuade and impress an unbelieving audience while at the same time taking care not to betray his client. If the tales of Tōno startle and frighten the reader, the *minzokugakusha* has succeeded in transmitting the affective charge around which the core of folk life and belief is constellated. He has brought the experience of monsters, the unforeseen encounter with alterity, into the citadel of the same. The problem that follows is whether folk studies thus conceived as the study of an often disturbing economy of affects would also, like the monsters who threaten the village, be ritualistically placed at the periphery and thus harmlessly incorporated into the presiding order of things, or else be accepted as a new resident who could potentially change the makeup of the neighborhood. In other words, would the mainstream academic community accredit the writing of folk studies as "real" (i.e., "scientific") knowledge or deprive it of this status and abandon it as the bastard offspring of too much feeling, fiction, and imagination? This concern was in retrospect apparently very much on Yanagita's mind as he sought to dissociate his "serious" work from his youthful romantic literature by purposefully excluding his poetry from his collected works, *Teihon Yanagita Kunio shū*.[72]

This question, however, appears irrelevant or at least misconceived when one remembers that it is the very lack/loss of "real" written knowledge that allowed the writing of this "unreal" field in the first place. This situation comes about when Yanagita embarks on an interpretive analysis of spoken forms or, if necessary, of written forms that most resemble the spoken, which for him offered the best "traces" of the folk heart. Moreover, Yanagita was drawn specifically to *fushigi na hanashi,* things that, unsupported by a commonsense material reality, existed only in language. One could even make the argument that Yanagita's style of folk studies in general boiled down to an interpretive analysis of certain modes of language usage. The particular relationship between the supernatural and language is, in any case, neither coincidental nor arbitrary. As Todorov puts it in his study of the literary fantastic: "The supernatural is born of language, it is both its consequence and its proof: not only do the devil and vampires exist only in words, but language alone enables us to conceive what is always absent: the supernatural. The supernatural thereby becomes a symbol of language, just as the figures of rhetoric do, and the figure is, as we have seen, the purest form of literality."[73] Within these terms, folk studies as Yanagita conceived of it is the study of absence par excellence: of passions absented from academic consideration; of beliefs and practices absented from official discourse; of a hidden world of beings absent from view; of Japanese absent from written histories. The goal of folk studies—its "fantasy"—is to make present these absences, so the hidden world, as absent presence, is the perfect figure or theoretic fiction around which to weave this discourse. This discursive operation properly belongs to a poetic, not referential, function because the scientific inexplicability of *fushigi na hanashi* as such breeds the need for a poetic knowledge of them, which involves a tactful linking of traces of the folk psyche as they appear in the literality of language, not in the reality of the empirical. In this respect, Yanagita again betrays his roots to the nativist concern for Japanese poetics as a source for a knowledge incommensurable to classical academicism.

Few will deny that *Tōno monogatari* is a literary text before being in any way a systematic treatment of the belief system among the residents of Tōno. Yet the impulse to seek in this text the beginnings of a scientific discipline of folk studies persists. This appropriation of *Tōno monogatari* in the name of science invariably seizes upon the "raw data" of its content and the impersonal aspects of its presentation while remaining blind to the literary forms and personalized aspects that empower Yanagita's text to entertain any scientific pretensions. Among the proponents of the Yanagita school of folk studies, the literary is sacrificed to sanctify the scientificity of the discipline. Curiously, the reverse move, equally plausible, is scarcely considered; namely, that the literariness of *Tōno monogatari* or even the poetry Yanagita wrote prior to it opened a way to an alternative form of human science. The only notable attempt at this kind of reading of *Tōno monogatari* and its relationship to folk studies is that of Yoshimoto Takaaki. Invoking an early poem by Yanagita ("Why did I wake to this floating world at its dusk? / Let me return once more to that beautiful world of dreams"), Yoshimoto, for example, states that "awakening from such a sleep, he [Yanagita] never stopped to analyze obscure folk legends in the light of logical reasoning. His system was more like a flow of dream-like visions which exist between sleep and awakening. And in fact Yanagita felt a strong attachment to the world of shared fantasies [*kyōdō gensō*] which float through the dim sensitivities of the villagers of Tōno."[74]

It was this kind of interstitial imagination that was the enabling scheme and productive force in Yanagita's writings. It operated between a world of dreams and a world of wakefulness; between an unknown and uninscribed world of folk beliefs and a known, inscribed world of urban reality; between an invisible history of unnamed masses and a visible history of "great events and great human feats" as Yanagita imagined them. To sustain these conditions of textual productivity, there had to be a ceaseless positing of an "other world" to travel to, to read, to write. This necessity impelled Yanagita to place his object of discourse at an ever increasing distance from the reductive sameness of the center, from the orthodoxies of literary, political, and academic discourse, *and from the products of his own writing*. Yet at the same time, to gain credibility and respectability for his writings as a knowledge of a particular object, he also had to work to make them acceptable to the central institutions of knowledge that conferred the status of reality to objects of discourse.

Begun as a turn, a trip, to the deepest geographical interior of Japan, to "the depths of Tōhoku" in Tōson's words, Yanagita's travel/writing eventually turned inside out to Okinawa, beyond "the edge of Kyūshū," as the alterity of the deep mountains diminished as he wrote about it. Concomitantly, the mountain people of Yanagita's earlier writings vanished into the abstraction he called "the abiding folk," and the ancient origins of the Japanese were placed beyond Okinawa and their essential beliefs concentrated in ancestor worship. Each of these articulations—representing temporal, spatial, and ontological otherness capable of inflections to infinity—generated the kind of self-reproducing structure by which *Yanagita-gaku* could be carried on and on and . . .

Without an invisible world to make visible, without an incredible world to make credible, Yanagita could not have written as he did, with imagination and authority. His valorization of the fantastic in an increasingly rationalized world guaranteed his place in the writing world as someone who disclosed and transmitted a hidden knowledge of the Japanese "essence" in an apparently modern science of and for the folk while doing little more and no less than cleverly and carefully weaving together the legends of Japan and his own experiences as traveler-writer into "garments of belief."

Revenant

What is concerned is an actual repression of some definite material and a return of this repressed material, not a removal of the *belief* in its objective reality.
— Sigmund Freud, "The 'Uncanny'"

One of the most written about topics in commentaries on the development of Yanagita's folk studies has been his "great shift" from writing about *yamabito* (mountain people), itinerants, and the popular beliefs in the supernatural associated with them—especially *tengu* and the hidden world of *yūmei*—to writing about *jōmin* (the abiding folk), rice-cultivation-based culture, and ancestor worship. This topic has been cast as a great mystery to be solved, for Yanagita did not explain explicitly in his writings the motivations behind his shift, which is sometimes even described as a radical break in his thinking about the determinant core of Japanese culture.[75] Certainly it is true that by the mid- to late 1920s

(Nagaike Kenji offers the 1925 text *Yama no jinsei* and others have suggested the 1926 essay "Yukiguni no haru" as the beginning of this turning point) Yanagita changed his focus from mountain people as vestiges of an aboriginal race on the Japanese archipelago to rice-cultivating and ancestor-worshiping plains people as the mainstream of a Japanese race whose ancestors originally came from the southern islands. Despite this undeniable change of subject, Yanagita's earlier construct of a *tengu*-filled hidden world lingered on, like an unappeased spirit, in the repressed form of a theoretic fiction that functioned to provide a foundation from which to write about his later construct of ancestor worship.

Why a *repressed* form? Because, among other possible reasons, Yanagita likely felt pressure from his on-again, off-again colleague Minakata Kumagusu to submerge his views on *yamabito* and *tengu*. Among the many approaches to the mystery of Yanagita's conversion to *jōmin,* one that has gained growing attention centers on Minakata's severe criticism and ridicule of Yanagita's belief that folk tales about *yamabito* and *tengu* referred to the descendants of a real, separate aboriginal race of people who were long ago forced into the mountains by the Japanese who then populated the plains.[76] The argument goes that this "farewell to mountain people," as Akasaka Norio has dubbed it, had its first impetus in a spirited debate over the real or imaginary status of *yamabito* that took place in the correspondence between Yanagita and Minakata around 1915–1916. Yanagita had earlier initiated their correspondence with a letter to Minakata requesting information about mountain people stories in the Wakayama region, where Minakata was living. Minakata confirmed the existence of numerous such tales circulating in the area among the general populace there and provided Yanagita with useful examples, but differed with Yanagita in their interpretation. Simply put, Minakata's view was that popular tales and beliefs about mountain people, *tengu,* and the like — such as the ones collected and retold in *Tōno monogatari* — did not refer to the "real mountain people" that Yanagita believed they did.[77] In one famous letter to Yanagita dated midnight 23 December 1916, Minakata relates an instance when he and an assistant, while collecting insect specimens half-naked in the countryside one hot day eight years earlier, came charging down a mountain slope waving their sticks and insect nets as their momentum sent them hurtling toward some village women at the base of the mountain. The startled women turned and ran, screaming that "strange beings have descended from the heavens" (presumably a reference to *tengu*). That, Minakata suggested, was your *yamabito*.[78]

Even if it were this prodding from Minakata that eventually led Yanagita to drop his view that tales of mountain people and *tengu* referred to a real entity, and therefore to drop mountain people and *tengu* from his folk studies agenda, it does not necessarily follow that Yanagita made a clean and complete break from everything associated with them. In particular, the common belief in a hidden world in which the likes of *tengu* resided as invisible overseers whose felt presence instilled a fear of punishment for misconduct would prove useful to Yanagita as a theoretical foundation for the same moral effect in ancestor worship. Considered in this light, Yanagita's "great shift" from *yamabito* and *tengu* to *jōmin* and *senzo* (ancestors) retains its status as an important break in the history of folk studies without denying the tactical (re)use to which Yanagita would put the figure of the hidden world—and the fantastic—in his theory of ancestor worship. To round off this chapter I will now demonstrate, with a linkage of texts that span this acknowledged break in the content of Yanagita's writing, that Yanagita never really exorcised the spirit of the hidden world that continued to lurk behind the scenes since the Meiji period.

In his later work, Yanagita displayed an explicit preoccupation with the articulation and theorization of a concept of ancestors and ancestor worship as the basis of Japanese social and cultural experience. This work is perhaps his best-known legacy. It is not that concern for the origins and the contemporary practice of spiritual belief was missing in his previous studies; on the contrary, this concern furnished to a large degree the motivation for Japanese folk studies from its inception. What distinguishes a text such as *Senzo no hanashi* (*About Our Ancestors,* 1945) from Yanagita's earlier researches on folk beliefs, however, is the overt drive to provide a now theoretically unified subject, the abiding folk, with a theoretically unified ancestry as object of worship. Yanagita's first attempts at describing the various religious practices of the folk—not yet theorized as the abiding folk but treated rather as a more heterogeneous body often associated with mountain people and itinerants—appear more tentative, more piecemeal, more hit-or-miss as he was still groping for a coherent theory of what constituted the object of awe and devotion for the everyday rural Japanese. This characterization of Yanagita's early texts is one common reading of his movement toward the notion of an abiding folk whose spiritual worship is centered on ancestors who have metamorphosed into a kind of collective deity (*kami*). But this metamorphosis is of a second order. A previous metamorphosis took place within the "hidden world" in Yanagita's writing: the transformation from *tengu* to *senzo*.

What I wish to detail in delineating this metamorphosis of the hidden world's inhabitants is a consistent theoretical ground, or more precisely, space of textual production, in Yanagita's view of spiritual awe and its subsequent social ramifications. The genealogy of *tengu* to *senzo* that has gone unrecognized in studies of Yanagita's project brings to the fore the theoretic function that the fantastical space of the hidden world (*yūmeikai*) played throughout his writing of the folk's lore. In fact, from his earliest attempts at a study of folk culture, Yanagita grounded his writing practice in a structurally unchanging theoretical framework while the agent of spiritual otherness, not the system in which it was deployed, changed shape.

This genealogy of *senzo* demonstrates that the hidden world, operating along with the unlettered sphere of the ordinary rural Japanese as the unsighted site toward which the affects of beliefs are directed, presented for Yanagita a productive "nothingness" from which the beginning of a "poetic" writing of these beliefs could issue throughout his folk studies. This explication of Yanagita's writing further points up the common relationship among theory, belief, and fantastic literature insofar as these discursive forms are generally unsupported by an empirical reality. It also provides an angle of analysis on the tension apparent in a study of the folk which, though relying largely on perishable sources (oral transmission and memory) and directed toward an intangible object (beliefs and sentiments), constantly appeals to the presence of an experienced empirical reality and strives for academic respectability within an institution of knowledge that prizes empiricism. In addition to the impetus he received from Minakata's criticism on the question of *yamabito* and *tengu,* it is my hypothesis that as Yanagita recognized under the gaze of the institution the suspect character of the fictive literary authorization of his writing, he worked to suppress this fissure in the real while still attempting to maintain the space of theoretic production that the poetic loss of rationalist knowledge of the real permits.

This formulation of theory, belief, knowledge, and fiction is again informed by Certeau's characterization of Freud's oscillation between literary and scientific discourses in which Freud "maneuvers between the 'nothing' of writing and the 'authority' that the institution furnishes the text. . . . The more he perceives a dangerous kinship and a disquieting resemblance between his discourse and the ancient legends, the more he institutes and restores from day to day an institutional place which authorizes this discourse in the eyes of his followers and posterity."[79] The scientific institution's unceasing insistence on a referentiality to the real for its legitimizing force in a realist narrative is at odds with the poetic gesture demanded of both Freud and Yanagita in order for them to access as a serious object of study the intangible realm of "the workings of the heart and mind" (*kokoro no hataraki*). In both late-nineteenth-century Europe and Japan the affects of the human psyche had been for the most part banished to trivialized, fictional, "unreal" forms (literature, folktales, myths, and legends). Such forms were resuscitated as valid knowledge in Japan only by strands of nativist (*kokugaku*) discourse that was preoccupied with Japanese literature, ancient myths, legends, and, as in some texts of Hirata Atsutane, stories of strange events and creatures from the hidden world.[80] Consequently, the conflict that arises in the formation of knowledge about the psychic realm turns on the source of legitimization of the investigator's discourse: Is it in the name of the other (the patient's unconscious, in the case of psychoanalysis; the "hidden world" along with the "folk heart," in Yanagita's folk studies) or in the name of the real (via the institution)?

Yanagita began writing on *tengu* and the hidden world from a lack. The lack to which he was responding gaped from what he otherwise regarded as an admirable, albeit biased, first attempt at a serious study of strange tales and the beliefs that generated them, namely, Hirata Atsutane's miscellaneous texts concerning monsters and the other world. Despite other of Hirata's texts that might suggest otherwise, Yanagita claims in "Yūmeidan" that in *Honchō yōmikō* Hirata placed *tengu* outside of his discourse on the hidden world and questions the wisdom of this exclusion.[81] Yanagita attributes to Hirata's strong prejudice against Buddhism this banishment of *tengu* from native Japanese conceptions of an invisible world that existed coterminus with the visible world. This view of *tengu* and *yūmei*, Yanagita insisted, was born of Hirata's passions rather than any theory of the old texts and legends.[82] Developing a different interpretive tack, Yanagita sought to enfranchise *tengu* as the principal denizens of the hidden world in Japan and thus fulfill a lack in theoretical insight that Hirata's blinding passions had introduced. Ironically, what Yanagita seems to have been after in these early attempts at folk studies was, as I previously described, a theory of passions.

Yanagita did accept from Hirata's school of nativism what he identified as "the gist of the theories on the hidden world" (*yūmeiron no kosshi*): "Within our world, what is called the phenomenal world [*gense*] and the hidden world [*yūmei*]—namely, this world and the other world—has been established. Although this world can be seen and heard from the other world, the other world cannot be seen or heard from this world. For instance, two persons sitting face-to-face can't recognize the empty space between them as the other world" (247). Because both punishments and rewards derive from the hidden world under this system of beliefs, the result of this invisible surveillance, Yanagita continues, is a fear of committing a social transgression: "Since people who believe in the discourse on the hidden world of the theologists recognize the fact that there is an other world and fear the other world, they, to put it in Confucian terms, restrain and moderate themselves—they abide by morals" (248). Where Yanagita differs from Hirata is in specifying the agent of surveillance existing in the hidden world that metes out these punishments and rewards. Whereas Hirata, according to Yanagita, saw *tengu* only as corrupted Buddhist priests, Yanagita argues that *tengu* should be considered one major form in which this agent of surveillance manifests itself in popular tales and legends. Because what interests Yanagita is the moral and social effect that this belief in *yūmeikyō* instills through a sense of fear and awe, the definition of the agency toward which these feelings are directed becomes important.

In the same movement by which he fills in this lack of *tengu* in Hirata's discussions of the hidden world, Yanagita produces another by stripping the word *tengu* of its literality before attempting to define it. In what would become a familiar interpretative move in Yanagita's style of ethnological analysis, all reference to the written form of a Japanese word whose origin and meaning is under investigation is denied. Its (Chinese) characters are erased. This methodological imperative shifts the basis of definition of *tengu* from a literal interpretation of the Chinese characters used to represent it to its association with a native notion of monsters. Casting off the characters for *tengu* frees the "substance" of *tengu,* which "has existed from the beginning [in Japan]," from any foreign (Chinese Buddhist) determination of meaning (242). Given Yanagita's opinion that the spoken word conveys thought more fully than the written word, this erasure of the written form opened up for Yanagita a space for a hermeneutics of the "spoken" Japanese psyche. This disposition toward supplanting meaning based on the written directly engaged Yanagita with the Hirata school of nativism, but at the same time he sought to go beyond Hirata's treatment of *tengu*.

In Yanagita's formulation, *tengu* becomes theoretically abstracted. It is merely one manifestation of a generic *obake,* which Yanagita in turn designates as any unexpected, chance communication with the other (hidden) world (248). In this articulation, "monster" is understood not so much as a kind of creature as an unforeseen event, an epiphany. Thus it is fundamentally formless but takes on various forms in narrative accounts of strange, unexpected, and inexplicable encounters. For Yanagita, *tengu* are not limited to "long-nosed, winged goblins," as they tend to be narrowly described in pictorial and narrative representations; he generalizes them to include, in theory, monsters made manifest in the forms of ordinary people, *yamabushi,* wandering monks, and so forth (252). The otherness of the other world whence these forms are believed to come is generated by the inexplicability of their chance appearance from the point of view of this world. In other words, the hidden world consists of everything that lies beyond rational control, comprehension, and predictability, but traces of its workings can be glimpsed in accounts of inexplicable "monsters." Narratively, the epiphanies of *tengu* thus represent breaks and discontinuities, and as such share in Minakata's sense of *fushigi* which upset the notion of unilinear progression in natural and human history.

"Yūmeidan" contains Yanagita's earliest published conceptualization of the hidden world, its inhabitants, and its social utility. It is a concept that derives fundamentally from the Hirata school of nativism via Yanagita's first literary and nativist mentor, Matsuura Shūhei.[83] What distinguishes it from Hirata's formulations is its insistence on the inclusion of a type of monster called *tengu* as the chief native administrator of this realm and as at least one of the figures feared and revered by believers in the existence of the hidden world. This fear and reverence seems due to the common inscription of *tengu* as messengers of the gods and the semidivinity that this position implies. In fact, it is probable that Yanagita's acceptance of this notion of *tengu* (and consequently of monsters in general) as an intermediary between *kami* and humans led to his well-known but now generally discredited assertion that monsters originated as fallen deities.[84] In any case, beginning with this 1905 essay, Yanagita appropriated and refined a paradigm of a popular religious belief in a hidden world in which *tengu* figured as its most immediate object of fear and respect.

As much as twenty-two years later, Yanagita reasserted this paradigm of popular belief during a roundtable discussion with Akutagawa Ryūnosuke, Kikuchi Kan, and Osatake Takeki. The topics of discussion included ghost stories, monsters, inexplicable phenomena, and the imaginative powers of the Japanese. In response to an inquiry by Akutagawa regarding the mutability of the physical forms of supernatural beings (especially *tengu*) as they are depicted over the ages, Yanagita replied:

> While the forms depicted in pictures gradually change, the notion that an invisible spirit exists here does not. My *kokugaku* teacher Matsuura Shūhei would say that if it ever happened that this belief were stripped from our notions of Japan, Japan would be ruined. He said that even when we are speaking together like this and we think that only two people are conversing—and may say some inappropriate things—an other unseen entity is present. Moreover, because of the belief that this unseen entity is passing judgment on us, we cannot be imprudent. This entity, who possesses all the same observational powers and the same above-mentioned judgmental powers as humans, is invisible to our eye and yet exists here incorporeally. If we think that the hidden world and the phenomenal world adhere closely we cannot do things that are inappropriate. He [Matsuura] would repeatedly say that to put it in Chinese Confucian terms, this would be an example of a person of inner discipline. It seems that this notion exists even now in the Japanese view of life.[85]

I cite Yanagita's response to Akutagawa in full to display the extreme similarities between this articulation of the hidden world and that which he made in his 1905 essay "Yūmeidan." In both he recognizes the instruction in nativist learning that he received from Matsuura, schematically describes the workings of the visible/invisible world setup, relates its moral effect on believers in Confucian terms, suggests that this belief is still active today, and, most important, introduces this conception in conjunction with an explanation of an abstract notion of *tengu* ("*Tengu and divine kidnappings*" being the heading of this subsection of the published discussion). Except for minor differences in phraseology, Yanagita's summary of Japanese beliefs in the hidden world, its *tengu* inhabitants, and its social function remained essentially unchanged over the twenty-two-year span separating "Yūmeidan" and this exchange with Akutagawa. What this consistency suggests, if nothing else, is that any theory of popular Japanese religious experience in its social context that Yanagita may have entertained did not develop appreciably during this period. This is a modest point, but one that gains significance when one considers the notable change that would occur in Yanagita's thinking about the hidden world over the next twenty-year span.

The next important discussion of the hidden world that appears in Yanagita's writing occurs in the sixty-fifth section of his 1945 publication, *Senzo no hanashi,* entitled "Ano yo to kono yo" (The other world and this world). In this instance, Yanagita initiates his inquiry with the explicit question: "And so, first of all, where is the other world?"[86] He then offers two related views, one "olden" and the other a more modern update of the older idea. The gist of the difference between the old and the new ideas revolves around the frequency, cause, and sentiments of the meetings between this world and the other world. In recent times, Yanagita suggests, the number of spirits in the nearby but invisible other world has increased to the point that they have gotten out of hand and so proper reverential observances have become difficult to maintain. Subsequently, a greater sense of fear developed toward these unappeased spirits as well as toward those who for other reasons had become dislodged and wandering. This enhanced feeling of fear paralleled a heightened sense of invisible surveillance present at all times around the visible world.

What interests me in this passage is not so much the differences that Yanagita hypothesized between old and new ideas concerning beliefs in the hidden world, but rather the subtle differences in the uncanny repetition of the now familiar motifs in Yanagita's general account of the hidden world. As in "Yūmeidan" of forty years previous, Yanagita once again credits Hirata with the first scholarly inquiries into the problem of the hidden world. He then similarly ranks his own *kokugaku* teacher Matsuura among those scholars who believed in providing reliable personal accounts of encounters with the denizens of the hidden world and cites his words as follows: "Although invisible to our eyes, even this space between you and me is the hidden world. What we say is heard by an unseen entity. What we do is seen by an unseen entity. Because of this, we cannot do evil." [87]

This paraphrase of Matsuura's thumbnail sketch of nativist theories on the hidden world is once again immediately compared to notions of Confucian morality by means of an allusion to the "Four Knows" story in the biography of Yang Chen, which Matsuura cited frequently. This story tells of how when Yang Chen was offered money clandestinely by a man one dark evening he refused, stating, "Heaven knows this secret, Earth knows it, I know it, and you know it." Like Matsuura's notion of the behavioral effect of belief in the hidden world, the "Four Knows" story emphasized the moral influence of an omnipresent, invisible surveillance. What is notably absent from an otherwise simple repetition in *Senzo no hanashi* of Yanagita's understanding of the hidden world in popular Japanese religious beliefs is any mention of *tengu*. Whereas on the previous occasions the hidden world was always brought up in the context of reported encounters with *tengu,* by this time the context is that of ancestral spirits and the worship of them. *Tengu* have been evicted from the hidden world, but Yanagita does not yet explicitly say that *senzo,* or ancestors, have moved into their place. In *Senzo no hanashi* Yanagita is focused, rather, on sorting out the origins and objects of an assortment of seasonal folk observances and detailing how spirits of ancestors achieve a divine status through these practices. The hidden world as such is touched on only tangentially, and hesitantly, amid this discussion of ancestor worship, as if Yanagita himself is not quite sure how he would reconcile his earlier work on *tengu* with his developing theory of *senzo.*

Part of the problem that generates this uneasiness seems to be the location of the other world in which *senzo* reside. Although the hidden world of *tengu* has been established as being immediately among the living, the beliefs concerning ancestors that Yanagita details in *Senzo no hanashi* could suggest that the invisible world from which *senzo* survey the living is transferred to the mountains as they eventually become ancestral deities. This relocation of ancestors to a more distant other world, one possibly distinct from the hidden world, however, does not in any way preclude the possibility of overlap, confusion, or even an amalgamation in Yanagita's thinking about the two (if they are indeed two separate) conceptions of an invisible space filled with spirits of one sort or another. Such an overlap would especially be expected during the transition period that Yanagita describes (typically, thirty-three years in most regions), when the spirits of the recently dead must be accorded the proper ritual observances in order to "become an ancestor" (*go-senzo ni naru*).

Although the personal stakes involved in respecting familial spirits might extend beyond death (i.e., a person would be motivated to carry out rituals for deification not only out of respect for the spirit of a dead relative who might then bestow beneficence to the living family, but also so that these rituals might likewise be performed for oneself after death), the effect of this invisible surveillance in instilling moral conduct during life remains the same as that furnished by *tengu*. In spite of conventional views about ancestral spirits that one could derive from *Senzo no hanashi,* their status is by no means a cut-and-dried issue with Yanagita while he is writing about it. The mere evocation of his earlier articulation of the hidden world attests to a greater fluidity, uncertainty, and complexity in his thinking about *senzo;* at the very least it indicates that the hidden world of his earlier writings on *tengu* still lingered wraithlike in his discourse on *senzo.* The reconciliation of *tengu* and *senzo* is a problem that would be dealt with at a later date.

Actually, the problem is rather repressed than dealt with. Although Yanagita separately related both *tengu* and *senzo* to the hidden world, he seems never to have discussed the two together. After *Senzo no hanashi,* ancestors clearly preside and *tengu* are sidelined in Yanagita's thinking about the moral agency that invisibly exerts influence over the Japanese. The clearest statement to this effect occurred during a 1958 interview entitled "Nihonjin no dōtoku ishiki" (The moral consciousness of the Japanese) in which Kuwabara Takeo asked Yanagita to provide an example of a meritorious trait that the Japanese in particular possess:

> *Yanagita:* You probably couldn't go so far as to call this a meritorious trait, but the Japanese have up until now taken punishments to heart. We have thought that if one commits an evil, punishment for it is a natural consequence. We have absentmindedly believed in the existence of something called a kind of "hidden world" [*yūmeikai*] that existed in "the olden days" of the late Tokugawa

and early Meiji periods. Even as I speak to you, there in that cor-
ner an unseen entity is listening, and I cannot bear being said of
me "Listen to that! Saying things foreign to his heart."

Kuwabara: In the case of Westerners, is this what is called "conscience"? Is it different from a conscience based on monotheism?

Yanagita: Since God can't go about like that, it's ancestors. What is
watching us at hidden places is our ancestors.[88]

In this exchange, the vestiges of Yanagita's previous description of the
hidden world remain. The comparison to Confucian terms such as *shin-
doku* (inner discipline) or *shichi* (the Four Knows) is notably absent and
replaced by the more neutral word *seisai* (sanction, punishment). Gone
too is any acknowledgment of Yanagita's nativist teacher, thus distancing
himself from a previous source of authority. Stripped of these elements,
the essential component—an invisible mechanism that instills a sense of
self-restraint and moral awareness—remains structurally unchanged. It is
important to emphasize here that Yanagita still conceives of the moral
consciousness of the Japanese as deriving from an unseen entity that is
believed to watch over the living. This conception of an invisible moral
surveillance appears in Yanagita's writing as an idée fixe that demands the
kind of theoretical backdrop that *yūmeikai* provided.

What substantially differs within this later statement concerning the
source of moral authority among the folk is the subject of action; it is
explicitly named as being *senzo* rather than *tengu*. As in *Senzo no hanashi, tengu*—previously the acknowledged focus of most past studies of
the hidden world, including Yanagita's—have no place in the discussion.
They have been completely displaced by a conception of an ancestral
spirit that Yanagita emphasizes "isn't a single person. It is precisely this
part that is difficult to explain. It [*senzo*] takes a continually accumulative
shape."[89] Just as he identified *bakemono*, of which *tengu* was but one of
many types, as a shapeless collectivity that is given individualized form
in the singularity of an emotive, narrative event, Yanagita associates ancestors with a nebulous accumulative collectivity that, as he explains in
Senzo no hanashi, receives a divine form through the ritual observances
punctuating the agricultural calendar. By this move, Yanagita has perhaps
chosen to discard his previous ideas about *tengu* and the hidden world
(which might help explain why he excluded "Yūmeidan" from his col-

lected works) or has conveniently forgotten them to avoid the conflict (embarrassment?) they would pose in an ancestor-based theory of Japanese moral consciousness that he espoused in his later years. Or perhaps *senzo* and *tengu* did fit together in Yanagita's theoretical otherworld as the one displaced the other.

The juxtaposition of the above four articulations of the hidden world, articulations that span over five decades, produces two immediately interesting observations about his position on the concept of the hidden world: (1) his position radically changed, and (2) his position radically remained the same. Both points—the internal changes and the internal consistency of Yanagita's view on folk beliefs in the hidden world—deserve extended analysis, but what I wish to highlight, perhaps contrary to my penchant for discontinuities, is the structural continuity of the hidden world as a theoretic fiction throughout Yanagita's thinking both within and beyond discussions of the hidden world and how it enabled the writing of folk studies. The shift from *tengu* to *senzo* is still ultimately important because this metamorphosis itself becomes a metaphor for the flux and pull characteristic of Yanagita's desire to make the invisible visible (i.e., "fantasize," the Greek root of which, *phantazein,* means to make visible or manifest) while at the same time denying flights of fancy in favor of empirical observations grounded in the bedrock of reason.

This process of transformation, of bringing the unknown and unreal into the known and real, was itself bound to change the shape of folk studies as it worked toward disciplinary status. The absence or lack at the origins of the discourse on the folk cannot be doubted; it also could not be discovered if folk studies was to survive as a legitimate form of knowledge within mainstream scholarship. Here is where I contend that the curious metamorphosis of *tengu* into *senzo* within the realm of the hidden world in Yanagita's writing can be productively read as a sign of the drive that aims to discipline, to "tame" folk studies without full attainment of the goal.[90] The empathetic study of the folk, as Yanagita theorized it, demanded an undisciplined discipline of the absent presences that the folk evoke. In the pursuit of this (unfulfillable) goal, the economy of affects returns, like an ancestral apparition, in folk studies as the economy of the hidden world, and the figure of the hidden world itself repeatedly returns throughout Yanagita's writing to help and to haunt him. It is very much a return of the repressed, a revenant, that manifests itself uncannily in familiar yet slightly altered forms.

This economy can be imagined as comprising a circuit of displacements within the theoretic fiction (the hidden world) that had initiated a reproducible writing space for Yanagita's folk studies. In "Yūmeidan" Yanagita generalized the definition of *tengu* (under the umbrella of "monster" as chance encounter) to include various liminal human types, most notably wandering monks and *yamabushi*. In "Tengu no hanashi" he also identified stories of *tengu* with sightings of Ainu and other mountain people. The result is that the other of the other world, although still unusual, attained a more human form as it became more rationalized in Yanagita's explanations. Yet, rather than continuing this line of rationalization until the hidden world is explained away, Yanagita retained the theoretical framework of the hidden world, which was necessary for his conception of moral consciousness based on an invisible surveillance, and placed "our ancestors" in it. With this move he thus achieved a degree of credibility for his object (it acquires a reality to which all Japanese, not just "superstitious" rural folk, can respond) without completely abandoning the "unreal" space that (re)produced and supported it in his writing. He has also, in effect, transformed the heterogeneous alterity of monsters into a temporal other as the Same for a history of "the Japanese folk."[91]

The first half of the circuit of agents in Yanagita's hidden world, then, goes like this: monsters (*tengu, obake*) to strange humans (*ijin*) to ancestors (*senzo*). The complementary half is formed by connecting Yanagita's view of the respective relations of monsters and ancestors to a fourth term, deities (*kami*). Given that he believed monsters had descended from a previous divine status and that ancestors could theoretically "ascend" into deities, the second half of the circuit appears thus: ancestors to deities to monsters. Together the two sequences of relations form a network of exchange (monsters to strangers to ancestors to deities to monsters) that accounts for each of these major objects of Yanagita's research within the same economy of the hidden world. Each can be staged against the same *theoretically* unified background that in practice appears piecemeal and disparate or, at best, sutured. In Yanagita's writing one can thus see the specific conception of a hidden world originally derived from Hirata's nativism broadened to furnish a general theoretical grounding for the entities occupying a hidden folk heart that preoccupied Yanagita's brand of folk studies.

This theoretical arrangement—itself "hidden" in Yanagita's writing as he is aware of the "surveillance" of the academy over himself—is a crucial mechanism for the generation of folk studies. The theoretic fiction of the hidden world sets in place a reproducible space for textual production by means of continual absences and displacements of signification which will always offer themselves for filling and completion; there will always be something hidden among the folk that will require revelation. That this foundation for writing rests on beliefs, fantasies, and theories that are referenced to "nothing" is irrelevant as long as it can appear and be accepted as "real." This legerdemain is enacted not only by the rhetorical and hermeneutical techniques enumerated earlier in this chapter, but also by the second stroke that the circuit of relations within the economy of the hidden world enables: the hidden world as a fantastically imaginative realm of *tengu* returns as a relatively rationalized realm of *senzo*. This move may or may not have been sufficient for folk studies' masquerade as an accepted scientific discipline, but at the same time may have ironically paved the way for its ideological co-optation by state apparatuses attached to the very same institution of knowledge from which folk studies sought disciplinary acceptance. Spiritual belief in ancestors would serve powerful interests in mobilizing patriotic spirit during Japan's war effort and imperial expansion of the 1930s and 1940s. In this context the shift from *tengu* to *senzo* marks important movements in the formation of Yanagita's mode of folk studies: movements between state and local interests, empirical observation and theory, disciplined knowledge and radicalized imagination, science and fiction.

PART III

MODERN MYSTERIES

CHAPTER 5

Transforming the Commonplace:

Fushigi as Critique

By pounding a firm metal anchor into the ground of reality and never being able to

forget the height of the tether, one can never idly walk the other side beyond the

white clouds. And moreover, what one can see is limited to what one wants to see.

—Yanagita Kunio, "Shoko Kyōka kan" (This view of Kyōka)

The tension between science and fiction at the heart of Yanagita's study of Japanese folk life should not be thought of as a simple contest between reality and unreality, truth and falsehood. Rather, it is better understood as the difference between two modes of observing, knowing, and organizing social existence to produce a world. Chapter 3 outlined how the Meiji government set out to undermine worlds organized by folk knowledges while constructing a world on epistemological foundations more suited to the ordering of citizens subjected to a modern nation-state. In large part, this program of civilization entailed, in Lafcadio Hearn's words, "the conquest of superstitions" through the institutionalization of modern education and medicine. Inoue Enryō was a principal spokesman in this crusade and was influential in forming late Meiji educational policy that specifically targeted folk beliefs and practices under the rubric of *meishin*. Although Minakata privately criticized the narrowness of Inoue's attitude toward folk ways from early on, it was not until Yanagita publicly challenged the basis of *yōkaigaku* that a sympathetic and sustained alternative approach to the subject of the folk appeared. In Yanagita's case the opening to this approach came largely through the gates of literature. In particular, his opposition to the credos and creations of the Naturalists during the final decade of Meiji found him in alliance with fiction writers of quite a different bent from this mainstream literary movement. Yanagita's mode of conceptualizing the realities of social existence within his experimental "science of the folk" was much closer to that of the practitioners of what has become known as *gensō bungaku* (fantastic literature) than that of the Naturalists who espoused norms of scientific objectivity in writing.

From mid-Meiji the literary fantastic ranged from classic stories of ghosts and the supernatural re-emplotted as modern moral allegories to more subtle inventions of a mode of writing which Todorov has characterized as "that hesitation experienced by a person who knows only the laws of nature, confronting an apparently supernatural event."[1] In other words, the hallmark of the fantastic is an ambiguity, an indeterminacy, a doubt concerning the explanation of an event that appears to defy scientifically discoverable laws of nature as understood by a "reasonable person" (i.e., one who is familiar with and accepts the truth according to scientific discourse). But, by situating itself in what Lance Olsen describes as an "ellipse of uncertainty," the fantastic in its most critically edged form demonstrates that no laws are "natural" and that the juridical standard of the "reasonable person" too is a man-made fiction, more often than not informed by a conservative ideological concern for civil control in the name of a Truth sanctioned by "reality." In this context, the fantastic conceived of as "a mode of writing which *enters a dialogue with the 'real' and incorporates that dialogue as part of its essential structure*"[2] valorizes within a historical time and place texts that might otherwise be discarded as transcendental or escapist indulgences of a minor literary tradition. In dialogue with a socially constituted reality, the fantastic is attached to that reality while at the same time putting the foundations of what constitutes the real into question. Thus imagined, it can become a mode of social and political critique.

Without doubt the most conspicuous practitioner of this genre of critical ambiguity during the Meiji period was Izumi Kyōka. With themes and motifs derived from ages of Japanese folk beliefs and literary ghost lore, Kyōka wrote tales that, though akin to traditional genres of ghost stories and legends, often furnished in their reinvested forms the basis for a penetrating critique of the route Japan's rationalized modernity was taking. His aesthetics of *chūkan*, of the in-between, proclaimed in his praise of twilight discussed in the prologue, indeed operated on the interstices between the categories that ordered a reality commonly accepted as a natural and true reflection of Reality. So situated, *chūkan,* the chronotope that informs fantastic tales, marks a critical register while the folk beliefs and communal imaginary (*kyōdō gensō*) that fuel them are consequently infused with new importance.

This chapter takes this conception of the fantastic as critique to late Meiji and Taishō period writings by Kyōka and Yanagita that possess an ambiguous sense of time and feature figures of *fushigi* associated with specific topoi: mountains and bridges. In Kyōka's texts such scenes congeal into a "chronotopic motif" (to use Bakhtin's phrase) and create a defamiliarizing moment through which to expose and critique the arbitrary foundations of social order in a modernizing Japan. The same chronotopic motifs reappear in Yanagita's writings on folk beliefs, not as scenes in a fantastic tale but as objects of knowledge in a scholarly discourse. These congealed events of *chūkan* narratives are not wholly detached from their previous literary incarnations, but they do undergo certain transformations when ultimately inscribed as objects of knowledge. To explore the effects of identity and difference between Kyōka's and Yanagita's respective writing practices is one aim of this chapter.

In the twilight of modern Japan, Kyōka and Yanagita shared the same discursive terrain—folk tales and legends—which they mined for the semantic treasures that enriched their respective writing practices. Because this kinship arose in no small measure from their shared opposition against the theory and practice of the Naturalists, it is first useful to detail Kyōka's critique of that movement, his own theory of literature, and his specific points of literary contact with Yanagita before engaging the critical fantasies they employed to transform the commonplace, to "walk the other side."

In Praise of Fantasy

I seem to hear the philosophers disagreeing. This is really unhappiness, they say, this life of folly, error, and ignorance. No, indeed; this is to be human. . . .

Still, it is a sad thing, they say, to be deceived. No; the saddest thing is not to be deceived. The notion that happiness comes from a knowledge of things as they really are is wrong. Happiness resides in opinion. Human affairs are so obscure and various that nothing can be clearly known.

—Erasmus, *The Praise of Folly*

The writers who rallied around Tayama Katai's cries for a literature that described the surface of physical surroundings with a scientific objectivity, that putatively curtailed the subjectivity—the thoughts, feelings, opinions, imagination—of the writer, derived their happiness and their truth from a knowledge of things "as they really are." In his numerous essays in response to naturalist theories of literature, Izumi Kyōka, like Erasmus's goddess of Folly, flatly asserted that this approach to a knowledge of things, especially of the human heart, was misguided. There was no room at all for human sentiment in the ideal of descriptive writing that the Naturalists had preached. Kyōka also would have agreed with Folly when she pointed out that "everyone admits that all the emotions belong to folly. Indeed a fool and a wise man are distinguished by the fact that emotions control the former and reason the latter." And he would not have felt a need to make apologies for his position, because Folly, as the purveyor of emotions, is also the wellspring of "imagination, inventiveness, and therefore pretense and make-believe."[3] As a reading of Kyōka's critical essays will reveal, the gist of his view on the sources, practices, and goals of literature echoed Folly's pedigree: for him, the essence of literature was the mediation of a given "factual reality" by an imagination that flowed from the writer's *kibun* (feeling) to invent new worlds with an artistry and skill that would make the reader believe in their reality. I will provisionally suggest that this view of Kyōka's was not too far from the theory of writing that Yanagita was at the same time attempting to formulate and apply to a cultural history of the "folk heart." A reading of Yanagita through this Kyōkaesque filter opens a new angle from which to reevaluate the writing of folk studies.

In a series of essays from mid-1908 to just after the publication of Yanagita's *Tōno monogatari* in 1910, Kyōka took the proponents of naturalism to task and he did so in no uncertain terms. The form of his twofold critique was simple and direct: first, mercilessly explicate the fallacies and contradictions implicit in naturalist manifestos; second, challenge the value, literary or otherwise, of writing produced according to such manifestos. Throughout these essays it is apparent that Kyōka's attack on the Naturalists was an aggressive defense of his practice of writing about the supernatural, which the Naturalists typically dismissed as being a form of antiquated, frivolous, and errant romanticism that had no place in an age of modern science. After all, the supernatural could not be properly measured, its surface could not be precisely described "as seen, as heard, as smelled, as touched, as tasted." But it was this very imprecision and incommensurability of the feelings conjured by supernatural themes placed in a modern context that Kyōka valorized in the creative transformation of what one ordinarily saw, heard, smelled, touched, and tasted.

In one of his most vituperative essays, "Romanchikku to shizenshugi" (Romanticism and naturalism, 1908), Kyōka makes a point-by-point parry and riposte against the harsh criticisms that the Naturalists had laid against him in particular and romanticism in general. He begins by derisively noting all the hubbub that the Naturalists have stirred up in the media and calls such advertisements "pointless and stupid," saying that the Naturalists would better prove the worth of their "ism" through their literary works rather than through debates.[4] But Kyōka preempts even the possibility of such worth being demonstrated by dissolving the grounds of the Naturalists' literary position with a definition of literature that excludes their form of writing and discredits their standards of literary critique. He considers the Naturalists confused and ignorant of the nature and goals of literary art: "Now then, I wonder if the Naturalists, who castigate romantic works as being 'art for art's sake' and advocate artlessness or the non-use of artistry, can really produce excellent works by means of artlessness, without using a single bit of artistry? It is extremely doubtful. If one pursues this 'artlessness' to the extreme—no, not even to the extreme —doesn't artlessness itself end up destroying the very substance of narrative fiction [*shōsetsu*]? Assuming that one doesn't use any artistry at all in a narrative fiction, what kind of narrative fiction would result?" (28:685).

Kyōka's answer to this largely rhetorical question is, None. The naturalist discourse on truth derived from objective descriptions of empirical reality is out of place when forced into the form of narrative fiction. Consequently, what they write is not literary fiction, or even art for that matter: "Wouldn't it be better," he suggests, "for the Naturalists, who attack artistry while proclaiming 'artlessness' in depicting so-called 'truth,' to publish scholarly essays [*ronbun*] instead of borrowing the form of narrative fiction which uses artistry?" (28:685). Kyōka is quick to point out that this does not mean that narrative fictions do not deal with truth of some sort. Indeed, he admits that art in the form of novel writing can probably be considered a *ronbun,* but one that attempts to depict and examine through artistic technique "feeling that can be transmitted neither by mouth nor by scholarly essay. If one can transmit feeling accurately [in fiction] it gives birth to something of deep flavor" (28:686).[5]

This transmission of a form of nonempirical truth, which is represented in feeling and conducted through an artistry derived from the writer's sensitive *kibun* or *kokoro* (Kyōka uses both words interchangeably), constitutes for Kyōka the ultimate goal of perfected art. In particular, he states that the best works of literature are those that "make the reader feel . . . feelings not felt by ordinary people." As long as this goal is effectively achieved it does not make any difference whether it is done by romanticism or naturalism, which is why, Kyōka explains, despite being labeled a "Romantic," he has no connection to any "ism" (28:684). What he is connected to, knowingly or not, is Yanagita's position concerning the depiction of "factual reality" (*jijitsu*) in the "sketch-from-life writing" (*shaseibun*) and "flat description" (*heimen byōsha*) advocated by the Naturalists.

It will be recalled from the preceding chapter that Yanagita came out against the Naturalists in a series of essays written at just about the same time as Kyōka's. In his 1907 "Shasei to ronbun," for example, Yanagita's line of argument begins at a different angle from Kyōka's, but their trajectories conjoin. Whereas Kyōka suggests that naturalist concerns for empirical truth were better suited to *ronbun,* Yanagita points out that because the ideal of *shaseibun* implies the banishment of authorial subjectivity and intervention, it is not even suited to thoughtful, speculative essay writing. This observation leads Yanagita to his declaration of what he thought to be the essence and strength of writing: "Writing is achieved by the spirit [*ki*]; that is to say, it produces texts through the author's feelings [*kibun*]."[6] In other words, the Naturalists could not possibly practice what they preached; it would go against the very nature of writing itself. Kyōka could not have agreed more. The way he put it was that "to employ writing itself is a kind of artistry," and to conceal this artistry is difficult (28:687). He strongly suggests here that even the Naturalists' attempts at artlessness constitute "artistry," but one of a low quality that is better identified as artifice disingenuously posing as nature. This brief comparison of Yanagita's and Kyōka's ideas about writing during this period is noteworthy for presenting two aspects of Yanagita. On the one hand, he seemed attracted to the notions of scientificity surrounding naturalist discourse because he was struggling at this time to apply that aspect of their theories to scholarly writing on folk culture. On the other hand, he was deeply impressed by the techniques, the "artistry," of conveying feelings in narrative fictions, particularly in those that achieved a fantastic effect in describing supernatural or invisible subjects.

Kyōka too analyzed the naturalist notion of *shaseibun* in another essay of this period, "Jijitsu no kontei, sōzō no junshoku: Jijitsu to sōzō" (The foundations of factual reality, the embellishments of imagination: Factual reality and imagination).[7] In a vein quite similar to Yanagita's argument for the application of *shaseibun* to speculative writing, Kyōka emphasizes the necessity to supplement *shaseibun* with imagination in order for it to come alive. He takes the term *shasei* in the literal meaning the Naturalists gave it (sketch from life) and reverses the value it held for them in relation to imagination: *shasei*, as a description of factual reality, he says, is only "a sketch, an incomplete picture. . . . What is interesting is one's completion of the sketch, the filling in of one's own shades and colors by adding imagination." But Kyōka does not completely discount the value of sketching observed reality. In fact, he goes so far as to concede that "one cannot attach a relative importance to observational powers toward factual reality or to imaginative powers" because "both are valuable in writing a piece" (28:732). Yet despite this claim of impartiality toward these two faculties, it is apparent that Kyōka privileges imaginative powers, which, significantly, are not mentioned as being "toward" anything, whereas observational powers are "toward factual reality." The implication is that *shaseibun* is by nature limited (or is limited by nature), whereas imagination is limited only by the limits of one's desire to see the supernature lying "beyond the white clouds," as Yanagita described the impulse behind Kyōka's vision in this chapter's epigraph.

The principle subversion of the Naturalists' valorization of the technique of *shaseibun* comes, however, in Kyōka's enumeration of the functions and effects belonging respectively to observational and imaginative powers. Observational powers are important, he states, in allowing the author "to bring out places not yet able to be brought out by others and to know scenes not yet able to be known," but in addition to these functions "it is necessary to have imaginative powers such that you think up things not yet thought by others" (28:732). Such thoughts for Kyōka are not mere diversions of idle fancy, for he asserts that it is only by the exercise of imagination that the true nature and complexity of "factual reality"—that is, its ultimately *subjective* constitution and existence through heterogeneous human experience—is brought to light. Kyōka implies that the homogenizing tendency of naturalist writing is not only lifeless and boring, but is supremely *un*natural by draining human history and experience from its object. Recognition of this effect in the logic behind naturalism is what was really at stake in both Kyōka's and Yanagita's praise of imaginative powers that dared to fantasize beyond the visible.

Kyōka illustrates the homogenizing and dehistoricizing effects of the Naturalists' ideal writing with a few simple examples that bear an immediate relation with Yanagita's early efforts to depict the heterogeneity of regional folk cultures in Japan. In "Jijitsu no kontei" Kyōka mocks the pseudoscientificity of a typically naturalist description of a bell ringing. Regardless of where or when a bell rang, a Naturalist, he says, would probably write, "the air oscillated so many times per second." But writing just the fact of having heard a bell has no "zest or interest at all" because it fails to move the feelings of the reader. Not only that, it homogenizes experience. By not evoking the "different shade and tone" that the sound of the same bell would have in a different place at a different time one actually fails in depicting the full reality of the object in its particular context. Its "reality" therefore changes according to context. The function of the writer's sensitivity and imagination is to evoke such different shades and tones through whatever artistic technique necessary to arouse the reader's own sensitivities and imagination to the point where what is read is thought to be a "true thing," a "factual reality" among many possibilities (28:730). Under the banner of scientific objectivity, naturalism sought to obliterate these differences, and consequently the possibility of thinking "otherly," by amputating the faculty of imagination from the human heart or, perhaps, by eliminating altogether the creative imprecision of human thoughts and practices.

This kind of homogenization of experience Kyōka dramatizes in a late 1909 essay that again questions the sterilizing effects of a naturalist style of writing that seeks to achieve a scientific precision at the expense of the gray areas, of the in-between, of human experience. In "Jijitsu to chakusō" (Factual reality and ideas) Kyōka compares a weather forecast that one might receive from a weather station with one produced by a sea captain. Rather than the meterologist's report ("Low atmospheric pressure at such-and-such an east longitude and such-and-such a north latitude"), it is the sea captain's announcement—"The clouds are at the cape so it's a storm"—Kyōka notes, that "moves our hearts to an unknowable degree."[8] He does not try to analyze why such a scene is more emotive, but the kind of folkic wizardry that derives from the sea captain's practical knowledge and experience, imprecise as it might be, is a good example of Minakata's notion of tact (*kotofushigi*) and the role of chance and hunches in the production of human culture.

Kyōka then indeed continues this essay with a discussion of how chance encounters can jog ideas and memories of things that on the surface might seem unrelated to the thing encountered. As a practical example of such a phenomenon, Kyōka notes: "By an unfamiliar place, the charm of one's native place clearly comes to mind for the first time." This rather prosaic comment becomes provocative when considered in the context of Yanagita's joint interest in curious local practices and fantastic tales. It might provide a clue to why the latter are so prevalent in Yanagita's first attempts at folk studies but then slowly fade to the background as he began to define a core native Japanese culture in his later work. That is, Yanagita might very well eventually have used the strange and unfamiliar represented in fantastic tales as a backdrop for the eventual mise-en-scène of the main character, an authentic core of "Japanese culture." This kind of spatial and, Kyōka adds, temporal distancing is an important technique to create an effect of defamiliarization that works within many of Kyōka's stories to generate a critical angle on one's given historical predicament. He emphasizes that sticking to the surface of factual reality as the Naturalists recommend does not allow any thoughts—critical or otherwise—to arise at all (28:748).

Perhaps the one comment from Kyōka on naturalist style with the most direct bearing on Yanagita's method of folk studies occurs in the essay that began this discussion, "Romanchikku to shizenshugi." In it Kyōka accuses the Naturalists not only of homogenizing varieties of human experience, but also of dehistoricizing the objects about which they write by seeing them only in terms of an abstract and universalized scientific outlook: "Seeing characters of a place-name, for example, conjures associations of places, history, and legends; whereas Naturalism, in the name of 'truth,' will give you the geometric dimensions of the place." Faulting the Naturalists for sapping literature of its proper creative function by reducing it to a pseudoscientific discourse, Kyōka then rhetorically asks: "Wherein would lie the difference between narrative fictions [*shōsetsu*] and geometry?" (28:687). As noted in the previous chapter, a key component of Yanagita's "hermeneutics of the heart" involved the linking of words, often place-names, to a network of historical and legendary associations to ascertain the meaning or origin of a particular folk practice or belief. Despite Yanagita's plea for a rigor worthy of a serious discipline, his method was far from being scientifically precise and required more artistic "tact" than geometric measurement. He emphasized the analysis of the spoken rather than the written form of a word, but I imagine that he could only have appreciated Kyōka's comment here about remaining sensitive to the history and folklore embedded in the characters of a place-name. Both enunciations spoke to a similarly conceived analysis of linguistic associations that brought to the surface buried layers of the mental and spiritual life of the folk. Indeed, sections of Yanagita's research on Japanese place-names, carried out from late Meiji to early Shōwa and collected in *Chimei no kenkyū* (A study of place-names, 1936), read like a relatively "disciplined" (I hesitate to say "scientific") realization of the more poetic conjuration of myth-historical geography that Kyōka suggests.[9] Yanagita and Kyōka were back-to-back facing opposite sides on the same line dividing and joining scientific and fictional discourses.

And they both were trying to listen to and record a polyphony of voices that naturalist theory could not hear. Three months after the publication of "Romanchikku to shizenshugi," Kyōka sought to clarify his position in the disputes between naturalism and romanticism in his essay "Yo no taido" (My position, July 1908). After denying membership to either the Naturalist School or the Romantic School, whose wrangling reminded him of rivalries among local barons and "is a very interesting phenomenon . . . a new field" in itself, Kyōka reaffirms his commitment to an art the goal of which is to depict and proliferate differences among people.[10] In this instance, he directly addresses the issue of accurately portraying different spoken voices and regional accents in writing, a problem that Yanagita too was wrestling with during this period. Kyōka describes his desire to nuance voices in different settings to achieve different effects because, he explains, "people's character depends on time and place." Much of what is contained in dialogue, he continues, is lost in printing, "so it takes skill to nuance it" (28:695), the same kind of skill that was required of Yanagita to interpret folk sentiment as it was ex-

pressed in spoken (or pseudospoken) words. The nuances of voices and
the subjective feelings they carry, like the history and lore associated with
written words and objects, were annulled by the theories of the Naturalists: such polyphony and sentiment constituted an excess in need of
excision in order to maintain the rigor of a writing that aspired to a scientific objectivity. Kyōka's point, however, is that it is this very excess,
identified (negatively by the Naturalists) with imagination and artistry,
that animates the core of human life and its portrayal.

The "different effects" that Kyōka had in mind are none other than
effects of defamiliarization wherein the extraordinary is brought out
from the ordinary, momentarily transforming "everyday reality" into a
glimpse of another world. Yanagita observed this effect of Kyōka's work:
"As a matter of fact, when led by Kyōka one notices that there is still
poetry in these modern times. Even in the hallucinations of people, tired
and lingering at the crossroads, reveries of distant ancient times passing
by are sometimes felt. The hardships of everyday life are not necessarily
commonplace and the sorrows of vagrancy are not necessarily vagrant
and in passing."[11] In effect, the thrust of Kyōka's fantastic fiction was to
make the reader think otherly about the same, to see the uncommon
within the common, but to do so in a credible fashion. He emphasized
the importance in maintaining a dialectic with the real in order that the
real may be set askew by the imagined. The perception of extraordinary
feelings within ordinary reality did more to plumb the depths of human
psyche than either naturalist scientificity or romantic sentimentality. It is
also what distinguished both Yanagita and Kyōka from these two literary groups. In his review article of *Tōno monogatari* (a book he loved and
"reread three times without tiring of it"), Kyōka noted with relish that
reading it makes one feel "not only the strangeness of things and the be-
witchment of objects. One can also hear among the silences local scenery,
customs, and floral colors."[12] The ability of *Tōno monogatari* to intimate
the supernatural within the natural and to stir the feelings and imagination of the reader is the aspect of this text that Mishima Yukio too will
later praise. This ability is also, as a commentator on Mishima's comments
has noted, a key characteristic of Kyōka's form of fantastic fiction.[13]

Kyōka ends "Romanchikku to shizenshugi" by severely reprimanding
the Naturalists' attacks on non-Naturalist writers. He calls them "cow-
ardly," "unmanly," and "shameful," like a bunch of "loose geisha trying to

make a quick buck without any artistic effort" (28:690). He challenges them simply to write well, to produce good stories rather than vacuous isms. But for Kyōka, as for Yanagita, to write well required the creation of a field of feeling and imagination among object, writer, and reader which the Naturalists theoretically expunged. He never believed that even in describing something "as it is" the Naturalists could in practice produce good literature without permeating their works with feelings and imagination. "Without feelings," he bluntly states elsewhere, "it's no good."[14] Not only would it be no good, it simply would not be literature. To the Naturalists' criticism that Kyōka's literature was out of touch with modern reality in its preoccupation with monsters, Kyōka responded, "In a word, monsters [*obake*] are the concretization of my feelings. There is no reasonable way to explain it." And when told that he should at least keep monsters in their natural settings of dark woods and mountains and out of Tokyo, he cryptically replied, "I want to put them in a place where a train's bell is audible in the middle of Edo."[15]

Dislocating Reality

Kyōka was not the only person responsible for bringing monsters to Tokyo. Sasaki Kizen's diary entry for 4 November 1908, the evening that Mizuno Yōshū introduced him to Yanagita, reads: "When I had returned from school Mizuno showed up and together we went to Mr. Yanagita's place. I told spook tales [*obakebanashi*] and returned back home."[16] Inoue Enryō had unwittingly attracted to Tokyo in 1905 a one-man *hyaku monogatari* in the body of Sasaki.[17] As previously mentioned, Sasaki quit Inoue's school and for a while wrote fantastic tales under a pen name derived from Kyōka, "Kyōseki." But what had brought notable attention to Sasaki was not so much his written tales—often based on themes of tales from Tōno—but the oral tales of the supernatural that were part and parcel of his Tōno upbringing. These formed a basis for much of Mizuno's creative writing in the period 1908–1909, from his novella *Kitaguni no hito* to his collection of "Kaidan" that appeared in *Shumi* magazine. And these tales from the fellow from the North Country, in turn, led to Yanagita's meetings with Sasaki that culminated in the writing of *Tōno monogatari*.

An interesting network of associations, to say the least, one that by

May 1908 had coalesced into the Kaidankai (Ghost Story Association), a literary group organized through *Shumi* magazine and dedicated to the research and recounting of supernatural tales that circulated among the Japanese populace. At the center of this group was Mizuno and, although he was not a direct member, Yanagita stood at its periphery. Several of Yanagita's friends from the literary group the Ryūdokai, of which Yanagita was a founding member, had joined the Kaidankai.[18] Despite its connections with key figures of the naturalist movement, the Ryūdokai saw among its members a growing interest in the literary fantastic, no doubt encouraged by Yanagita, who at the time was writing polemics against naturalism and offering in its stead forms of fantastic fiction (recall his praise of Maeterlinck's play *The Intruder*). It is reported that at the 28 October 1908 meeting of the Ryūdokai, in which Yanagita participated, the main topic of discussion was tales of ghosts and monsters.[19] The research of the Kaidankai was clearly in line with Yanagita's own research interests at the time and, barring any sense of competition over this material, Yanagita was likely pleased to witness its formation.

The first concrete result of this group's efforts was the publication in October 1909, just eight months before *Tōno monogatari,* of a volume simply entitled *Kaidankai.* Its preface was written by none other than Izumi Kyōka:

> Most of the books on supernatural marvels handed down to this day relate—for the sake of ethical education and admonitions—moral allegories and they become nothing more than material for didacticism. They presumably press these spirits into service for the sake of a lesson. How can human faculties grasp the likes and dislikes of the spirits? Attached to the mores of this world, they all miss the truth of the matter. The things that are recorded here in this book are all facts [*jijitsu*], I hear. Reader, do not be at a loss on account of that rushing thing not resembling a train, that flying thing not resembling a bird, that swimming thing not resembling a fish, and that beautiful thing not resembling a worldly, chic schoolgirl.[20]

In a subtle critique of the mistreatment "spirits" (*kishin*) have received as objects of moral allegories and the neglect they have received in contemporary literary discourse on "factual reality" (*jijitsu*), Kyōka exposes in this passage the implicit complicity between Inoue-inspired "superstition bashing" and naturalism-inspired "sketch-from-life writing." In a complementary fashion, they both work in the name of a truth determined by reason to obliterate deviancies derived from the experience and imagination of the folk. He asks the reader not only to be open to the unusual material that follows and to consider it a part of a factual reality (prefiguring Yanagita's similar plea in the preface of *Tōno monogatari*) but also to be sensitive to and appreciative of differences within similarity without dismissing them as confused inaccuracies on the part of the writer.

Just as Kyōka's comments here prefigured a crucial point in Yanagita's preface to *Tōno monogatari,* one of Mizuno's contributions to Kaidankai was a "pre-retelling" of one of Sasaki's Tōno ghost tales that would find its way into Yanagita's book as tale number 100. But even this early publication of a Tōno tale was predated by several months by seven of the stories in Mizuno's June 1909 "Kaidan." One of those seven was the one Yanagita himself said "recalls Maeterlinck's *The Intruder.*"[21] It appears in *Tōno monogatari* as tale number 22:

> When the great grandmother of Mr. Sasaki died of old age the relatives assembled to put her into her coffin. Everyone slept together in the parlor that night. The daughter of the dead woman, who was insane and had been cut off from the family, was also in the group. Since it was the custom of the area to consider it taboo to let the fire die out during the period of mourning, the grandmother and the mother sat up alone on both sides of the large hearth. The mother put the charcoal basket beside her and from time to time added charcoal to the fire. Suddenly, hearing the sound of footsteps in the direction of the back door, she looked up and saw it was the old woman who had died. She recognized how the bottom of the old woman's kimono, which dragged because she bent down a lot, was pulled up as usual into a triangle and sewed in front. Other things were also the same, and she even recognized the striped kimono cloth. Just as she cried, "Oh!" the old woman passed by the hearth where the two women sat and brushed the charcoal scuttle with the bottom of her kimono. The round scuttle turned round and round. Being a stouthearted person, the mother turned and watched where she went. Just as the old woman drew

close to the parlor where the relatives were asleep, the shrill voice of the mad woman screamed out, "Here comes granny!" The others were awakened by the voice and it is said they were all shocked.[22]

In his brief comparison of Yanagita's retelling of this tale with Mizuno's, Nagaike Kenji notes that although the basic story is identical, there are noticeable differences in presentation. What he keys on is that Mizuno's shorter version goes almost straight to the appearance of the dead spirit without stressing the verisimilitudinous details of everyday life that serve to enhance the fantastic effect of the scene.[23] For example, the keeping of the fire during the wake is not explained as a local custom; there is no mention of the women actually sitting next to the hearth nor of the hearth itself; no details of the dead woman's kimono are given; and there is no attempt at characterizing the mother as "stouthearted." Another intriguing detail of Yanagita's version missing in Mizuno's is the insane daughter who had been "cut off from the family." (As the daughter of the dead woman, apparently it would have been her duty to keep the fire.) As a "mad woman," her "abnormal" awareness of the ghost's approach to the parlor parallels the similar ability of the blind man who senses a ghostly presence in *The Intruder*. Nagaike's point is that the context of everyday reality is insufficiently described by Mizuno so that the contact made between the natural and the supernatural, epitomized by the turning charcoal scuttle, lacks in the fantastic effect—that subtle ambiguity and commingling between the natural and the supernatural—achieved by Yanagita.

The basis of Nagaike's critique of Mizuno's version of this tale is Mishima's characterization of the function of the charcoal scuttle that is sent turning by the brush of the apparition's kimono sleeve in Tōno tale 22. Mishima describes the turning scuttle as "a hinge for the dislocation of reality."[24] It is one of his examples of an effective and powerful realization of another world. Through an everyday object another world is signaled, and through this signaling the everyday is transformed. This technique, observes the noted writer and critic of fantastic fiction Shibusawa Tatsuhiko, was the essence of fictionalization in Mishima's view of literature.[25] It was also the dynamic of much of Kyōka's fiction and at the heart of the genealogy of Yanagita's folk studies.

This shared concern of Kyōka and Yanagita for intimating the fantastic through the ordinary so that one's view of a given reality is altered—which is tantamount to "the dislocation of reality" itself—comes across strongly in their mutual praise of one another. In his review of *Tōno monogatari*, Kyōka had noted the uncanniness felt behind the depiction of Tōno's local life and scenery. He was also particularly impressed by Yanagita's ability, in tale number 9 for example, to instill a chilling sense of supernatural presence by the description of a disembodied voice in the valley shouting compliments to a passing flute player under a cloud-streaked moon: "The transformation of this mere voice is much more unearthly than a monster; that is to say, it makes you feel as if something formless, on the contrary, has form."[26] Such a·technique complied precisely with Kyōka's own suggested formula for depicting things that are *fushigi*. In an April 1909 essay entitled "Kai-i to hyōgenhō" (Monsters and methods of expression), Kyōka states that the first rule for conveying the *fushigi* of monsters is by not writing in a *fushigi*-like fashion: "To depict the fantastic, one must not write sounding fantastical [*Fushigi o egaku ni wa fushigirashiku kaite wa ikemasen*]." A descriptive phrase such as "The head of a demon-woman appeared from inside the tatami mat" is, he says "rather exorbitant" and has less "ghostliness" (*sugomi*) than the direct words or actions of the fantastic being itself. "It is easy to make the form of a ghost appear," Kyōka continues, "but to make one talk becomes quite difficult." And the reason for this difficulty comes back to that same problem that Yanagita was grappling with at this same time: "This is because among monsters there are regional distinctions [*chihōteki tokushoku*]."[27]

The attempt to deal with spatially and temporally generated otherness within Japanese history and culture is the one general aspect of Kyōka's texts that Yanagita lauded and identified with in his eulogistic tribute "Shoko Kyōka kan" (This view of Kyōka). Although not actually a eulogy (Kyōka was alive and well at the time of its writing), the style and tone of the piece, written in 1925, clearly expresses a sense of loss over a vision of the world that has passed away amid the business of modernization.[28] To Yanagita, Kyōka's work represented a desire to go beyond the boundaries of commonly accepted reality, to stretch the tether that binds one to it. Only by such action, Yanagita implies, can there be any progressive discovery and creativity in human life. The mysterious "other side of the white clouds" that he invokes is consonant with "the hidden world" (*yūmeikai*) of unseen things that preoccupied Yanagita's early research.[29]

I would specify it further as being a metaphor for other worlds, just as real as the visibly present but existing on an affective, not observational, level. Outside of one's own personal experience, or perhaps using that experience as a rudimentary guide, access to this realm of mental, emotional, and spiritual life of others required more than the physical senses could provide. It also required the sensitive use of a faculty that both Yanagita and Kyōka conveniently referred to as "imagination." Given the way Yanagita begins this essay—situating Kyōka as a "literary oddity," who with his creations "transcended" rather than represented his age—echoes of Yanagita's earlier critique of the Naturalists are easily heard.

But this curious and subtle piece by Yanagita does not stop at simple praise for Kyōka and disdain for the Naturalists. From Kyōka's peculiar treatment of space and time, Yanagita garners clues for a model of writing a history of the Japanese folk for whom past written documentation is largely nonexistent. "Chronology," Yanagita points out, "was futilely unable to bind this author" to its unilinear standard: "Moving and turning from the eternal *Tamayori-hime* in the age of the gods and reaching the gourd-flowers of Taishō, the ages were to Kyōka merely one shining round jewel. To pierce it using a bright scarlet thread was insufficient. He did not always need to inquire of the notches in time such as 'Edo,' 'Momoyama-Azuchi,' and 'Muromachi' in the manner of historians."[30] Is this an intimation of an alternative vision of the past and the passage of time? A veiled plea for a revision of historiographical periodization? Perhaps. Knowing Yanagita's expressed discomfort over the inadequacies of conventional historical periodization that was based entirely on "great men and great events," it is not difficult to imagine him experimenting with even the vaguely circular sense of mythic time evoked in this passage. Indeed, the diffusionist model of concentric circles of time that Yanagita hypothesized to examine historical change emanating from cultural centers across the countryside appears as an inverted reflection of the concentric spatiotemporal circles that structure Kyōka's narrative in "Kusameikyū" (Grass labyrinth), the story to which Yanagita was most likely alluding in the passage quoted above.[31]

Makita Shigeru succinctly explains the basis of Yanagita's concentric circle theory: "He indicated that it is possible to establish interchangeable relationships between distances in geography and distances in time."[32] In other words, forms of cultural practice—religious rites, tales, words, even the use of material objects—that were spatially more distant from the theoretical center were also temporally more distant. Yanagita grafted this concentric spatiotemporal ordering onto his famous icicles image of the working of time throughout Japan as a whole: "Previous ages are hanging down here and there, like icicles, are they not? . . . In Japan things changed only like drippings and saggings which are so gradual and slow that it is not very easy to discern when they changed if they changed at all." [33] Two components of this metaphor of historical time upset historical chronology as conventionally conceived of in Yanagita's day: first, as in Fernand Braudel's *longue durée,* there was a level of change that was glacially slow and largely unresponsive to great persons and great events; second, there was a plurality of disparate times, "hanging down here and there." The immediate ramification of this view of historical time and change is that, for Yanagita, unilinear time in and of itself ceased to be a unifying principle around which one could construct a general narrative of "the Japanese people" without severely excluding a majority of the population or imposing an arbitrary norm that distorted it. Rather, one had the obligation to consider many narrative sites, each with its own standard of time. The problem for Yanagita was first how to access such a spatiotemporal heterogeneity and then how to relate it meaningfully in writing as a legitimate part of "Japanese cultural history." Kyōka had had some practice in dealing with this kind of situation in literary creations that drew from folk narratives. His solution was simple: Believe in their facticity.

Following Kyōka's advice was one thing for literary creations, but what could be the nature of the facticity of folk tales for a cultural history of Japan? This question was, as pointed out in the previous chapter, the focus of the exchange that took place between Yanagita and the cultural historian Nishimura Shinji around 1926–1927. This period, it should be recalled, marked a crucial turning point in Yanagita's work. It was around this time when he began to take stock of his previous research and seriously organize the object, sources, and methodology for the disciplined practice of folk studies. It was also the period during which his focus of study shifted from the marginal, wandering, and heterogeneous complex of Japanese cultures represented by *yamabito* and the folk tales associated with them to the homogeneous unity represented by a *jōmin* (abiding folk) that was characterized by ancestor worship, rice cultivation, and a fixed domicile. His effort to define a researchable object and to lend his research of it an air of academic (i.e., "scientific") respectability may help explain both his shift of focus and the interesting reconciliation between historical "fact" and folkloric "fiction" that he offers Nishimura.

Nishimura was steadfast in his position that tales and legends did not in any way reflect historical facts and therefore they were of little use to the historian of Japanese culture.[34] His attitude stemmed from a positivistic urge common throughout historiography (both then and now) which assumes that historical sources serve only to reflect an empirical historical reality on the level of their content. Even if he were to accept an allegorical reading of folk narratives as an oblique reflection of historical facts, the primary assumption about the reflective relationship between the content of such a narrative and the presumed historical reality lying outside of it would still be in effect. In other words, the historian's job when confronted with such a source would be to cull it for kernels of "factual" referential content and jettison the "fictional" husk.

Yanagita launched a harsh criticism of the trained narrowness of Nishimura's position by arguing that indeed the contents of folk tales and legends were not "historical facts," but that they were believed and passed down among people *is* a historical fact.[35] His criticism can be taken as directed at the positivistic bias of institutionalized historiography as a whole. What Yanagita urged as a remedy was a redefinition of historical "reality" to include beliefs and the feelings that sustained them. He also urged a recognition that folk narratives—from mythical legends to harvest ditties to fantastic tales of *tengu*—were part and parcel of such beliefs. His position here was not far from that of practitioners of the so-called ethnographic history of *mentalités,* a "kind of cultural history," Robert Darton notes, that "belongs to the interpretive sciences. It may seem too literary to be classified under the *appellation contrôlée* of 'science' in the English-speaking world, but it fits in nicely with the *sciences humaines* in France."[36] And, I would add, it fits nicely with the interpretive historical ethnology/folk studies that Yanagita was developing in Japan.

The effect of Yanagita's inclusion of folk narratives themselves into the field of historical reality was twofold. First, it placed in toto such sources into history as constitutive of historical reality rather than selectively seeing tidbits of them as reflective of some preconstituted historical reality or, even worse, banishing them from any historical consideration whatsoever. Second, and more interesting, his practice tends to reverse the historiographical process and its results: instead of turning a set of facts (or events) into a historical narrative, he turns a set of narratives into a historical fact. For example, from comparisons among variations of a particular legend and its possible associations with other textual sources, he would attempt to derive (i.e., interpret) the "core" or "original" meaning of that legend in folk knowledge during some period of time (a process that, as folk studies became more disciplined, unfortunately became more homogenizing of the heterogeneity from which it began). The meaning of the narrative then constituted a "fact." It becomes a "historical event" in a form of cultural history that comes closest to what has become known as *seishinshi* (spiritual history, history of mentalities) in recent Japanese historiography.

The relative lack of historical specificity and the lack of a clear diachronic narrative in Yanagita's writing—the charges most commonly leveled against his work by "scientific" historians—likely result from this inversion of event and narrative. A multiplicity of folk narratives whose spatial distribution would, according to the concentric circle theory, indicate a certain swath of time, congeals to form a synchronic "fact" or "event," which is then set relative to similarly derived "facts" thought to represent earlier or later beliefs. Rather than a chronology with detailed "notches of time," one ends up producing wide plateaus of "long past," "recent past," and "present" beliefs. The agency of change from one such slow and vague plateau to another is itself slow and vague. Even when Yanagita is writing about recent changes in a modernizing Japan he hesitates to credit modern technology with affecting the deepest core of folk beliefs and practices among ordinary people. For example, even in a more ostensibly historical text such as *Meiji Taishōshi sesō hen* (1930), Yanagita is concerned with, as he puts it in the introduction, a "cross-section of recent everyday life" in which "facts" come and go before our eyes (suggesting empirical historical change).[37] But he seems reluctant throughout his analysis to give up the notion of a slower moving core of feeling among the common folk in which "facts" are not coming and going before our eyes and are not heavily affected by the external changes of modernization. This enduring quality, in short, becomes the basis of the abiding folk.

Another way to explain the "unscientific" style of Yanagita's writing is to consider seriously his attraction to a writer such as Kyōka rather than the Naturalists, who had stated scientific pretensions that seemingly would have been more appropriate to someone trying to formulate a "science" of the folk. As late as 1928 Yanagita was, after all, still exchanging fantastic tales face-to-face with Kyōka and others in roundtable discussions.[38] In light of Kyōka's prescriptions for fantastic literature, with its essential mediation of imagination to work on everyday reality and transform it into a credible glimpse of another world, Yanagita's engagement with Kyōka's works can be understood as being driven by the same desire to depict the reality of an other that seemed alien to, but no less "truthful" than, the reality of the modernizing center of Japan. Kyōka's imaginative writing, which challenged conventional orderings of time, space, and even species, offered an opening through which Yanagita could attempt to present the place of the other that everyday folk beliefs represented for him within the hegemony of modern historical, pedagogical, and political discourses of late Meiji and Taishō Japan. The antiestablishment impulse apparent especially in Yanagita's early writings should be placed in the context of this effort to translate, through an interpretive analysis, the content and form of folk space and time as he imagined it existed. This practice did not mean a true replication of that alterity nor its complete distortion, but entailed processing the message received from the encounter with the other.[39] This processing in Yanagita's folk studies produced a "Japanese culture." Kyōka's vision furnished Yanagita with a model by which to access this folkic other across spatial and temporal boundaries and to produce an alternative enunciation in the discourse on the folk and the fantastic which seemed to speak from a position closer to the place of the other. But, as demonstrated in writings by Yanagita and Kyōka that dealt with the same folk figures, entering into the place of the other is tantamount to entering madness.

Mountains of Madness

The 1910–1916 survey of Japanese mental asylums noted in chapter 3 revealed that among the reasons for confining a patient was simply "Goes into the mountains" (*Yamanaka ni hairu*). This phrase is certainly the most conspicuous in Yanagita's 1925 series of essays collectively published as *Yama no jinsei* (Life in the mountains).[40] And, in all of the legends and alleged true stories that he recounts, several of which are from Sasaki, to enter the mountains indicates in the popular imagination a mental deviancy. Yanagita is fascinated by the frequency and mystery of these accounts in Japan and urges that "because it [the phenomenon of taking to the mountains] is today still inexplicable [*fukashigi*], all disciplines should take it under their jurisdiction in the future. To throw it out and not take notice of it would be rather inappropriate."[41] Whether madness leads one to take to the mountains or whether one becomes mysteriously lost for some time in the mountains and returns mentally changed, the narrated action *yama ni hairu* in these accounts configures a chronotope of abnormality. More specifically, it becomes a sign of division and exclusion: division between the sane and the insane; between the citizen and the criminal; between the commonality of "plains people" and the alterity of "mountain people"; and between men and women.

In his comparison of the function of the (mountain) forest as fantastic space in *Tōno monogatari* and in the works of Kyōka, Kasahara Nobuo invokes, with a reference to *Yama no jinsei,* the notion of mountains as sites of madness because of their symbolic relationship between this world and the other world.[42] For him, the "madness" associated with entering the in-between space of mountains that Yanagita relates in *Yama no jinsei* (as well as in *Tōno monogatari*) is a kind of "divine madness" given the popular belief in mountains and forests being sacred sites, topoi of epiphanies from *kami* and *tengu* alike. Such a designation neatly weds the two sides of abnormality, super- and subhuman, that spin ambiguously from *yama ni hairu*. I mention it here to prefigure the discussion that follows on the nature of the social divisions that this chronotope marks in late-nineteenth- and early-twentieth-century Japan.

In *Yama no jinsei* Yanagita is not content, as the keepers of *yashikirō* were, with simply labeling those who go into the mountains as "insane." In several accounts he does not deny that the behavior of these people, often described by fellow villagers themselves as possessed by *tengu*, fox spirits, or deities, can be identified in modern psychological parlance as the results of *seishinbyō*, but he seeks to explore more deeply the circumstances surrounding such supposed mental illnesses. In the section of *Yama no jinsei* that was originally given as a lecture in 1917, one hypothesis Yanagita offers is that going off to the mountains is not the voluntary or natural consequence of insanity, but rather has been part of a long history of "hidden coercion" that has for a variety of reasons ostracized people in the name of "possession" or "insanity" (4:253). There is a hint in Yanagita's statement that the classification of deviant behavior of any sort (true mental derangement or otherwise) as *seishinbyō* under the auspices of modern medical knowledge is the state-sponsored extension of this folkic form of exclusion. Unfortunately, he did not pursue this provocative suggestion any further during this lecture, but elsewhere in *Yama no jinsei* he did relate the distinctions among mountain madness stories that circulated in modern Japan.

The most notable distinction is that between men who go into the mountains and women who go into the mountains. In the preponderance of stories that Yanagita relates, the mental transformations that men undergo while in the mountains and their motivations for going are generally characterized as positive, whereas in the case of women both the result and the motivation are generally characterized as negative. In section 4 and later in section 11, Yanagita recounts old legends and recent reports of men who, world-weary or in pursuit of secret knowledge, take to the mountains to train to become *sennin* (a mountain wizard or hermit-sage). Although in some cases they are described as returning (if they do return) "crazy" or in an "unusual mental state" after their mountain ordeal, it is usually attributable to the harsh conditions of their ascetic practices and may still indeed denote in the folk imagination a divinely inspired madness (4:90–91, 117–25).

In contrast to this male-dominated phenomenon, Yanagita comments on a late Meiji "true story" of a wandering woman who ends up being beaten to death by a group of laborers: "Of course among women there are no cases of hiding in the mountains on account of dissatisfaction and weariness of life. Anyone looking at her conduct understood that it was the result of having gone mad" (4:92). This "fact" is stated as if there were naturally no good reason for women to leave their village for the mountains; therefore, it must be motivated by unreason. Interestingly, a large number of such cases of women's madness are reported as having occurred immediately after the trauma of childbirth (the same affliction, one will recall, that purportedly struck Deguchi Nao's daughters), thus feeding the classical notion of the hysterical woman.[43] The other common explanation for a woman's leaving the village, one that becomes part of Yanagita's interpretation of the phenomenon known among the folk as *kami-kakushi* (the kidnapping of women and children by a deity), is that the woman is forcefully abducted by a lonely "mountain man" seeking a companion; that is, she is raped. In one way or another, then, the woman who enters the mountains is victimized by her sex.

It remains unclear how much of this gender bias resides in the facts of the reported cases, how much in the folk mentality from which these stories come, and how much in Yanagita himself.[44] Judging, however, from his discussions of the spiritual powers of women as shamans, who in their training and peregrinations have strong ties to mountains, Yanagita does try to resuscitate the positive aspects of the type of woman who commonly appears in folk tales as well as in many of Kyōka's stories as a *yama-hime* (mountain princess) figure. Just three months after the completion of *Yama no jinsei,* Yanagita's essay "Imo no chikara" (The power of women) appeared. As part of the studies on Japanese shamanism he had begun in 1913 with "Miko kō" (On shamans), "Imo no chikara" describes behavior that was branded "hysteria" in modern times, but a privileged power in former times. He emphasizes that the most important aspects of folk spiritual life had been under the jurisdiction of women, who provided what a worldly and male-dominated Buddhism lacked in easing otherworldly anxieties. The reason women were thought to serve best as shamanistic mediums of divine spirits, according to Yanagita, likely resided in the fact that "being easily moved, they could, as if there were something happening, spontaneously display the effects of an abnormal mentality [*ijō-shinri*] and relate mysteries [*fushigi o katarieta*]." He adds that women's "special physiology" and ability to bear children "had a strong influence on mental operations."[45] Hence, all young women naturally possessed greater aptitude for shamanistic skills, but usually only those who had further marks of spirituality (i.e., abnormality, blindness being a classic example) were selected for the ascetic training that developed these skills. In most cases this training took place in the mountains.[46] Although amounting to a somewhat backhanded compliment, Yanagita's research on shamanism does strive to understand *yama ni hairu* stories within the spiritual life and mentality of a premodern folk. It implies that wandering insane women of modern times were in former days wandering spiritual purveyors.

The late Meiji true story of a wandering woman who was beaten to death was set in a village near Mt. Nakino in Sakushū (present-day northeast Okayama prefecture), an area that Yanagita introduces as famous for sightings of a red-haired, blue-eyed, half-naked *yama-hime*. The woman is first assumed to be this *yama-hime*, and the startled laborers respond by attacking her, but "when they closely examined her, they realized that she was a woman from a nearby village who long ago went mad and left home." Thus, an "autopsy" reveals that a legendary supernatural figure is reduced to a sublunary lunatic. The pessimistic lesson to be drawn from this story and Yanagita's related work on mountain-centered shamanism is that the supernatural privilege of the woman who could literally speak the fantastic wanes woefully in the rational light of the modern world. The optimistic lesson is that if set at the proper angle, a shamanistic *yama-hime* could provide critical leverage on that modern world.

This critical potential certainly existed in Yanagita's initial concern for the marginalia of humanity represented in wandering shamans and mountain monks, peddlers and minstrels, *yamabito* and *tengu*. Yet Yanagita, forever denying any political involvement, did not pursue a politics of the marginal or even fully press the issues of discrimination that his research had brought to light. Indeed, he had a sympathetic attitude toward regional folk beliefs and the marks of difference they represented, but he ultimately worked to unify those differences under the abstract sign of *jō-min*.[47] Despite gender biases and differing interpretations concerning the phenomenon of people running off for the mountains, *yama ni hairu* had, as a chronotope of a mountain-based abnormality in Yanagita's writing, a formative role in a discourse on a plains-based normality. The object of folk studies turned from an emphasis on mountain people, mountain ascetics, mountain gods and goddesses as traces of difference to an emphasis on them as symptoms of communality within folk spirit. The path to the mountains, site of magical men and mad women, was a path to a spatial, temporal, and cultural alterity within the geographical boundaries of the archipelago. But, rather than seize upon and develop this past as a site of critique of the homogenizing effects of rationalization in modern Japan, Yanagita used it to define and accent a spiritual commonality among all Japanese as the other of rational society. Yanagita's pivotal 1926 essay, "Yu-kiguni no haru" (Spring in the snow country), is a prime example of this dynamic. In it Yanagita demonstrates that despite climatic and environmental conditions that seemingly would make impractical the practice of rice cultivation rites brought originally by settlers from the warmer southwestern regions of Japan, such rites persisted due to deeply felt, unchanging beliefs.[48]

Kyōka, on the other hand, did seize upon the folk figure of the *yama-hime* to cast clouds of doubt on the Meiji enlightenment. Whatever boundaries Yanagita may have approached in writing about *yama-hime* as objects to be grasped by knowledge, Kyōka broached in writing about them as possibilities to be caressed by imagination. Placed within fantastic tales set in contemporary times, they could be excused as quaint and beautiful romantic anachronisms or invited as serious dialogues on the nature of modernity in Japan. Too many people have done the former; I will attempt the latter.

Probably the most well-known of Kyōka's *yama-hime* figures is the mountain woman that a traveling priest encounters in the marvelously eerie novella *Kōya hijiri* (The Kōya priest) published just at the turning of the twentieth century.[49] Part innocent country woman, part erotic temptress, part beneficent healing goddess, and part vengeful sorceress, the woman in this story is a classic example of the *chūkanteki* character, in between simple classifications of good and evil, that Kyōka claimed as the focus of his métier. The work as a whole exudes this quality of ambiguity in the style of its narration and description, constantly maintaining a tension between the natural and the supernatural in its intimations of otherworldly powers permeating the priest's path over the mountain pass in Hida. Like other commentators, I could spend pages detailing this aspect of the text in its many unforgettable scenes: the forest of leeches; the woman's strange intimacy with the horse and the idiot-boy; the Walpurgis Night that a menagerie of men-turned-beasts bring to the restless priest.[50] However, the captivating power of these fantastical elements has, understandably, occluded discussion of the equally important ties this text has to the social reality in which it was produced. When read in such a context, *Kōya hijiri* displays a critical relationship to a modern medical discourse that is embedded within this harrowing tale of a youthful pilgrimage, set sometime in early Meiji, that the now middle-aged traveling priest relates to a young traveling companion one night at an inn in Tsuruga.

Disease flows subterraneously throughout the priest's tale, springing up at crucial points. He begins his narrative with a description of a "strange and disgustingly perverse" Toyama medicine peddler whom he meets while resting at a foothill teahouse before crossing the Hida Mountains. The obnoxious peddler, whose trade suggests a bastardization of folk cures, capitalism, and modern quackery, was in the area apparently to take advantage of an epidemic that the priest mentions as having hit a nearby village. The priest, about to drink from a stream flowing by the teahouse, is concerned that the contagion might have infected the teahouse water and so asks the hostess its source. The medicine peddler insolently jokes at the priest's worldly concern for his own life, saying that the only reason he became a priest was because no woman would have him. He then offers his advice about the water: "Just go on and drink 'til you're flooded. If your life's endangered, I'll give you some medicine. That's why I'm here, you know; isn't that so, Miss? Hey, but it's not for free! With all due respect, it's the sacred medicine 'Mankintan'—300 *mon* a pop" (14). The scene ends with the medicine peddler making lewd passes at the hostess in front of the young priest. The intertwined motifs of water, disease, and desire have been introduced for the rest of the story.

The flustered priest quickly leaves the teahouse and starts up the path toward the mountains. The medicine peddler overtakes him, but then is forced to make a detour up a twisting fork in the path because the main path is flooded. After learning from a passing peasant that the lower main path is in fact passable despite the flooding and that the upper path is dangerous, the priest decides that it is his duty as a holy man to go after the medicine peddler and warn him. The peasant also tells him that thirteen years before, an enormous flood destroyed a village that used to be in that area, taking with it a "doctor's big house." The story behind this past flood and this doctor, which gives the mysterious mountain woman her critical edge, will be revealed in the final two chapters of the story.

In the meantime, on his way after the medicine peddler, the priest stumbles across increasingly large snakes up the "serpentine path" and has a chilling encounter with a nest of enormous forest leeches that, like so many medical treatments by nineteenth-century doctors, nearly suck the life out of him until he finally comes upon the house where the woman and the grotesque idiot live.[51] The priest has seen no sign of the medicine peddler, but hears the neighing of a horse behind the house as he tries to question the unresponsive idiot, who sits awkwardly in front of the house playing with his abnormally large navel. The woman appears and agrees to allow the priest to spend the night as there is no other lodging about.

She then leads him down to the flooded stream behind the house, where she proceeds to wash his perspiring body and leech wounds in a nervously erotic bathing, during which she suddenly but casually disrobes the embarrassed priest against his protestations and unexpectedly strips herself naked, displaying her "glossy silk" body before him. On the way to and from the stream the priest witnesses several strangely familiar exchanges between the woman and a variety of animals—toad, bat, monkey—who accost her. She chides them like a mother, saying "Don't you see there's a guest?" After returning to the house, he watches her calm down the boisterous horse by ritualistically and seductively caressing the animal and passing naked under its body. In the priest's eye she has in this scene transformed into "a goddess or a demon." By the next morning he has survived both a night of shrieking beasts around the house and the woman's temptations, but after he departs he has a lingering desire to remain with her as he hallucinates her figure within one of a pair of intermingling waterfalls that he later learns are called the Man and Woman Falls.

The reader then learns the full truth of the woman through the story that an old man who, on his way back from selling the horse for the woman, tells the priest as a warning against succumbing to his desire to return to her. The woman, he reveals, is a powerful sorceress who has developed her supernatural powers over the years by practicing none other than *tengudō,* the occult mountain asceticism and sorcery associated with *yamabushi* and *tengu* that Yanagita writes about in "Yūmeidan." The old man gives an example of her powers in a clever wedding of economic exchange with supernatural metamorphosis: "You saw the horse I led away, right? Didn't you say you met a Toyama medicine peddler on the mountain path coming to the house? There you have it! That lecherous guy was instantly turned into a horse and then into money at the horse market, and the money transformed into this carp" (69). And the carp, the woman's favorite dish, will soon be consumed by her. Kyōka pointedly uses the verb *bakeru* (to transform), commonly used to describe the metamorphosis of *bakemono,* to characterize the money transforming into a carp. The driving force behind both forms of transformation, that of modern capitalist consumerism and that of premodern monsters, is, as Kyōka suggests here, unbridled desire. By thus associating the two in this fashion Kyōka evokes the monstrosities that can arise from within a desire-driven economy.

Through the old man's explication Kyōka has even more to say about
the monstrosities created by a modern medicine that is motivated more
by profit and professional prestige than by genuine concern for the well-
being of fellow humans. The woman's sorcery, the old man details, grew
out of response to the profiteering debacles of her father, the doctor
whose house was washed away by the flood thirteen years earlier. The
doctor specialized in treating an epidemic of eye diseases, no doubt associated with the same *torahoomu* (trachoma) that the Education Ministry
would soon exploit in their elementary school ethics textbooks stories
to stigmatize folk cures in the light of modern medical treatment.[52] The
character and medical expertise of this doctor are, however, described
in harshly derogatory terms. He is a "haughty poseur" who had a smat-
tering of knowledge about eye diseases, but who in cases of internal
medicine (*naika*) and surgery (*geka*) was utterly incompetent. Nevertheless, "his practice prospered rather well in this region lacking in other
country doctors since even the head of a sardine, if believed in, can be
turned into a deity and those not already fated to die could recover" (70).
In other words, despite his incompetence, the doctor was able to bam-
boozle the locals with an air of knowledge and a promise of recovery.

But his practice did not really flourish until the popular belief spread
that the "jewel-like" (recalling a *Tamayori-hime*) and "extraordinary" (*fushigi*) daughter unbelievably born to this despicable doctor and his disgusting wife was none other than an incarnation of Yakushi, a deity of
medicine, sent to save the people. This belief began innocently enough
when the daughter, upon coming of age, started to take a polite concern
for the villagers who came daily to the doctor's office for their treatments. It was discovered that with her touch she could cure rheumatism
and that by holding their shoulders with her breasts pressed tightly to
their backs she could ease the pain of patients who came to have boils
sloppily butchered by the doctor's rusty knife. She uses the same position
to treat the priest's leech wounds in the stream. Gradually her powers
approached the miraculous when a young man demonstrated that one
touch from her "divine hand" (*kamisama no te*) would make one's skin
impenetrable to hornet stings.

One day, news of her powers of healing brought a man from the
mountain down to the village with his son, who was afflicted with a particularly bad tumor on his leg. The doctor prepared an elaborate opera-

tion and, in a scene reminiscent of Charles Bovary's botched operation on a clubfoot, cut wrong and the boy bled profusely for three days. The daughter's presence eased his pain and the boy managed to escape with his life, but the great loss of blood rendered him permanently retarded and deformed. The boy's whimpering at his grotesque condition irritated the doctor, who considered it an affront to his professional standing. Because the boy would not leave the daughter, who pitied and comforted the boy during this entire ordeal, the doctor ordered her to take the boy back to his home on the mountain. She is entreated by the family to remain a few days with the boy, and during that time a terrific rain begins, eventually flooding out the doctor's village below. Only the boy, the daughter, and an old man miraculously survive.

The mysteries of identity in the priest's tale are now clarified. The woman's house is the boy's family house and the idiot with whom she lives is the boy whom the doctor had maimed thirteen years before. The stream behind the house created in the flood's aftermath is "an enchanted stream she received from Heaven to lure men" and to replenish her body after the ascetic disciplines of *tengudō,* which she commenced after having moved to the mountain with the boy. Since that time her supernatural powers have increased to the point where she can control the flora, fauna, and climate around her and like a Circe seduce any man who comes her way, transforming him into a beast once she tires of him. For this reason the old man urges the priest to quit his desirous thoughts of the woman and continue on his pilgrimage, for he is the first man to return from the enchanted stream without being transformed into a beast. Blessings from heaven or perhaps his innocence appears to have miraculously spared him. Once the old man passes out of sight up the mountain, a terrific thunderstorm erupts and the priest runs down the path under a torrent of rain. This is the final episode of the story that he tells his traveling companion at the Tsuruga inn.

Kōya hijiri ends with the priest leaving the inn the next morning without having made "any commentary or sermon concerning this story." But within this story, which stands on its own as a terrific fantastic tale, Kyōka has embedded a critique of the adverse effects of modern knowledge gone amok. The doctor, more concerned with his personal and professional well-being than with that of his patients, exploits the bit of medical knowledge he has acquired to extract his living from the suffering bodies of villagers. As a counter to him, the charmed daughter, a kind of faith healer, does not, however, seem to represent a viable alternative in modern times to the destruction that the doctor has caused. After all, the village is washed away by the flood, as if to suggest that the only solution is a dissolution and restart from a slate washed clean. The daughter's power is a temporary salve that eases suffering, but with age it turns into a lustful means to exact revenge on lustful men. There is something Dantesque in the damnation these men receive: just as the doctor has transformed the boy into a deformed idiot (a monster of sorts), the mountain woman turns men into dumb beasts, which perhaps they have been all along. And is that not the purpose of critique, to reveal the *shō-tai,* the true form, of the monsters that modernity has spawned?

Bridges of Alterity

In tandem with the *yama-hime,* Kyōka also enlisted her roadside cousin, the *hashi-hime* (bridge princess), to dissect modern rationality. But rather than directing criticism at the Meiji medical institution, he made use of the *hashi-hime* figure in his 1897 short story "Kechō" (Chimera) to carry out a subtle deconstruction of enlightenment within the typical Meiji elementary school classroom.[53] As is typical in his fantastic tales, Kyōka juxtaposes signs of modernity with a reinvested folk figure who embodies an alternative—not necessarily antiquated—mode of thinking. In this case, the *hashi-hime* figure, abundant in tales across Japan from the Middle Ages, is reincarnated as the character of a female bridge-keeper in mid-Meiji.[54] It is this thoroughly *modern* placement of such folk tale characters and motifs that keeps Kyōka's fiction from being simply romantic fantasies while lending them their critical power. The Naturalists' disparagement of such an invasion of supernatural creatures into the streets of modernity belied their lack of any critical awareness with regard to the sources and effects of that modernity as they trumpeted the values of "objective" descriptions done in the name of a modern science and rationality.

The protagonists of "Kechō" are a young schoolboy and his mother, who live together in a hut at the end of a bridge "on the outskirts of the dirty town." The two eke out a meager living by collecting tolls from those who must cross the bridge daily to work in the town. These people constitute a heterogeneous mélange of marginal types: "day-laborers, construction workers, coolies, people who play shamisen and drums, people who sell candy, Echigo lion dancers, monkey showmen, people who sell spill, people who sing songs, and people who do odd jobs such as making paper hair bands and match boxes."[55] Conversely, the bridge is also the point of passage for the townspeople who make trips out to view the famously beautiful seasonal flora—cherry, plum, and peach trees, irises—as well as a variety of birds in the hills and valleys out beyond the bridge. In its position as both divider and commingler of an inner town area and outer surroundings, the bridge is thus immediately identified as *chūkan,* in between.

Initially, the temporal impression conveyed by the description of the ragtag troop in the opening section of the story is vaguely olden, definitely rustic. But at the end of the first section the appearance of the boy's "sneaky" schoolteacher, a woman, who passes without leaving the toll in the box, suddenly injects a temporal proximity and familiarity that throws the position of time on the bridge into the same kind of ambiguity that is experienced in its space. This commingling of past and present is confirmed in the temporal viewpoint of the now older boy (adult?) who narrates the story; increasingly he seems to exist simultaneously in both the "past" he is narrating and in the "present" from which he is narrating as he approaches his final line of the story: "Because mother is here; because mother was here."[56] In this sense, the bridge becomes a fully chronotopic motif of the in-between, a spatiotemporal incarnation of what writer and folklorist Orikuchi Shinobu called "Mr. Izumi's pet theory of twilight-time [*tasogare-toki*]."[57]

The worldview that the chronotope of the bridge generates in the *hashi-hime*-like mother, who subsequently transmits it to the boy, creatively confounds the categories that structure the rationality of the teacher's reality. After the boy questions his mother about the teacher's morality, he is prompted to relate a classroom incident that he feels is evidence of the teacher's dislike of him and disrespect for his mother's teachings (therefore leading to an intentional snubbing of the bridge toll). It also implies moral hypocrisy on the teacher's part. The incident in question took place recently during the teacher's *shūshin* or ethics lessons, the same kind of *shūshin* lessons that Inoue Enryō and others helped standardize in Education Ministry textbooks within six years of the publication of this story. It is significant that Kyōka sets this scene during a *shūshin* lesson, for it not only attests to the central place of ethics in the Meiji educational system, it also allows Kyōka to lay bare the arbitrary and self-serving foundations of these lessons that professed to be mere reflections of a natural evolutionary norm.[58]

The boy reports to his mother that during a *shūshin* lesson the teacher told the class that "people are the most superior thing [*ichiban erai mono*] in the world." The boy, as if he has been taught otherwise, objected, "Uh, no, teacher, that's not so. People, cats, dogs, and bears too, all are the same beasts [*kedamono*]." After calling the boy's assertion "ridiculous," the teacher engaged him in a questioning that sought to demonstrate the error of his statement and the truth of her own. Defining the ability to speak as a sign of human superiority, she first asked him, "Do dogs and cats work their mouths to say things?" To which the boy replied, "Don't birds all talk together 'cheep, cheep, cheep, cheep' with their mothers, fathers, children, and friends?" Again the teacher dismissed his point by saying that in the case of birds it's only unintelligible chirping; you cannot understand anything from it and therefore they do not "say" anything. Again the boy countered, this time with a lengthy response in which he pointed out that, for example, when people are in a group talking at a distance from him he cannot understand a word they say; it is "the same as the sound of a rushing river." Likewise, he noted that when a party boat passes by the bridge where he lives, the polyphony of singing on board "is in the end no different at all from birds crying out loud and long. And when something howls way down river, I don't know whether it's a person or a dog." He then told the teacher that his mother said the reason he could not clearly understand the meaning of the birds' conversation was because his ears were small and therefore could not yet take in everything, but he would understand more as he grows older (3:119–20).

At this remark the teacher, whose duty it is to dispel such foolish thinking, became annoyed and scowled in disgust. She renewed her attempts at correcting the child by condescendingly granting that animals may talk, but they do not have the mental capacity to reason and contemplate things. As proof of this natural order of things she asserted that with reason and cunning humans can successfully trap fish and game. The animals' lack of such capacity dooms them. The boy's response to this example was a redescription of such fishing and hunting from an altered point of view based on an entirely different but nonetheless internally consistent set of descriptive rules which in its apparent absurdity worked to relativize the teacher's absolute and self-centered position.

First he took the case of people fishing with nets in a river. When standing they are indeed "humans that have faces," but when they dive in the water and swim about, the inadequacy of their legs compared to the graceful tails of goldfish becomes immediately visible. Thus in this context fish are superior to humans. Additionally, when submerged with only their legs showing above water, "you can say that it's a human, but if you try to imagine that it's legs growing out from inside the river—now that's interesting. It's not at all disgusting, so it's far better than going to see some trashy freak show [*misemono*]. Since that's what my mother says, I think so." He then described to the teacher a person pole-fishing: "It's not a human; it's a mushroom, please see for yourself. A figure standing still with hand in pocket and sedge hat on is the same as a single mushroom growing on the riverbank." This conclusion, he explained, is based on one's perspective (i.e., point of view): humans fishing at a distance are mushrooms growing near at hand. Beyond a general similarity in shape, this judgment is also based on a coherent application of observable common traits or taxonomic rules. He was very specific about their being mushrooms: trees and grass sway in the wind, mushrooms and humans do not. When viewed by this standard, the mushroom and the fisherman "who has intelligence" are classified together in contrast with the fish "who are swimming about all the while" (3:122).

Extending this kind of counterlogic to the case of hunting, the boy observed that the smart bird-trapper is the one who, while stalking his prey, remains silent. How, then, can not speaking be a sign of an animal's stupidity, he queried the teacher. Increasingly more angry and flustered by the child's persistent subversion of her categories of reason and unable even to begin the lesson, she finally pulled out what she thought to be an unassailable basis for her original point. "Fine," she said, "I will provisionally grant that all of what you have said so far is as you think. However, even you will certainly recognize the fact that humans are more splendid and superior than trees or grass. So let's begin the lesson with this as its base." "But, teacher," the boy hesitantly interrupted, "flowers are more beautiful than you" (3:124). She turned red with embarrassment. The teacher of lessons had been taught one.

The mother, after listening to her child's account of this classroom incident, explains that out of politeness one should not say such things in front of others. She does not, however, dispute her child's viewpoint and reasoning because she is the source of this way of thinking and finds it perfectly valid. It is a product of the diverse in-between life on the bridge. She sums up the lesson: "Flowers are inaudible to the ear because they don't say things, but in place of that they are beautiful to the eye" (3:126). In other words, the definition, order, and value that one attributes to things are dependent on the categories and characteristics of comparison that one applies, as well as on the relativity of one's position, ocular or social. There is nothing "natural" about this arrangement.

This lesson is constantly being put into practice throughout the story through the boy's habit of viewing people according to the characteristics they share with particular animals. For example, another toll scoffer, a haughty gentleman decked out in Western clothing and whose business card practically identifies him as the Meiji establishment incarnate ("City Health Association Member, Executive Secretary of the Education Symposium, Life Insurance Company Employee, Pawnbrokers' Association President, and Arts Promotion Association Trustee, Ono Kitarō"), is identified by the boy as simply "Mr. Frogfish" (*Ankō-hakase*) because of his fat stomach (3:140, 136). On one level such appellations are merely an innocent childish game. But on another level, given the source of the child's proclivities (his mysterious *hashi-hime* mother) and the nature of his previous classroom confrontation (the disruption of a *shūshin* lesson), calling a figure representing enlightenment medicine, education, business, and culture "Mr. Frogfish" is not an innocent gesture at all. Kyōka is able to cloak criticism in the innocence of the child's imagination.

Kyōka exploits this same alibi in the critique of modern reason that is carried out during the classroom scene. This veritable dialogue between reason and imagination, in which the boy innocently turns the teacher's questioning back on itself, exposes the arbitrary categories that ground the truth that she delivers as natural and self-evident. The fixity of the teacher's categories is loosened as their borders are blurred by the boy's alternative ways of perceiving, understanding, and organizing things. This action is a prime example of the critical effect of the "twilightization of life" that Kyōka advertised as the goal of his fantastic fiction. However fantastic or impractical the boy's taxonomy may seem, it does signify possible alternatives that work to confound absolutist and transhistorical claims. The entire episode is not unlike a dramatization of Borges's imagined "Chinese encyclopedia" that Foucault invokes as a foil in the preface to *The Order of Things.* The absolute Order and universal Reason to which the teacher appeals are shown as being socially and historically constituted forms of ad hoc organization and contingent rationality, the goals of which were ideological. *Shūshin* education was not to reveal ethics, but to keep concealed in a robe of reason this contingency of Meiji order. In this respect, the red-faced embarrassment of the teacher in "Kechō," her failure, was not at placing second in beauty to a flower, but at being disrobed by the hands of a child.

Granted, it was by an atypical child whose fantastic imagination was fed by a mother who inherited and transmitted the enchanted ambiguity of the *hashi-hime,* a divine medium—or roadblock—amid the traffic of assorted souls crossing a bridge between worlds. Raised on this boundary line, an atopic topos, this child could witness a carnival of unaligned creatures and imagine "interesting" (as his mother would say) alignments among them, creating connections and combinations that cut across conventional taxonomies and lines of analysis. His was a taxonomy guided by a logic more poetic than scientific, leading to discoveries of the extraordinary within the ordinary. And that process, I would emphasize, was the "spinning jewel" in the labyrinth of Kyōka's artistic practice that Yanagita found so alluring.

Yanagita too was drawn to tales about *hashi-hime,* but his treatment of them differed from Kyōka's. He first introduced his interest in the *hashi-hime* figure in a brief 1911 essay written for *Shinshōsetsu,* the same journal that published *Kōya hijiri* eleven years earlier. Fittingly, he begins this essay by responding to Kyōka's query, which appeared only a few months earlier in the latter's review article on *Tōno monogatari,* concerning the archetypal quality of many of the tales of Tōno. Yanagita agrees with Kyōka that many of the tales are of a more or less set pattern and can be found elsewhere throughout Japan. He indicates that when he was writing *Tōno monogatari* he did not believe they were restricted only to the Tōno area.[59] As examples of tales with a set pattern, he recites several involving characters that in a later essay he will identify as *hashi-hime.*

The core of the tales he relates centers on a traveler suddenly encountering, either at the foot of a mountain pass or on a bridge, a beautiful woman who asks him to deliver a written message to her counterpart at another bridge or mountain. The traveler takes up the charge and along the way to the destination opens the message and sees that it says "Kill this man!"[60] Frightened, he rewrites it to say "You should not kill this man!" Upon his arriving at the destination, another beautiful woman suddenly appears and looks angrily at the man. He nervously passes her the message. After she reads it she smiles and thanks the traveler, who is allowed to pass. Yanagita's short commentary at the end of these examples presents the phenomenon of this type of tale, a product of "unexpected fancy," as an "arcanum of humanity" that scholars, even those practicing *yōkai kenkyū* (undoubtedly an allusion to Inoue Enryō), will never be able to elucidate in its entirety. The only conclusion that he can offer at this time is: "Sure enough, the greatest mystery [*fushigi*] in the universe is man himself."[61]

His final comments not only read as a subtle swipe at Inoue and the Meiji academic institution that produced him; they also sound like a self-posed challenge for the field of study, *minzokugaku,* that Yanagita was in the midst of formulating. And sure enough, this is what they prove to be. In a lecture he gave at a girls' school in late 1917, published soon afterwards in *Jogaku sekai* as simply "Hashi-hime," Yanagita renders comprehensible the incomprehensible mystery he had posed less than seven years earlier. The first notable aspect of this essay is that he begins it with a repetition of the main tale from the previous piece, but this time clearly contextualizes it within a network of old beliefs concerning a goddess that was enshrined at the foot of bridges, the *hashi-hime.*

To solve the mystery of the meaning of this cycle of tales Yanagita turns to several variations of this story and focuses on a certain detail. This detail is the belief that if any mention of a certain bridge is made while on a certain other bridge, it will provoke a strange or frightening event. In some cases, the appearance of the *hashi-hime* who requests the delivery of the message to the other bridge is itself specified as the frightening event. In other cases, it is simply believed that some undetermined bad luck will occur. There are also versions that further detail that certain songs ("Aoi no ue" and "No no miya") were forbidden to be sung on the bridges in question. By associating these clues with related versions of this story in other sources, Yanagita slowly pieces together an interpretation of the *hashi-hime* narrative. The real linchpin to his interpretation springs, however, from a reference to the ninth chapter of *Genji monogatari* (The tale of Genji), "Aoi," in which the bitterly jealous spirit of the Rokujō lady leads to the death of Genji's wife, Aoi. Anyone familiar with this chapter, Yanagita says, knows that the song "Aoi no ue" describes jealousy between women. "No no miya" too, he explains, takes rivalry among women as its subject.[62] By association with these songs that are said to be forbidden on certain bridges, the *hashi-hime* in folk tales are thus determined to be full of *netami,* which commonly means "jealousy" or "envy" in contemporary usage. It is out of *netami* that the *hashi-hime* of one bridge becomes angered by the mention of another bridge. The deep structure of *hashi-hime* stories and their mountain-related counterparts revolve, then, on the feelings this word *netami* describes.

Always desiring to go beyond the results of conventional character-based philology, Yanagita cites evidence suggesting that originally the spoken word more generally meant resentment, dislike, or disapproval (*ikidōri, kirai,* or *fushōchi*). With this clue he cracks the conundrum: "So then, if you ask for what reason one would enshrine at the side of a bridge a deity who had this kind of disposition, it was for the purpose of wanting to have the deity fully exhibit this characteristic toward enemies, demons, and harmful people who come along from outside" (6:368). Yanagita interprets *hashi-hime* (and male-female pairs of mountain pass deities) as being boundary guardians. This interpretation is not far from Kyōka's modern incarnation of the *hashi-hime* as bridge-keeper in "Kechō," but the emphasis in Yanagita's explanation is clearly on the *hashi-hime*'s function as divider and discriminator between groups, not as facilitator of potentially creative intermingling among them. The former is likely more representative of conservative rural mentality, which was after all the object of Yanagita's research. In this respect, "Hashi-hime" offers a persuasive example of folk studies' hermeneutical method, its imaginative application, and the fruits it could bear in representing folk beliefs. It also throws into relief Kyōka's own imaginative rewriting of this folk figure as a pivot of progressive critique; his interest (besides writing a good story) was not in representing what folk feelings were or still are, but in strategically utilizing them to question what modern feelings had become.

Critical Feelings

In *Shōsetsu shinzui* (The essence of narrative fiction), a landmark essay in the development of modern Japanese fiction, Tsubouchi Shōyō argued that the aim of modern fiction was to explore the phenomena of thoughts and feelings that existed on the inside (*naibu*) of humans. It was a kind of laboratory for the study of human emotions (*ninjō*).[63] However, this study of human emotions was not to be conducted by imagination (*sōzō*), but, according to Tsubouchi, by a realistic application of the principles of psychology (*shinrigaku no dōri*). Tsubouchi's advocacy of the scientificity of psychology over the fantasies of imagination was no doubt an effort to define the writing of prose fiction as a legitimate pursuit of educated gentlemen in the Meiji period. Prior to that time, the practice of prose fiction (as opposed to that of highbrow poetry) was generally looked down upon as a vulgar undertaking. The direct source of Tsubouchi's appeals for *shinrigaku* was in all probability Inoue Enryō, for Tsubouchi was one of the original members of Inoue's Fushigi Kenkyūkai, which was founded in the midst of *Shōsetsu shinzui*'s serialization between September 1885 and April 1886 (the Fushigi Kenkyūkai was formed in January 1886). Because Inoue was a principal proponent of psychology in Tokyo at the time and given his association with Tsubouchi in this group, it is difficult to imagine that the style of Tsubouchi's thought in this passage could come from anywhere else.

It becomes understandable, then, that Kyōka made appeals for the powers of imagination and not psychology despite his shared interest with Tsubouchi in exploring human sentiment. Kyōka was not content with a mere diagnosis and subsequent description of a predictable "natural progress" of fictional characters based on that diagnosis, as Tsubouchi advocated: "After the author has presented [the protagonist] in the world of the narrative fiction, he cannot animate him as he, the author, desires. He must consider him as a real person and depict his life as it would naturally progress."[64] That would ultimately have been a mechanical, uninteresting, and conservative procedure not unlike the Naturalists' misappropriation of literature to represent empirical truths. He instead attempted in many of his essays and stories to fabricate and mobilize a subjective *kibun* against the onslaught of objectivist discourse that was emanating from institutional sites spreading to all quarters of Meiji thought and culture. *Fushigi na hanashi,* as products of feeling and imagination (a point on which he agreed with Yanagita), offered the richest raw material for the formation of this *kibun* from the largest group of Japanese, whose basic structure of everyday life and practical knowledge was being affected by enlightenment ideology.

In discussing the antiestablishment tendencies of Kyōka's early so-called thought stories, Kawamura Jirō agrees with Muramatsu Sadataka's evaluation that they were "not written from a frame of mind that seeks awakened liberation in the modern ego; rather, they have originated in Edo commoner feeling (in something similar to the resistance that Edo townspeople felt toward the samurai class)." "In other words," Kawamura restates, "it is not ideology, but a kind of feeling [*kibun*] or emotion [*jō-cho*]." But this *kibun,* he goes on to point out, is not a powerless component in an empty formalism, for "in the sphere of power relations in reality, and in the realm of art and ideas, the power to carry out radical change is in fact more often the power of feeling [*kibun*] than the power of ideology."[65] If the potentialities of the affects, of the possibilities entertained in imagined worlds, could not be directly translated into a concrete reality, they at least could serve as a site of critique of the given reality—that is, the socially and historically constituted reality—into which one has been thrust. Feeling that is mobilized in this fashion therefore carried a critical power aimed at bringing about change in the "real world." The Meiji establishment certainly recognized this threat by instituting what Kawamura Kunimitsu has called its mass "sentimental education" that was geared to channel feeling vertically (ultimately toward the emperor) in the formation of a national body. The effect of this process, like that of Inoue's monsterology and psychology, was to rationalize feeling, thus exorcising its monstrous potential.

In the context of late Meiji Japan, then, the use of imagination as Kyōka defined it (the working on the given world to create, through the *kibun,* believable other worlds) amounted to critical thinking. For both Yanagita and Kyōka such an imagination was key in approaching the place of the Other, whether it be cast as an ethnographic *yamabito* or fantastical *hashi-hime.* Imagining other possible worlds through one's *kibun* was, in the least, an implicit critique of the contemporary world and, if empowered in the way Kawamura Jirō suggests, could potentially effect change in that world. Kyōka's fantastic fiction did strive to empower the products of folk sentiment in a critique of the unquestioned assumptions of the rationality ordering the modern world. Although he was an ally of Kyōka on many fronts, Yanagita's folk studies, despite its implicit "critical nostalgia," for the most part fell content to describe, decipher, and to some degree preserve the products of folk sentiment in the development of a new field of study. There was a limit to his spiritual kinship with the writer he so admired. Still, both writers were thoroughly engaged in a discourse of Japanese modernity even as they deployed the fantastic to critique the particular effects that Japan's modernity was producing or to offer alternatives to it.

It is easy to try to explain this limit by saying simply that Kyōka was essentially a fiction writer whereas Yanagita was essentially a—what? scientist? folklorist? ethnologist? ethnographer? anthropologist? Perhaps this way is not so easy after all. Perhaps it would be more fruitful to attribute their differences to their respective discursive positioning around their shared object. This articulation of their differences is slightly different from one based on a comparison of essences. In my view, Yanagita placed himself as a kind of archaeologist in a field of would-be knowledge, collecting and interpreting shards of folk sentiment. Despite his opposition to the pseudoscientific rationalizations of *fushigi* that Inoue undertook, Yanagita's own will to knowledge necessitated carving shapes of reason from the shapelessness of *fushigi* in the tales and beliefs he examined. This tension between reason and imagination would persist in folk studies, a science that has more than a few poetic skeletons in its closet.

Kyōka, on the other hand, situated himself as a kind of parodic actor in an interlude of *chūkan*, donning the carnivalesque makeup of folk sentiment and performing in the twilight between reason and feeling, the real and the imagined. The "ellipse of uncertainty" thus generated from this interstice scattered the light of reason into a penumbra of possibilities. In Kyōka's play, the monsters of imagination lurking in the wings would always cast—and be cast as—amorphous shadows on the center stage of reason: "*Tare so, kare?*" [Who is that?]

Thus for Kyōka sentiment became the engine and fantastic literature the vehicle by which to develop a critical perspective on the process and effects of modernization in Japan. If, as the Naturalists declared, this form of writing practice constituted romanticism, then, Kyōka replied, "all art is 'Romantic.'"[66] It was the discourse on modern rationality that stigmatized "romantic" sentiment as a kind of madness, much as it had done in stigmatizing folk cures in the "Avoid Superstition" stories propagated in *shūshin* lessons. Its growth and survival depended on this parasitic relationship. The "will to transcendence" in Kyōka's writing, which is often isolated out of context as proof of a flighty metaphysical romanticism akin to that of the German Romantics, is in fact simultaneously counterbalanced by a deep attachment to the stuff of everyday reality that is lacking in the German Romantics.[67] This aesthetics of the in-between, necessarily tethered to reality while at the same time idly walking beyond the other side of the white clouds, indeed configured Kyōka's writing as a practice that "enters a dialogue with the 'real' and incorporates that dialogue as part of its essential structure." And in the genuine spirit of critique, it gave neither side of that dialogue the final word.

CHAPTER 6

Supernatural Ideology

Ideology is not ideas; ideology is not acquired by thought but by breathing the
haunted air.

— Lionel Trilling, *The Liberal Imagination*

Throughout the history of modern Japan, control of spirits has meant the
control of Spirit. Japanese spirituality was reorganized into the Japanese
Spirit, where spirits were relegated to the realm of folklore and superstition in what I call supernatural ideology. The qualification of such an
ideological operation as supernatural is perhaps, as Trilling's remark suggests, redundant. He continues: "Ideology is not the product of thought;
it is the habit or the ritual of showing respect for certain formulas to
which, for various reasons having to do with emotional safety, we have
very strong ties, of whose meaning and consequences we have no clear
understanding."[1] The political, social, and economic cataclysms leading
to and in the wake of the Meiji Restoration and the rapidly spreading
contact with strange things and strangers among the populace at large
disturbed the emotional safety of many. This dis-ease was in part to be
expected given the consequences of foreign threats and internal political upheavals, but it was also in part nurtured by the rulers of the Meiji
state so as to create the need for a cure that they could administer under
their own control. Playing on common fears, Meiji educators and ideologues initiated the ritualization of respect for new formulas for emotional safety, often, but not always, with impressive results.

Despite certain successes of the Meiji state at rationalizing power and
knowledge in Japan's modernization, a tension persisted in this late Meiji
struggle over spirits, one that pitted bureaucratic reason against alter-

native visions of community, nation, and national community. Yanagita himself acutely embodied this tension. As a bureaucrat in the Agropolitics Section of the Department of Agriculture under the Ministry of Agriculture and Commerce during the last decade of Meiji, he criticized the prevailing views of key policymakers who insisted on Tokyo-centered heavy industry, arguing instead for a more even distribution of local industries that would complement agricultural production and stimulate regional consumption. Kawada suggests that Yanagita's ultimate disillusionment over the course of official agricultural and industrial policy led him to fashion an approach to local rural society in the form of a *minzokugaku* that extended and supplemented his own agropolitics.[2] Both articulations can be seen as arising out of a concern for rural people in the face of modern capitalist expansion and a concern for Japanese national survival amid international competition. Yanagita similarly criticized the artificial and state-centered quality of the morality that the central educational system and the Imperial Rescript on Education imposed. Although recognizing the limits of village spiritual and moral beliefs for the foundation of national morality, he nonetheless imagined the possibility of adapting them for the nation in modern times. Yanagita's dual concern for the fate of the local and of the nation explains in part the ambiguous legacy of his writings in the twentieth century: on the one hand, it presented a critique of the state's path of modernization; on the other, it produced a concept of the Japanese folk that could lay the ideological bedrock for that path.

This concluding chapter takes up the tense and ambiguous legacy of the folk and the fantastic as figures of resistance to bureaucratic reason, which itself had occasion to rely on fantastic effects. My approach is first to consider a case of "applied folk studies" deployed by Minakata against the state in the battle over community spirit(s) in late Meiji and then to evaluate the promise and pitfalls of applications of Yanagita's folk studies since. In this context, late-century "booms" in *Yanagita-gaku, nihonjinron* and native-place-ism, *yōkai,* and, most recently, Minakata studies[3] offer, perhaps, symptoms of a renewed crisis in Japanese national-cultural identity which summon mysteries and mystifications that triangulate with the *fushigiron* that formed around the century's beginning.

The Bureaucratization of Spirits

As exemplified in the efforts of Inoue Enryō, the state builders of Meiji Japan programmatically worked, particularly through the ideological apparatuses of nationalized education and medicine, to redirect the spiritual sentiments of the masses away from heterogeneous complexes of local beliefs in the supernatural and toward a homogenized belief in a unique *kokutai*. The notion of civilization and enlightenment (*bunmei kaika*) and of the mythical divinity of the restored emperor of the Enlightened Rule were instrumental in this process. As demonstrated in chapter 3, enlightened education that made tactical use of Western science and technology was not aimed to liberate free thinking among benighted individuals who had relied on local, folk knowledges to conduct their everyday lives. Rather, it was deployed to break down regional resistance to a network of national power that was being constructed through new knowledges manipulated and institutionalized by an elite caste who were formally and informally associated with the Meiji government. As a popular educator, religious philosopher, ethics textbook consultant, superstition basher, and folklorist, Inoue is just one pivotal example within a wider discourse. As early as 1873 orders issued through the Ministry of Religion (Kyōbushō, which was terminated in 1877 and whose functions were transferred to the Ministry of Home Affairs) proscribed against shamans, faith healers, exorcists, fortune-tellers, and the like who "blinded the people" with their practices. The following year the Ministry further ordered the control of "those who with talismanic prayers [*kin-en kitō*] impede doctors and who commit acts disruptive of government."[4] Items 11 and 12 of Article 427 of the 1880 Meiji Criminal Code, enacted in 1882, made the use of such talismanic prayers a crime. In the revised code of 1908, items 16 through 18 of Article 2 went even further in enumerating the practitioners of "superstitions" who were subject to criminal punishment:

> 16. Those who spread gossip and wild rumors or false alarms which deceive people.
> 17. Those who without authority tell fortunes; or who conduct exorcisms and incantations; or who otherwise mislead people by conferring on them things resembling talismans.

18. Those who conduct spells, exorcisms, and incantations for the sick; or who impede medical care by giving amulets and holy water.[5]

These new codes were instituted amid the domestic crises—economic, social, cultural, intellectual, and political—that marked the latter years of the Meiji period following the Russo-Japanese War of 1904–1905. As an officially codified application of Inoue's earlier *yōkaigaku,* they were designed to remove obstacles to state power and reduce oppositional political critique and action that might derive from the mobilization of malaise among people distraught by lost war dead, inflation, poor working conditions, and both physical and spiritual dislocation. The complement to these sanctions against unauthorized "superstitions" during this same period was an enhanced bureaucratization of spirits under the aegis of the authorized superstition of the divinity of an unbroken imperial line descended from the *kami* Amaterasu enshrined at Ise. A concerted resystemization of the respect and sentiment that common folk felt toward ancestral spirits as well as toward the spirits of the immediate familial war dead was conducted by the Meiji government through two tightly related actions: the national enshrinement of the spirits of war dead at Yasukuni shrine and the shrine mergers of 1906–1912.

Although it is generally said that at the time of the Russo-Japanese War the Japanese masses felt the nation to be an ethnically joined community for the first time, there was no guarantee that this feeling would persist once the war was over. In fact, an abundance of evidence—soldiers' letters, wartime songs, newly created local practices—suggests that even throughout the conduct of the war one's family and hometown held greater concern for soldiers and their kin than one's country.[6] The most prominent point of conflict between such localism and nationalism was over the enshrinement of the spirits of the war dead. From 1905 to 1910, 88,243 soldiers who "died for the sake of the Emperor" were "jointly enshrined" (*gōshi*) as Shintō *kami* at Yasukuni shrine in Tokyo as part of an effort by the state to fasten the would-be wandering spirits to itself. Such joint enshrinement would, it was thought, be a particularly effective means by which to unify and bind the nation at a fundamental spiritual level: "The dead were decorated, and by transcending individual differences they were homogenized."[7]

This "honor" meant on the other hand that 88,243 spirits were not, strictly speaking, allowed to repose with the ancestral and clan *kami* of their respective home regions; nor could their spirits be properly memorialized as *hotoke* (a Buddha). Interestingly enough in the case of the Tōhoku region, memorialization was an activity conducted by local village shamans. Such local rites were important for the "emotional safety" of villagers and townspeople because properly memorialized ancestral spirits were thought to watch over and provide bounty for one's family, whereas unattended spirits were feared to exact revenge in the form of disease, famine, harsh weather, infertility, and the like. Spirits of dead family members were not, for any reason, to be abducted from their home regions and housed in a strange, faraway place, which Yasukuni shrine represented to a farmer or fisherman in the provinces. National enshrinement was strictly incompatible with folkic thought and practice. In other words, through this use of Yasukuni shrine the state usurped, for its own ideological purposes, the people's local management of spirits— its spiritual economy—and attempted to place the emotional investment of peoples from diverse areas into state hands when ancestors became associated with national entities and with the ancestors of the imperial family itself. Once the national enshrinement of heroic spirits, blessed by the emperor at Yasukuni, had been firmly established, it began to be preached in the 1910 revised edition of elementary ethics textbooks as part of the "family state" (*kazoku kokka*) ideology.[8]

The other half of the Meiji government's spiritual management policy was a massive program to streamline the hodgepodge of "people's shrines" (*minsha*) throughout the country and focus their organization toward the big central government shrines (*kansha*), which had Yasukuni as its pinnacle with the Grand Shrine at Ise hovering above the entire shrine system in a category of its own. Government officials preferred to refer to this initiative by the wonderfully bureaucratic term *jinja seiri* (shrine consolidation), although it was also called *jinja gappei* (shrine merger) or simply *gōshi* (joint enshrinement), the last being the same term often used in the case of the national enshrinements at Yasukuni. In its ideal form, a merger in a particular locality was to result in the establishment of one shrine per administrative village or town (*gyōsei-son*) by combining the multitude of small ungraded shrines (*mukakusha*) and the several village shrines that served respective hamlets (*buraku*) within the administrative village units that had been drawn up by the Meiji government in the late

1880s. What an actual merger entailed was the transfer of the *shintai* (god-body), the sacred object that embodied the *kami* of a particular shrine, to the receiving shrine and the subsequent dismantlement of the old shrine compound. In most cases, the property of the dismantled shrine, including most importantly its surrounding forests, were processed and sold, with the proceeds going to the receiving shrine (or unscrupulous officials and priests). The official rationale for the policy was to enhance the reverential aspect of shrines by consolidating the resources of smaller shrines that were unable to maintain an appropriately dignified appearance and investing these resources in one well-kept shrine central to the area. In addition to establishing local organs of greater administrative control between the state and the masses, the merger policy possessed the ideological aim of channeling the people's respect for local Shintō deities and ancestors toward the imperial nation-state. The "one shrine per village" (*isson issha*) ideal was rarely achieved, but on the whole about 41 percent of the ungraded and village shrines throughout Japan were merged, with most success coming at the lowest level of ungraded shrines.[9]

As Wilbur Fridell explains in his monograph on the shrine mergers, the plan looked great on paper and made bureaucratic sense in the attempt to foster a strong familialism and patriotism through a pyramid structure of shrines that directed faith and reverence toward the emperor as spiritual symbol of the state. Where government officials miscalculated, however, was in assuming that the consolidation of smaller neighborhood shrines into a larger, materially better off administrative village or town shrine would strengthen reverence in general among the populace. In the cases of merging ungraded shrines to the hamlet level (what Fridell calls "partial mergers"), some success in socioideological objectives were probably met, but in instances of total mergers at the village or town level, what was gained in administrative organization was typically lost in the spiritual violation of intimate community beliefs and practices—much in the same way that the enshrinement of war dead at Yasukuni shrine robbed families of the private care of the family spirits (98–103).

Such spiritual losses were the focus of the strongest direct questioning of the shrine merger program to be carried out by a member of the late Meiji government. In March 1910 and then again in February 1912, Nakamura Keijirō, Diet representative from Wakayama prefecture, sharply interrogated the government concerning the wisdom of the merger policy.[10] The thrust of his complaint was that the destruction of merged shrines was actually subverting the sense of reverence among the people toward ancestral spirits, local *kami,* and ultimately the emperor. The result, he argued, was a loss, not a gain, in patriotic spirit from the masses. In his reading of Nakamura's denunciation of the shrine mergers, Fridell emphasizes the assumptions that Nakamura and the government held in common ("that shrine reverence generated those very socio-ideological patterns which were most essential for the development of strong national rule"), while playing down the critical side of his speeches, which might have been indicative of popular sentiment within his constituency. Fridell takes at face value the terms and language of Nakamura's speeches—which do suggest assumptions shared with the government's motives for the mergers—without considering Nakamura's use of the official rhetoric of imperial reverence, filial piety, and patriotism as simply the necessary use of a common idiom to which the government would respond (76–79). I am not implying that Nakamura was not a reverent patriot, but I would like to suggest that when one looks deeper at the "grassroots" sources of Nakamura's statements, one finds a deeper and more broadly based criticism that he rephrased into terms that his audience in the Diet would appreciate and react to more readily. The need for this rephrasing becomes all the more apparent once one realizes that Nakamura's principal informant concerning the local damage being caused by the shrine mergers was the hot-tempered and rebellious Minakata Kumagusu.

Ecosystems of Protest: From Minakata to Minamata

For whatever reason, Fridell completely missed Minakata's participation in local resistance against the shrine mergers and only in passing cites Yanagita's comments about "strong opposition" in Wakayama (86).[11] After Mie prefecture, which contained the Grand Shrine of Ise, the neighboring Wakayama prefecture was the site of the most intensely enforced shrine mergers. According to Minakata's contemporary figures, the number of shrines in Mie had been reduced from 5,547 to 542 by June 1911 (a 90.2 percent decrease), and those in Wakayama had been reduced from 3,700 to 600 by November 1911 (an 83.8 percent decrease).[12] The shrine to which the Minakata family was attached, Oyama shrine in the present-day town of Kawanabe, was one of the shrines targeted for merging. The merging was eventually executed in October 1913 despite Minakata's efforts to stop it. It was thus as an individual personally affected by the destruction directed at provincial shrines and their surrounding lands that Minakata began his protest campaign.[13] In addition to enlisting the aid of Yanagita, who at the time had influential government connections and helped to produce and circulate a pamphlet of Minakata's views, Minakata made appeals to the Lower House of the Diet through his acquaintance Representative Nakamura. Much of the material of Nakamura's two inquiry sessions before the House are said to have been derived from his consultations with Minakata.[14] In his severe and systematic critique of the shrine mergers, Minakata states that Nakamura had even shown to Home Minister Hirata Tōsuke, who at the time was in charge of the execution of the mergers, photos that Minakata had taken of the pitiful situation that the mergers were creating in the countryside.[15]

Unlike Yanagita's opposition to the shrine mergers, which remained on the level of soliciting oppositional views and expressing sympathy for those people adversely affected by the program, Minakata engaged in direct action. On 21 August 1910 he forced his way into the Wakayama prefectural office and violently demonstrated his opposition against the merger policy. On the following day he was summarily arrested and incarcerated for the next eighteen days in the jail of his hometown of Tanabe. He kept a notebook while in prison and, in characteristic fashion, discovered growing there a rare variety of slime mold which he sent off to research companions at the British Museum.[16] In hopes of stirring up international pressure on the Japanese government, he later drafted a letter to his British friends concerning the ruthlessness of the shrine merger policy, but was ultimately dissuaded from sending it by Yanagita, who did not want international involvement over a domestic issue.[17] To carry on his protests after being released from prison, Minakata settled on engaging in on-site surveys of the impact that the mergers had on local areas. His conclusions were organized and published in his anti-shrine-merger statement of 1912. Yanagita's later unwillingness even to include the issue of shrine mergers as a relevant topic of discussion for the studies of rural life that he promoted in the 1910s as the editor-in-chief of the journal *Kyōdo kenkyū* (Community Studies) raised the ire of Minakata

and clearly shows their different conceptions of folk studies and the con-
tentious, experimental nature of the field at that time.[18]

Minakata begins his important and revealing essay by enumerating the
standards that the Home Ministry had set in 1906 for shrines to be designated exempt from becoming merged. These were shrines that for one
reason or another could claim a special lineage (*yuisho*), which typically
meant a connection with the imperial family or an important regional
lord, or being listed in the *Engi-shiki* (Procedures of the Engi era, completed 927) or the *Rikkoku-shi* (The six official histories of the country,
ca. early tenth century) as the recipient of official imperial offerings in
ancient times. Besides objecting to this elite bias, Minakata also protests the unreasonably high shrine maintenance standards—compound
dimensions and appearance, priest's salary, capital assets, and so on—that
the Ministry had set in order to force smaller shrines into merging.[19]
He also accuses the Ministry of making false promises to people to force
merging and the *Yomiuri shimbun* of misrepresenting the actual effects
of mergers by reporting a relatively smooth merging process (253, 255).
What probably irked Minakata most was that in many cases this fraud
was the result, he says, of priests cutting deals with powerful bureau-
crats and profiting from the sale of shrine trees (257). To counter these
official lies, Minakata offers testimony of *shintai* being left to defilement
or heedlessly burned by village officials without notifying local inhabitants. He also attests to smaller shrines simply being tossed into rivers.
His final general complaint in the opening sections of this essay is against
the reckless destruction of old-growth shrine forests that contained rare
plant specimens. Not only was it a loss of nature, but the resulting ero-
sion and disruption of local ecosystems would destroy the livelihood of
villagers as well (255–58).

The body of Minakata's essay then moves on to a detailed itemization
of the ill effects of the shrine merger policy on the general populace as
he has analyzed the situation over the prior few years. His remarkably
comprehensive observations cover moral, spiritual, cultural, social, economic, political, and environmental questions that are worth enumerating in brief. First, he says it is a deception on the part of regional bureaucratic officials to advertise that the shrine mergers will enhance reverence
toward *kami*. On the contrary, because many of the receiving shrines are

too far away for children and elders, they simply do not go to worship. Accusations of "Who has kidnapped our *uji-gami* [clan deity]?!" are also frequent among those whose shrines have been "consolidated." Mina-kata thus concludes that "the mergers have in actuality impaired the idea of reverence for the deities" (259). His second point is that the mergers "hinder the conciliation of people and obstruct the execution of the in-stitutions of self-government." Fighting and disputes have broken out among hamlets over whose shrine will be merged, and people (including Minakata himself) have been thrown into jail without due process. Pas-sions become particularly heated, Minakata notes, when local laborers in a risky profession such as ocean fishing have their guardian *kami* taken away (260). Point number three is that the mergers bring economic de-cay to the provinces. Not only is the money that is associated with the sale of shrine buildings and land often pilfered and diverted from neigh-borhoods, but the perpetual community assets that such buildings and land represented are gone for good. In addition, innkeepers and people who make a living selling food, drink, and festival items around shrines are severely hurt when their shrine is merged (261–62).

Minakata's next two points further specify the cultural and psycho-logical impact of the mergers: "Joint enshrinement plunders the solace of the people, weakens human feelings, and corrupts customs," and "Joint enshrinement damages love of one's home region [*aikyōshin*]" (263, 266). He argues that there is no need for large impressive shrines when people feel most comfortable and familiar with their own small shrines, how-ever decrepit they might be. What is important is the surrounding for-ests that set off the beauty and sense of repose of a small shrine's simple architecture. The spiritual security that such a setting provides for local peoples is severely disturbed by the mergers. This unsettling of a locus for community life in the provinces leads to a loss of "local patriotism" or *aikyōshin*. To cultivate national patriotism from local loyalties was the government's aim, and Minakata criticizes this attempt to exploit the reverence of individuals for nationalistic purposes. He cites even shrine priests who will sell out their local loyalties for personal financial gain in the name of *aikoku-chūko* (love of nation, loyalty and filial piety; 268).

The last two items on Minakata's list cover environmental, ecological, and related economic issues. For example, drawing on his experience and observations abroad, Minakata insists that public park space is essential for healthy communities and that shrine groves and compounds provide this function to some degree in Japan. Not only are shrines sites for special festivals and amusements, but children often play in the surrounding forests. Once these forests are cut down, sold, and turned into rice paddies, this space is lost. Their use as natural boundaries and landmarks (e.g., in navigation for fishermen along the coast) is also lost. Relying on the results of studies conducted by others as well as his own research, Minakata emphasizes that this transformation of the environment entails many other hidden costs. To begin with, when shrine groves are turned into paddy fields, the taxable land in the community increases. Paddy fields also attract harmful insects while at the same time there is a proportional loss of forest habitat that harbors wildlife that prey on insects. The combined result is a huge increase of pests and a proportional increase in the cost of insecticides (a government-supported chemical industry). In addition, the number of forest birds that eat termites and other pests harmful to human habitats also diminishes when shrines are merged and their groves cut down (268–70).

Minakata finally describes this destruction of scenic spots, historical and cultural sites, and popular practices as a kind of internal imperialist venture that *minzokugaku* must work against in order to elucidate and preserve the history of the common people. He pleads for a positive role for folklorists in Japan by pointing out that British folklorists, such as George Lawrence Gomme, who was awarded peerage by his government, have been instrumental in developing government policy toward the preservation and management of such sites. Preserving only those shrines associated with the recorded history of the Imperial House unjustly excludes the record of the common people which folk studies attempts to examine through oral histories, legends, and tales. As Minakata sees it, "Investigating outside written histories those things that are omitted by written histories is the task of folk studies." To accomplish this task, regional customs and practices, songs, slang, games, dialects, as well as the ancient architecture and utensils of extant shrines must be preserved and accessible for study (276).

As a critic of wanton degradation of local ecosystems, spiritual practices, and political economies for the sake of rapid industrialization and national ideological consolidation, Minakata shares an affinity with his better-known elder contemporary, Tanaka Shōzō (1840–1913), popular rights activist and Diet representative from Tochigi prefecture from 1890 to 1901. Both played roles in support of the principle of local self-rule, which was rapidly deteriorating under the centralization of state power since the Meiji Restoration. Although Tanaka kept within parliamentary procedure as long as he could, having faith in Japan's fledgling constitutional government, he ultimately quit the Diet and supported until his death direct action in seeking redress for the environmental damage caused by the Ashio Mine.[20] The postwar revival of Tanaka as patron saint of the protests against Chisso for its mercury poisoning at Minamata has enshrined him as Japan's first environmental activist, a title that he should perhaps share with Minakata. Indeed, the recent revival of interest in Minakata has, among other things, defined him too as an original environmental thinker ahead of his time (although a similar rediscovery of the comparably idiosyncratic Tokugawa-period intellectual Andō Shōeki has pushed that claim even further back). Tsurumi Kazuko's work on Minakata has been particularly strident in putting him forth as a prime example (along with Yanagita) of "endogenous creativity" and as an innovative theorist of "ecology."[21] It would be reasonable to speculate that attention paid to this aspect of Minakata's eclectic writings has been an indigenous cultural response to the range of postwar Japan's acute environmental problems and citizens' protest in general, as if to discover in Japan's own intellectual history individuals ("geniuses" and "heroes") like Andō, Tanaka, and Minakata who theorized and acted in such crises even if (or perhaps because) they were ignored or misunderstood in their own time. A certain nobility of failure does mark each of their respective stories.

In the parlance of environmental groups today, Minakata was of the "think globally, act locally" frame of mind. That is to say, what Tsurumi calls Minakata's "comparative" and "international" approach to folk studies was characterized by a free trade of concepts and ideas across national borders that were put to active use in scholarly as well as political engagements within a local community. Minakata studying regional slime molds (and taking notes in French, English, and Japanese) while in jail for protesting the shrine mergers is a wonderfully compact image of this attitude. Although his cosmopolitan attitude has not rendered him immune to cultural nationalist resuscitation as a made-in-Japan genius of international scope, the political and racial boundaries of "Japan and the Japanese" did not circumscribe his thought and actions as such. For him, the nation-state entity did not constitute the ground for folk studies, nor were these studies limited to the psychic realm of rural life. With this view he contrasted sharply with Yanagita's "one-nation folk studies" and its tendency to gravitate toward the interpretation of the spiritual beliefs grounding folk practices.

Fantasizing Folk Histories

Generated to some degree in response to government agricultural policy, Yanagita's fledgling folk studies shared with Minakata this appeal to foster folk studies for a constructive role in the development of modernization policies toward the cultural and economic resources of the provinces. They differed, however, in what they viewed as the essential aspects of provincial life around which folk studies should be formed. Yanagita's turn toward the spiritual, his concept of *jōmin,* and his call for nationally bounded folk studies would also harbor a potential for ideological co-optation by cultural nationalists in a way difficult to imagine in Minakata's case.

In his construction of a *jōmin* who possessed a fundamental spiritual unity transcending local differences, Yanagita, despite his overtures to otherness and warnings against assumptions of Japanese homogeneity, comes dangerously close in some of his theoretical writings to defining the nation-state (with an assumed racial and linguistic homogeneity) as *the* organizing category for "one-nation folk studies": "There is no need to lament over the lack of sources. It is even possible to actively collect sources in order to solve problems. This is because in relations between race and language, in Japan there exists a phenomenon: one nation, one race and one language. Therein exists the reason why there is a possibility that one-nation folk studies can be established in this country."[22] In such an articulation, the strangeness and unfamiliar diversity of provincial beliefs, language, and practices—the *fushigi* of folk cultures in Japan—which had offered sources and forms of knowledge that were alternative to those of conventional historiography, was transmuted into familiar forms of a basic Japanese Spirit that was constituted as fantastic in and of itself. The exuberant "critical nostalgia" of Yanagita's early writings, the kind of critical attitude seen in Kyōka's modern reuse of folk tales and literary ghostlore, diminished as folk studies was progressively disciplined from the 1930s. Organization and national prestige for the discipline meant giving up the local ghosts and goblins, whose manifestations were redefined as products of a common *Japanese* sentiment toward ancestors rather than particular manifestations of a universal sense of fear and awe toward the supernatural and unknown. In this instance, Yanagita's folk studies paralleled the trajectory from spirits to Spirit that marked the ideological machinations of bureaucratic reason in Japan's modernity. Yet perhaps its susceptibility of lapsing into a nationalist ideology of homogeneous and unique racial essence was always latent, even necessary, in the nature of folk studies. Yanagita had, after all, justified his study of *tengu* and *yūmeikai* after the Russo-Japanese War as important for understanding the spirit within the national body.[23]

The outcome of the Asia-Pacific War ironically nurtured the conditions for the redemption, popularization, and application of Yanagita's work. In the aftermath of a war defeat that shook faith in prewar forms of totalitarian control, there appeared under the banner of a new democracy a new encouragement of learning that at least theoretically sought to decentralize power and knowledge while at the same time reassembling the material and psychic unity of Japan the nation. Although in practical political and economic terms much remained centralized before, during, and after Japan's postwar "economic miracle," a range of local citizens' movements, amateur research groups, and new cultural political discourses have been born of a distrust of the old center and its narratives, modernist and Marxist. The concurrent centripetal and centrifugal forces implicit in such trends are not unlike tensions of alterity and sameness pulling at Yanagita's folk studies. As Igarashi lucidly demonstrates in a close analysis of Yoshimoto Takaaki's and Amino Yoshihiko's postwar readings of Yanagita's prewar writings, Yanagita offered, by dint of the very paradoxes of his hermeneutics, a discursive space from which postwar thinkers could imagine alternative histories that challenged the epistemological assumptions of conventional academic historiography.[24]

In addition to Amino's productive turn to Yanagita's prewar writings to open up questions of alterity and heterogeneity in historical representation and knowledge, Irokawa Daikichi has arguably been the most prominent proponent of drawing from Yanagita to challenge the centrism of the historical establishment in Japan. While Yoshimoto was busy describing the hallucinatory style of Yanagita's writings and finding the formation of imaginaries in them, Irokawa was involved in his own historiographical deployment of Yanagita's work from the mid-1960s. Taking as his inspiration Yanagita's call for a history of people unrepresented by tradition (written) sources, Irokawa set out to formulate and promote "populist history" (*minshūshi*).[25] After an attempt at a history of popular thought in the Meiji period with *Meiji seishinshi* (The spiritual history of the Meiji period, 1964), he came out with *Meiji no bunka* (1970), which was published in English in 1985 as *The Culture of the Meiji Period*. In the preface to the English edition, Irokawa reflects on its original publication and his role in Japanese historiography at the time: "It was my aim to discredit the prevailing mode of Japanese cultural history, which was centered on intellectual elites—great thinkers, scholars, educators, and men of arts and letters. In its place I sought to produce a cultural history conceived from the standpoint of the common people—a deep social stratum that was in basic opposition to intellectual elites—by exploiting methods used by Japanese folklorists and historians of popular thought. My goal was nothing less than a paradigmatic change in the field of Japanese cultural history."[26] Irokawa is modest in his appraisal of that goal's fulfillment, noting in retrospect that the book "failed to change the scholarly world in any drastic way because its thesis lacked sufficient coherence, lucidity, and theoretical formulation" (viii). Interestingly, the same criticism might also be applied to Yanagita's notoriously slippery writing style, which has been both derided as too loose and illogical and valorized as strategically opening discursive space onto glimmers (shadows?) of alterity.[27]

This comparison raises questions about the extent and status of Irokawa's appropriation of Yanagita's model for contemporary populist history: Does he go beyond the mere content of "the silent folk world" that Yanagita pointed to, attempting to emulate Yanagita's form of argument for counterhegemonic effect and subsequently lack coherency because he follows Yanagita all too well or not well enough? Do both writers by the same or independent routes reach the same representational and/or institutional impasses in efforts to give voice to nonelite, common people? Are theirs inherently impossible projects? If so, it did not keep Irokawa from developing populist history in the shadow and light of folk studies, composing twenty years later *Shōwashi sesō hen,* which he described as a "new history of everyday life and social conditions" consciously modeled after Yanagita's 1930 work *Meiji Taishōshi sesō hen*.[28] Like Yanagita and other practitioners of folk studies, Irokawa and other practitioners of populist history have been preoccupied with recovering a "voice" of the folk through largely, though not exclusively, extra-archival sources.[29] Ontological difficulties of this position aside, the assumption that this real or imagined orality of the folk possesses a truer and broader expression of Japanese history and culture runs into epistemological and representational binds. How is this "voice" recognized, defined, and known as such? Who can recognize, define, and know it? How can it be written about? What does it mean to "give voice" to the silent in written histories of them, or even to let the silent voice themselves? To some degree these are problems in any kind of historical representation. They become particularly acute, however, in writing histories of the folk. Yanagita's answer, as we saw, was to supplement empirical description of the material with techniques of fictional writing to represent a truth of the spirit in the folk's "voice." One needs "to become a *tengu*" (or a shaman) to channel that voice, to imagine other worlds, to fantasize folk histories. This requires a leap beyond the hermeneutical horizon that most scholars in established social sciences are not willing to take or accept even as they might unconsciously be doing so in their own writing.

Despite Irokawa's excessive zeal and occasional naïveté, his pioneering efforts at applying folk studies to shake up academic historiography, be it Marxist or modernist, deserve appreciation. Much like Yanagita himself, he was actively responding to perceived biases and blind spots in the conception and writing of history in Japan. His own modesty aside, Irokawa and other historians (such as Amino Yoshihiko) who have gained insights from folk studies have had notable impact on "the scholarly world" through their experiments in writing histories of the passed-over. In such work one can glimpse other histories. Yet, at least in Irokawa's case, a latent Japanism not unlike that which haunts Yanagita's folk studies sometimes surfaces in surprisingly frank terms. Perhaps only a hook to appeal to an economically confident yet culturally anxious audience at the time, the introduction to *The Culture of the Meiji Period* nevertheless exemplifies the kind of mystification—fantasizing—of Japan and its people typical of *nihonjinron,* complete with a totalizing view; loaded cultural, historical, and environmental comparisons vis-à-vis other countries; the "paradox" of nature (qua premodern) and industry (qua modern) cohabitating;

tropes of essentialism, continuity, homogeneity, uniqueness, and more. Entitled "Fushigi na kuni" (A wondrous country) but rendered "Japan: A Very Strange Country" in the published English translation, it begins:

Japan is a peculiar country. Seen from above, it resembles a long, narrow, arc-shaped chain of islands floating on the eastern edge of the Eurasian continent. In terms of Europe, these four islands, which are veiled in mists and fog for the greater part of the year, would extend from England to the tip of the Italian peninsula, or from the Russo-Polish border to the Franco-Spanish border. A central spine of rugged mountains divides the islands into two extremely different climate zones. The little valleys into which the islands are divided by seas and mountains prove to have paddy after emerald paddy, and little toy-like tractors move along their surface. Houses and villages resemble a miniature garden. The tranquillity of the fields and hills and the white sands of the beaches against which the waves roll all contrast sharply with the clusters of factories that fill the sky with black smoke.

But what is strange about Japan [*nihon no fushigisa*] is not that this overpopulated, resource-poor Asian island country has managed to compete for a place as the world's second or third largest industrial power. The fairy-tale aspect of this small island is to be found in its history. Despite its location a mere four hundred miles off the coast of China that boasts Asia's oldest and greatest culture, Japan has never once throughout its two-thousand-year history been incorporated within that empire; it has consistently maintained its national independence, and it has by and large preserved its distinctive culture.

The people who built the great Maya and Inca civilizations have been destroyed. The splendors of the Nile and Tigris-Euphrates are now nothing more than objects of tourist curiosity. On the island of Crete, on the isles of the Aegean, in Ceylon, in Indo-China, and in the oases of Central Asia cultures developed that dazzle the eyes of modern man, cultures that still sustain the spirit of their present inhabitants. But those are not part of a single web of history and culture that has somehow survived intact to become part of the modern life of a nation, to be absorbed into its industrial, scientific, and artistic strength, as is the case with Japan. In that sense, Japan seems a country filled with a strange wonder [*fushigi na kiseki*], at once ancient and new. There is not another case like it in the history of the world.[30]

Maybe so, but is this the only way to describe modern Japan? Why describe it like this? Why, especially, would someone like Irokawa, who is certainly no narrow-minded Japanist, feel compelled to describe it like this? What are we to make of this articulation in which the operative word is *fushigi*?

My purpose in citing this passage is not to impugn Irokawa and his work and, by association, Yanagita and his. Rather, it is to point up the internal tension of their shared discourse of Japanese modernity, a discourse that desires difference (from the past, from Tokyo centrism, from the non-Japan in the present) but needs identity (within itself and for a history of "the Japanese folk"). As is apparent in occasional "lapses" in both Yanagita's and Irokawa's writings, this tension is sublimated by positing something as a "native" principle of perpetual difference within the identity of Japan. "The fantastic"—surfacing in Irokawa's introduction as "strange wonder" and "fairy-tale aspect"—serves this function in being identified with Japan. More specifically, ancient and new things appearing together as *fushigi* in the historical scene of Japan's rapid modernization—and, most important, the people's capacity to weather this wave of wonder, even actively to generate it—are fetishized and taken to reflect a defining feature, a "spirit," of "Japanese history and culture" that the people as folk embody. The fantastic is thus rendered natural to Japanese modernity. And, positioning Japan in between the West and the rest of the East in discourses of modernity ever since Meiji, this fantastic nature of Japan and its people is also cast as exclusive. In this respect, the deployment of folk studies to challenge mainstream Japanese historiography constantly runs the risk of succumbing to Japanist configurations, especially insofar as the mainstream is identified as derivative of Western social sciences and the alternative is not identified as Eastern.

Fushigi *and Modern Japanese Identity*

One interesting revelation that arises from the examination of the discourse on *fushigi* offered in this present study is that the sundry assertions of knowledge about *fushigi* are always just that: knowledge about, around, circumscribing a presumed object rather than positive knowledge that "objectively" grasps the mystery and possesses it. Positive possession of things *fushigi* occurs under either of two conditions: the *fushigi* object is transposed onto something "real" (as in Inoue's *yōkaigaku*), in which case the object vanishes as part of a discourse on *fushigi* and enters a field of empirical science and bureaucratic reason; or the real is redefined to include the products of belief, imagination, and affectation (as in Yanagita's *minzokugaku*), in which case the science vanishes as empirical and enters a field of hermeneutics that feeds on a perpetuation of absences to be made present or conundrums to be cracked. Minakata's theoretical musings too led toward a rethinking of scientific principles of research and attempted to account for the roles that chance, uncertainty, hunches, feelings, and instinct play in human endeavors—from the production of knowledge about the natural world to the production and study of cultures. If applied to Minakata, "becoming a *tengu*" would be a metaphor for the creative accident, the dreamlike epiphany, the achronological disruption that frustrates simple categorizations of things and breaks up the determinism of a unilinear historical chronology. What he offered in their place were conditions that opened up alternatives for thought and action.

The *fushigi* that these intellectuals found among the folk thus gave rise to a "structure of mystery" (what Ivy calls a "structure of phantasm") whereby the object of study is always fleeting in one way or another, but eventually reappearing in a different guise. *Yōkaigaku* facilitated the redirecting of spiritual sentiment toward the emperor, a supremely enlightened (i.e., deified) human who in effect became the supernatural incarnate, a modern mystery of ancient lineage.[31] Originally formed in explicit opposition to *yōkaigaku, minzokugaku* wittingly or not created the possibility—but not inevitability—for the application to the whole of Japan what was first described as fantastic and mysterious among commoners in parts of Japan. In this application of folk studies, the national essence becomes *fushigi*. Thus, from the top down, Japan, having already titillated the imagination of foreigners with its "exotic" cultural oddities and having already astounded the world with its swift and "miraculous" industrialization, stands to be further mystified as *fushigi* in the quest for a modern identity. More often than not, the "found" identity is predicated on this essentialized notion of *fushigi* itself.

Both of these strands of the modern discourse on *fushigi,* so different in their attitude toward folk beliefs and practices, thus could potentially be affiliated with the warp and woof of *nihonjinron.* Even the fantastic literature of Kyōka, critical as it was of modern state institutions, can easily be turned into grist for a Japanese uniqueness mill that feeds the cultural essentialism abetting those same institutions. The critical power of the twilighted in-between that characterizes Kyōka's use of *fushigi*—a perspective that could actually serve as a means to break down the simple binarisms of inside/outside, Japan/West, traditional/modern that mark *nihonjinron*—evaporates when trivialized as just another expression of the mysterious paradoxes of a uniquely unique modern Japan.

Tanizaki Jun'ichirō's 1933–1934 praise for shadows, shadows being his emblem for a fading Japanese authenticity located somewhere between Western enlightenment and primitive benightedness, can be read in this light, so to speak. Even when discussing the aesthetics of discrimination in the relative "whiteness" and "darkness" of skin tones among the Japanese, Tanizaki is quick to point out that Japanese whiteness and darkness is distinct from the Western variety: "From ancient times we have considered white skin more elegant, more beautiful than dark skin, and yet somehow this whiteness of ours differs from that of the white races. Taken individually there are Japanese who are whiter than Westerners and Westerners who are darker than Japanese, but their whiteness and darkness is not the same."[32] It is because of the cloudiness of Japanese whiteness, he continues, that the cultivation of a "world of shadows" became necessary to enhance through contrast the "supreme beauty" of whiteness as embodied by an elegant and elfin Japanese woman: "It is whiter than the whitest white woman I can imagine. The whiteness of the white woman is clear, tangible, familiar; it is not this otherworldly whiteness" (33–34). In other words, the supernatural quality of Japanese whiteness (whatever that could possibly mean) renders it superior to Western whiteness. Its logical corollary would be that a similar supernatural quality in Japanese blackness renders it blacker than Western blackness. Seemingly innocent because of its aestheticization in Tanizaki's articulation, such spiritually charged assertions cultivate social and political ramifications that are potentially extreme and frightening. This kind of affirmation of superiority by an appeal to an intangible otherworldliness was not unlike that found in the 1937 propaganda tract *Kokutai no hongi* (The true meaning of the national body), an ideological bulwark of the Greater East Asia Co-Prosperity Sphere. Indeed, as Komatsu and Naitō suggest in passing, the "conversion" of intellectual activist Kita Ikki, for example, from the left to the ultraright wing quite possibly might have been catalyzed by a "terrifically sensitive feeling for the other world" gained through his association with one of Hirata Atsutane's *kokugaku* disciples, Satō Nobuhiro.[33]

Cornel West's comments about the racial politics of whiteness/blackness in America seem uncannily appropriate here for the case of modern Japan:

> One cannot deconstruct the binary oppositional logic of images of Blackness without extending it to the contrary condition of Blackness/Whiteness itself. However, a mere dismantling will not do — for the very notion of a deconstructive social theory is oxymoronic. Yet social theory is what is needed to examine and *explain* the historically specific ways in which "Whiteness" is a politically constructed category parasitic on "Blackness," and thereby to conceive of the profoundly hybrid character of what we mean by "race," "ethnicity," and "nationality." For instance, European immigrants arrived on American shores perceiving themselves as "Irish," "Sicilian," "Lithuanian," etc. They had to learn that they were "White" principally by adopting an American discourse of positively-valued Whiteness and negatively-charged Blackness. This process by which people define themselves physically, socially, sexually and even politically in terms of Whiteness and Blackness has much bearing not only on constructed notions of race and ethnicity but also on how we understand the changing character of U.S. nationalities.[34]

Meiji Japan did not of course have the same degree of voluntary immigration (although the Japanese government would later lure or forcefully bring to the homeland laborers from its colonies and treat them as "black"), but it did face the problem of constructing a pure (i.e., "white") and unified national race from diverse pockets of local cultures and dialects that spread southwest to northeast across the archipelago. And it carried out this project not only in relation to Western powers; definition of a national identity went hand-in-hand with colonial conquests abroad and at home.[35] As West notes, "Whiteness" is politically constructed in a parasitic relationship to "Blackness." This mechanism is basically what Komatsu is articulating with his theory of Japanese political authority being derived through the centuries from the management of "the dark-side of Japan." What we see occurring simultaneously with the colonization of the "outer territories" (*gaichi*) is an endocolonization of the demons and spirits of the "other world," a world conceived as other both spatially (rural periphery) and temporally (past beliefs). In the case of modern Japan, external *and* internal sources of blackness were thus at the disposal of the builders of a nation-state, the cultural, political, and social integrity of which would rely on an overdetermined spiritual ethnos to mask domestic differences *and* foreign similarities. The foreign took over the role of present Other while the *fushigi* of the folk was consigned to an anachronistic but respected past of national essence and origins.

Externally, the 1894–1895 war with a China perceived as politically and technologically backward provided Japan with its first colonies (Taiwan and the Pescadore Islands) and widespread opportunity to enhance the whiteness of the Japanese against the blackness of subjugated peoples. It comes as no surprise that white imperialists spoke glowingly of the Japanese effort.[36] Ten years later, war with an autocratic and constitutionally backward Tsarist Russia (the Meiji state at least had a constitution ostensibly based on Western models) furthered imperialist ambitions among Japanese leaders which led to the subsequent annexation and colonization of Korea in 1910. To coax without conflict Korean loyalty to the Japanese emperor, colonial propaganda actually emphasized the cultural and racial proximity of Koreans and Japanese, but in actual treatment they were brutally discriminated against and much conflict resulted.[37] This apparent paradox is perhaps expected, as it is not uncommon that the most extreme assertions of difference befall those who are closest to the same; consider the treatment of Korean colonial subjects as a purification of Japanese Spirit, the last bastion of difference. Finally, once the ideological use of "enlightened" Western knowledge had been completed by the Taishō period (its practical use persisted), old images of demonic, red-haired "southern barbarians" (Westerners) could be resuscitated as part of an international blackness over which the light of an ultranational Japanese whiteness could cast its rays in "overcoming the modern."[38]

Internally, the Japanese blackness upon which a parasitic Japanese whiteness could grow already had roots in the "nonpersonhood" of Japan's historical outcasts (*eta*) and the "primitiveness" of indigenous Ainu to the far north and of newly incorporated Okinawans to the far south.[39] Yet, as I have argued in this study, another principal foundry for forging a sense of modern national unity in Japan worked on otherworldly materials. In this respect, Inoue's casting common *yōkai*—and the "primitive" rural spirituality related to them—as signs of benightedness against which a spiritually healthy and unified national body could glow was instrumental. Recall his description of pious Japanese subjects "reflecting and glittering in the completely spiritual divine light of the [imperial] national body." The "monsters" that had belonged to an in-between twilight were blackened out and placed in the past. Regional cultural diversity and folk knowledges were concatenated to a chain of superstition and duly stigmatized or repressed, but this process did not mean the expulsion of the supernatural. Differences in class, gender, occupation, environment, lifestyle, and so on were transcended in a purified world of familial spirits presided over by the supernatural father-figure of the emperor.

Against this construction of binary oppositions, which seeks to exclude or benignly incorporate diversity, ambiguity, and chance possibilities by associating these with the "disorder" of blackness while associating purity of blood with the "order" of whiteness, a writing of twilight gray like Kyōka's or an assertion of unpredictable change like Minakata's achieves its deconstructive force. As I aimed to show in linking Yanagita's early work with that of Kyōka, Yanagita too, perhaps out of sheer fascination with the mysteries in the modern, had originally embarked on a similarly critical writing. But in this same juxtaposition of texts and also in comparison to Minakata's more explicitly marginal positioning toward the centers of institutional knowledge, the limits of a folk study that openly sought to establish itself as a serious, respected, and authoritative enterprise are thrown into relief. When the legitimation of knowledge is a function of institutions supported and sanctioned by the national government, that knowledge (in this case, Yanagita's folk studies) is forced to prove its practical application and national worth. Within the "haunted air" of ideology, Yanagita's shift—from a study of the "black" elements of Japan (*yōkai, yamabito,* wanderers) to the fabrication of a *jōmin* charac-terized by ancestor worship, fixed abode, and (white) rice cultivation—appears as a complementary, even predictable, move rather than as the profoundly mysterious break that it is often made out to be.

There is much about Japan that has been made mysterious since the days of *bakumatsu bakemono.* Modern mysteries—from Japan as *Kamiguni* (land of the gods) to economic wunderkind—have been produced and consumed both domestically and abroad. Ironically, foreign observers of Meiji Japan may have been the first to invite the *nihonjinron* trope of Japan as a unique and inexplicable *fushigi,* as the manifestation of a racial spirit felt in the Japanese blood and impervious to the foreign brain. The ex-oticization of a cultural other too often (or always, as disturbing as this might be) depends on and reinforces a cultural essentialism. And more often than not, the observations that fueled this process in the case of Japan focused on figures of the fantastic found among the spiritual be-liefs of the common folk.

Undoubtedly the most prodigious and well-known example of this genre of writing is the Irish-Greek-American writer Lafcadio Hearn (1850–1904), who has been hailed by Japanese and non-Japanese alike as the most sensitive and sympathetic foreign interpreter of Japan. Yanagita even had occasion to cite him—and perhaps not cite him when he should have.[40] Hearn's principal interest in Japan was the spiritual beliefs and ghost lore of its people, on which he wrote numerous essays and short stories in addition to collecting, adapting, and translating ghost tales from Japanese literary and oral traditions. His volume *Kwaidan* (Ghost tales) is actually more widely read today in its "retranslation" back into Japa-nese. Alarmed by the ill effects that Western-inspired industrialization was having on what he perceived as the core of Japaneseness—awe and reverence for the supernatural—Hearn appreciated and salvaged Japanese ghost lore in the same way that his contemporary Ernest Fenellosa appre-ciated and salvaged Japanese art. (One can only imagine that Hearn would have considered the bureaucratization of spirits in the shrine mergers program as the overt destruction of Japanese identity.) In this respect he too, like Yanagita, engaged in a study of the folk that aimed to elucidate the beliefs and sentiments associated with the other world. Likewise, his dedication to the other world harbored a critical nostalgia in relation to the present world.

In Hearn's case, however, the appeal to folklore "in ghostly Japan" (as he would name one of his volumes) possessed a deeply romantic, even erotic, longing that tended to fetishize the fantastic, reifying fragments of *fushigi* into whole cultural manifestations that could then be identified as authentically "Japanese" because of their unfamiliarity, their "strangeness and charm."[41] Constituted as such, Japanese history and culture can only be "felt" by a non-Japanese who is especially empathetic and sensitive to Japanese spiritual beliefs; rational analysis is unsuited to the study of Japan, or at best has only a secondary role, for modern rationality is understood as being a product of the West. Implicit in this formulation, which echoes Yanagita's conditions for Japanese folk studies, is that to know Japan one must become Japanese, a transformation Hearn legally if not spiritually accomplished by becoming a Japanese citizen and taking the Japanese name Koizumi Yakumo.

Thus hallowed as the key to understanding anything about Japan, the Japanese Spirit is somehow innately comprehensible to natives by what Peter Dale has called an "epistemology of the blood," while it is mystically cast as a *fushigi* fundamentally incomprehensible to foreigners.[42] This foreclosure or at least severe devaluation of any foreign (and even heretical "Westernized" Japanese) attempts to study Japan—though no such barrier is said to exist for Japanese studying foreign cultures—is a typical trait of the *nihonjinron* mystification of Japan and "the Japanese mind." Hearn's writing has a definite allure and many interesting insights into the culture and society of Meiji Japan that remain valuable to this day, but his fetishization of Japanese culture as manifest *fushigi* has not only fed similar exoticizing operations among other foreign observers of Japan, it also dovetails with the domestic production of a cultural essentialism that operates to undermine any critical discourse on Japan.

My own foreign foray into a historical critique of the roles that the folk and the fantastic played among a variety of discursive sites in late-nineteenth- and early-twentieth-century Japan has in part been directed at discerning some of the neglected roots of contemporary cultural essentialism in Japan. I think some have been discerned. At the same time, I have also directed my investigations at the disclosure of cultural productions that contested essentializing tendencies within the intellectual arena of modern Japan. I think some have been disclosed. Implicit throughout this study has been the question of the fantastic (as explored through and identified with the folk) putting the "Japanese" in Japanese modernity. Certainly a case has been made that the fantastic, as an object and even mode of discourse, was closely affiliated with the instantiation of modernity in Japan, and that it has been mobilized to assert a mysteriousness if not exclusivity for modern Japan ever since. This does not mean that Japan stands outside the modern or has in any way "overcome the modern" or has an essentially unique modernity (it is as unique as any other). It does mean that under particular historical circumstances, a discourse on the fantastic—in its negativity and positivity—fundamentally shaped modernity in Japan. It also suggests that such a discourse might have shaped other modernities as well, which have gone unrecognized without the defamiliarization of modernity that an examination of Japan's case performs.

Given that the impetus of this study was to cut through foregone conclusions concerning civilization and monsters, I will rest content knowing that I have at least brought *bakemono* into the history of modern Japan and have demonstrated the formative role of things *fushigi* in Japanese modernity. If nothing else, I hope to have impressed upon the reader that ancient monsters bred in twilight do not vanish in modern times—they merely change their shape.

NOTES

Prologue: Monsters in the Twilight of Enlightenment

1 Izumi Kyōka, "Tasogare no aji" [The taste of twilight], in *Kyōka zenshū* (Tokyo: Iwanami, 1940–1943), 29:683–84. Unless otherwise noted, all translations are mine.

2 Although most commonly thought to refer only to the time near dusk, the word "twilight" as well as the Japanese *tasogare* and *kawatare* could refer to both near dusk and near daybreak. Although synonyms, *tasogare* and *kawatare*, the *Daijirin* informs us, took up a popular pseudodivision of labor: *tasogare* came to refer to the evening phenomenon and *kawatare* came to refer to its morning counterpart. Kyōka's use of *shinonome* to refer to the morning phenomenon is in a way redundant, as *tasogare*, in its association with *kawatare*, effectively comprises both times at which this ephemeral shade occurs.

3 Yanagita Kunio, "Kawatare-doki" [Twilight time], in *Yanagita Kunio zenshū* (Tokyo: Chikuma shobō, 1989), 6:37–39.

4 Yanagita Kunio, "Yōkai dangi" [A discussion on monsters], in ibid., 6:20.

5 As will be discussed in chapter 4, a hierarchy of eye, ear, and heart (*kokoro*) as organs of collecting deepening levels of information about folk practices becomes important in Yanagita's method of folk studies. The heart is privileged in order to allow a stealthy, tactical opening for a subject who can to some degree identify (with) the feelings of his or her object while maintaining an image of scientific objectivity during an essentially hermeneutical procedure. But even this alternative method of forming knowledge must pass through the modern institutional eye to be accepted by the Academy.

6 Tidy English translations for *fushigi* and *yōkai/bakemono* are difficult to come up with given their context-determined nuances and the popular associations of possible English counterparts. As noun and adjective, *fushigi* ranges from "the marvelous, the strange, the mysterious, the uncanny" to "inexplicable, incredible, magical, miraculous." Taking a broad view of "the fantastic" (and *fushigi*) that encompasses these meanings, I use it to refer to what often liter-

ally appears as *"fushigi"* in many texts. I will, however, turn to any of the other possible renderings of *fushigi* or leave it in Japanese when it appears appropriate for a given context. *Yōkai* (which is used interchangeably with *bakemono* in many of the primary and secondary sources that I draw on) is often rendered as "ghosts and goblins" or "monsters and apparitions," which is perhaps the most inclusive, albeit a clunky, translation. The same can be said of the more generic "supernatural beings." "Ghosts"—in my view and that of many other commentators—is too limiting for the Japanese case. The word *yūrei,* which is considered one type of *yōkai,* is more appropriately translated as "ghost," as it most closely approximates what is understood by the English word. Although "monster" to an English-language audience might also generate limited and culture-bound images of Frankenstein's monster, of freaks of nature, and even of Godzilla, I have settled on it as a translation of *yōkai* and *bakemono* in most cases, with the understanding that it denotes a very wide range of Japanese monsters and apparitions, that is, supernatural beings. In any case, I am not so much concerned with literal translations as I am with conceptual categories.

7 The prolific output of Mizuki Shigeru (1924–) is a good example of the boom itself as well as of its crossover nature. Mizuki began his career as an amateur *yōkai* researcher and later became a popular comic book artist known for his supernatural characters and themes drawn from the folklore of Japanese monsters. He is perhaps best known for creating the comic *Ge ge ge no Kitaro,* which was turned into a television cartoon that was still being broadcast in the early 1990s. His extensive *yōkai* research and comics were the center—the hook, one might say—of an exhibition "Mizuki Shigeru to Nihon no yōkai" that toured Japan from the summer of 1993 to the summer of 1994 and featured a historical overview of monsters in Japanese culture. Published roundtable discussions among prominent academic scholars of *yōkai,* in which Mizuki himself has participated on occasion, is another medium whereby interest in Japanese monsters has crossed high- and middlebrow arenas.

8 By "folk" I do not mean to designate an identifiable homogeneous body of Japanese people. Nationalist ideologues in Japan and their unwitting apologists abroad already have a monopoly on that unfortunate activity. I should perhaps use the plural to emphasize the differences of age, class, culture, speech, physique, sexual orientation, occupation, gender, thought, lifestyle, and so on among "the Japanese." But even I will bend to convention at times and so will use throughout this study the term "folk" with the understanding that it signifies a heterogeneous collective that has been ideologically constructed during Japan's modernization as a unified and homogeneous subject with a single history.

9 *Minzokugaku* (民俗学) has been rendered more interpretively by Harootunian and others as "nativist ethnology" or "native ethnology," translations that

I find absolutely appropriate for the discipline designated by *minzokugaku*. I, for the most part, stay with the more literal and old-fashioned "folklore studies" and "folk studies" to foreground the subject of the "folk," which also becomes the focus in non-*minzokugaku* writings. Some of this fluidity in translation is no doubt the result of the overlapping meanings and disciplinary associations designated by the homonyms *minzokugaku* (民俗学) and *minzokugaku* (民族学). The *Konsaisu 20 seiki shisō jiten* (Concise dictionary of twentieth-century thought [Tokyo: Sanseido, 1989], 775–76), defines the former ("science of folklore") as the study of "folk culture of civilized races [*bunmei minzoku no minzoku bunka*—文明民族の民俗文化") while noting that its disciplinary form differs from country to country. On the other hand, it defines the latter ("ethnology") as classically denoting "theories of culture and research of culture based on comparative research of various cultures," pointing out that it used to refer specifically to the study of so-called non-literate societies but now can practically include study of any group for which ethnographic fieldwork can be done.

10 *Yōkai no minzokugaku: Nihon no mienai kūkan* [The folk study of monsters: Japan's invisible space] (Tokyo: Iwanami shoten, 1988) by historical ethnologist Miyata Noboru and several works by cultural anthropologist Komatsu Kazuhiko stand out as laudable efforts to rethink *minzokugaku* in the context of a historical study of Japanese monsters. Despite his own tendency to essentialize Japanese monsters as reflections of Japanese mentality, Komatsu in particular has offered convincing critiques of the shortcomings of both Yanagita's and Inoue's approaches to the subject. See his *Hyōrei shinkō ron: yōkai kenkyū e no kokoromi* [Thesis on spirit possession beliefs: Toward monster research] (Tokyo: Arina shobō, 1989); *Yōkaigaku shinkō: yōkai kara miru nihonjin no kokoro* [Monsterology reconsidered: The mentality of the Japanese seen through monsters] (Tokyo: Shōgakukan, 1994); and, with Aramata Hiroshi, *Yōkai sōshi: ayashiki monotachi no shōsoku* [with the English cotitle "Book of hobgoblins: A breath from the darkside of Japanese history"] (Tokyo: Kōsakusha, 1987).

11 Tsuboi Hirofumi's *Imo to Nihonjin: minzoku bunkaron no kadai* [Potatoes and the Japanese: Topics in folk culture studies] (Tokyo: Miraisha, 1979) and Akamatsu Keisuke's *Hi-jōmin no minzoku bunka: seikatsu minzoku to sabetsu mukashibanashi* [The folk culture of non-abiding folk: Daily life folk and folktales of discrimination] (Tokyo: Asahi shoten, 1986) are examples of such critique.

12 Sometimes simply translated as "the folk," *jōmin* (ordinary people) was the term that Yanagita eventually settled on by the 1940s to refer to the idea of rice-cultivating, ancestor-worshiping people of fixed domicile that he imagined as the core constituency of Japanese ethnicity and culture in the history of the archipelago. The *jō* (常) of *jōmin* implies both ordinariness and changelessness; the translation "abiding folk," first suggested by Harry Harootunian,

brings out this latter quality which Yanagita certainly had in mind in addition to the ordinariness of the folk.

13 Yoshimoto Takaaki's meditations on Yanagita's *Tōno monogatari* and, to a lesser extent, on *Yama no jinsei* [Life in the mountains] appear in *Kyōdō gensōron* [Thesis on collective imaginaries], which was serialized in *Bungei* from November 1966 to April 1967 before being published along with other essays by Kawade shobō in 1968. He also published other articles on Yanagita from the 1960s which have been collected in *Yanagita Kunio ron shūsei* [A collection of essays on Yanagita Kunio] (Tokyo: JICC, 1990). Akasaka Norio's essays on aspects of the early formation of *minzokugaku* have been collected in *Kyōkai no hassei* [The genesis of boundaries] (Tokyo: Sunagoya shoten, 1989); *Yama no seishinshi: Yanagita Kunio no hassei* [A spiritual history of mountains: The genesis of Yanagita Kunio] (Tokyo: Shōgakukan, 1991); and *Yanagita Kunio no yomikata: mō hitotsu no minzokugaku wa kanō ka* [Ways of reading Yanagita Kunio: Is another folk studies possible?] (Tokyo: Chikuma shinsho, 1994). Uchida Ryūzō offers an engaging treatment of historical representation, subjectivity, modernity, and alterity in Yanagita's early writing in *Yanagita Kunio to jiken no kiroku* [Yanagita Kunio and the recording of events] (Tokyo: Kōdansha sensho metier, 1995). Although not specifically related to the question of fiction and the fantastic, Satō Kenji's important theoretical work on Yanagita, modernity, and media, *Dokusho kūkan no kindai: hōhō toshite no Yanagita Kunio* [The modernity of textual space: Yanagita Kunio as method] (Tokyo: Kōbundō, 1987), deserves mention in the context of innovative approaches to the work of modern folklore studies.

14 Kawamura Kunimitsu, *Genshisuru kindai kūkan* [The hallucinating space of modernity] (Tokyo: Seikyūsha, 1990).

15 Matsuyama Iwao, *Uwasa no enkinhō* [The perspective of rumors] (Tokyo: Seidōsha, 1993).

16 Ronald A. Morse, "The Search for Japan's National Character and Distinctiveness: Yanagita Kunio (1875–1962) and the Folklore Movement" (Ph.D. diss., Princeton University, 1974); J. Victor Koschmann, Ōiwa Keibō, and Yamashita Shinji, eds., *International Perspectives on Yanagita Kunio and Japanese Folklore Studies* (Ithaca: Cornell University East Asia Program, 1985). Contrary to Morse's translation of the title *Tōno monogatari* as *The Legends of Tōno*, Marilyn Ivy rightly restores the sense of *monogatari* to "tale" in her rendering *The Tales of Tōno*, linking it with tale literature from the Heian period on, in *Discourses of the Vanishing: Modernity, Phantasm, Japan* (Chicago: University of Chicago Press, 1995), 66. I think, however, that she too facilely assumes that *monogatari* should be plural. *The Tale of Tōno*—also a possible translation—places emphasis on Yanagita's act of writing these tales of Tōno together in one work and thereby constructing a unified image of Tōno, its surroundings, and its resi-

dents. (The singular "tale" would also, for example, follow the precedent of Heian classics such as *The Tale of Genji,* to which Ivy alludes.)

17   Noriko Aso, Susan Burns, Alan Christy, Yoshikuni Igarashi, Tom Looser, Kentarō Tomio, and I made up the core of that group and have since researched topics related to nativism, folklore, and questions of national identity and the social sciences in Japan. Harootunian has provocatively related the ideological production of modern folk studies with early modern nativism (*kokugaku*) in the epilogue of *Things Seen and Unseen: Discourse and Ideology in Tokugawa Nativism* (Chicago: University of Chicago Press, 1988), and in his essay "Disciplining Native Knowledge and Producing Place: Yanagita Kunio, Origuchi Shinobu, Takata Yasuma," in *Culture and Identity: Japanese Intellectuals during the Interwar Years,* ed. J. Thomas Rimer (Princeton: Princeton University Press, 1990), 99–127.

18   Gerald Figal, "Yanagita Kunio writing in Wonderland: The Limits of Representation and the Representation of Limits" (master's thesis, University of Chicago, 1987); "The Folk and the Fantastic in Japanese Modernity: Dialogues on Reason and Imagination in Late Nineteenth- and Early Twentieth-Century Japan" (Ph.D. diss., University of Chicago, 1992).

19   Susan J. Napier, *The Fantastic in Modern Japanese Fiction: The Subversion of Modernity* (London: Routledge, 1996), 12–13.

20   Uchida's analysis of Yanagita's theory and practice of representation as it relates to the writing style of *Tōno monogatari* and the construction of *yamabito, jōmin,* and a modern historical subject is, in my opinion, textually richer and more sharply argued than either Ivy's or my earlier efforts.

21   Ivy, *Discourses of the Vanishing,* 72, 86, 25. Uchida makes a similar argument with respect to the "unbounded alterity" of the fantastic (evoked by the image of *yamabito*) being transformed into the other of the Same, "the Siamese twin of *jōmin,* as it were" (*Yanagita Kunio to jiken no kiroku,* 112–13).

22   Alan S. Christy, "Representing the Rural: Place as Method in the Formation of Japanese Native Ethnology, 1910–1945" (Ph.D. diss., University of Chicago, 1997), 399.

23   Picking up where Christy leaves off, Yoshikuni Igarashi, "Imagining History: Discourses of Cultural Politics in Japan, 1930s and 1960s" (Ph.D. diss., University of Chicago, 1994), has analyzed postwar critical interventions into Yanagita's writings (especially those of Yoshimoto Takaaki), arguing that "the widespread renewed interest in his [Yanagita's] scholarship in the 1960s (the 'Yanagita boom') was more than just a nostalgic longing for what Japan had lost in the process of history; it also contained a desire to free Yanagita from canonical readings" (77). Even Kawada Minoru, although keeping to Yanagita and limited in analysis, documents some of the practical concerns and historical contingencies that Yanagita faced, thus presenting a relevant, for-

mative historical context that Ivy elides. See Minoru Kawada, *The Origins of Ethnography in Japan: Yanagita and His Times,* trans. Toshiko Kishida-Ellis (London: Kegan Paul International, 1993).

24 Ivy, *Discourses of the Vanishing,* 22.

25 In his analysis of the construction of the public image of the Meiji emperor, T. Fujitani suggests ways in which popular folklore and the new emperor-centered "folklore of the regime" colluded and collided around beliefs in the emperor's divinity; see *Splendid Monarchy: Power and Pageantry in Modern Japan* (Berkeley: University of California Press, 1996), especially chap. 5, "Crowds and Imperial Pageantry."

Chapter 1 Bakumatsu Bakemono

1 Kajima's description is cited in Andrew L. Markus, "The Carnival of Edo: *Misemono* Spectacles from Contemporary Accounts," *Harvard Journal of Asian Studies* 45, no. 2 (December 1985): 509. The examples of the more grotesque forms of *misemono* attractions are enumerated on 527–30.

2 Komatsu discusses the details of this political use of *bakemono* (*yōkai*) with Naitō Masatoshi in *Oni ga tsukutta kuni, Nihon* [Japan, the land that demons built] (Tokyo: Kōbunsha, 1985), and outlines it with *yōkai* researcher and illustrator Mizuki Shigeru in "Yōkaidangi aruiwa takai e no manazashi" [A discourse on monsters, or, a glance at the other world] *Yurika* 16, no. 8 (August 1984): 124–25.

3 Whether the one form of manifestation is dependent on the other or in fact one and the same is a question open for analysis among semioticians and philosophers of capital far more capable than I.

4 Miyata Noboru, *Yōkai no minzokugaku: Nihon no mienai kūkan* (Tokyo: Iwanami shoten, 1988), 152.

5 Markus, "The Carnival of Edo," 518–21.

6 Hashizume Shinya, *Meiji no meikyū tōshi: Tōkyō-Osaka no yūraku kūkan* [Meiji's city of mazes: Amusement areas in Tokyo and Osaka] (Tokyo: Heibonsha, 1990), 100–104.

7 Ibid., 539–40.

8 The rise of department stores must also be considered instrumental in this redirection of urban crowds in Meiji Japan. Not only did they provide such crowds with the new entertainments of museum exhibits of cultural items and window displays of consumable goods within a fixed (and taxable) space, they also removed the masses from a popular economy outside government appropriation and inserted them into an economy of modern capital directed and profited on by the state. See Noriko Aso, "New Illusions: The Emergence

of a Discourse on Traditional Japanese Arts and Crafts, 1868–1945" (Ph.D. diss., University of Chicago, 1997).

9   Sasaki Miyoko and Morioka Heinz, "*Rakugo:* Popular Narrative Art of the Grotesque," *Harvard Journal of Asian Studies* 41, no. 2 (December 1981): 419. Only a handful of *yose* still exist in Tokyo today. From Taishō to the present, radio, cinema, television, pachinko halls, and video games have progressively forced them out of business.

10   Kawamura Kunimitsu, *Genshisuru kindai kūkan* (Tokyo: Seikyūsha, 1989), 103.

11   San'yūtei Enchō, *Shinkei Kasane ga fuchi*, in *Enchō zenshū*, ed. Suzuki Kōzō (Tokyo: Sekai bunko, 1963–64), 1:1–2.

12   Kawamura K., *Genshisuru kindai kūkan*, 104.

13   James A. Michener, *The Floating World* (Honolulu: University of Hawaii Press, 1983), 228.

14   Asai Osamu and Elizabeth Harrison publicized the view of *bakumatsu nishiki-e* as journalistic political cartoons in an article in the *Japan Times* 4 July 1982. The Asai Collection—a small portion of which, thanks to Elizabeth Harrison, I have been able to sample through a catalogue of reproductions and summary explanations of the "decoded" political content depicted—contains many satirical prints that make use of monsters and supernatural figures derived from common folk belief.

15   Some count as many as fifty distinct monsters. The confusion of the monsters depicted makes them difficult to distinguish, and in a few instances apparently distinct forms could be seen as different parts of a single monster. The count of forty-seven works nicely to suggest an aspect of revenge by the numerical association to the forty-seven *rōnin* who plotted the revenge on Lord Kira carried out on 30 January 1703. But perhaps it works a bit too nicely. One other probable allusion of this scene is to the old belief, dating back to the Heian period, of the *hyakki yakō* (nightly parade of one hundred demons), in which it was thought that in certain places a large number of ghouls and goblins paraded about at night and dispersed before dawn.

16   Research on the destructive late-Tokugawa-period peasant movements known as *yonaoshi* is extensive. Among English-language research, interesting perspectives on *yonaoshi* appear in the pieces by Harry Harootunian, Hashimoto Mitsuru, Stephen Vlastos, and George M. Wilson collected in Tetsuo Najita and J. Victor Koschmann, eds., *Conflict in Modern Japanese History: The Neglected Tradition* (Princeton: Princeton University Press, 1982). Also see Stephen Vlastos, *Peasant Protests and Uprisings in Tokugawa Japan* (Berkeley: University of California Press, 1986), 142–53; and George M. Wilson, *Patriots and Redeemers in Japan: Motives in the Meiji Restoration* (Chicago: University of Chicago Press, 1992), chaps. 5, 6.

17 Komatsu and Naitō, *Oni ga tsukutta kuni, Nihon,* 204. A detail from a repre-
    sentative *namazu-e* accompanies the text. For an extended analysis of these
    prints in English, see Cornelius Ouwehand, *Namazu-e and Their Themes* (Lei-
    den: Brill, 1964).

18 Komatsu and Naitō, *Oni ga tsukutta kuni, Nihon,* 26.

19 Komatsu Kazuhiko, Maeda Ai, and Miyata Noboru, "Ijin to yōkai," *Shizen
    to bunka, tokushū: Ijin to Yōkai* [Nature and culture, special ed.: Strangers and
    monsters] 16 (spring 1987): 36.

20 Yanagita Kunio, Osatake Takeki, Akutagawa Ryūnosuke, and Kikuchi Kan,
    "Shōka kidan," in *Yanagita Kunio taidanshū* (Tokyo: Chikuma sōsho, 1964), 263.
    Whereas *kappa* are mythical water imps second in popularity only to *tengu* in
    folk tales, *tanuki,* often translated as "raccoon-dogs," are real mammals who,
    like badgers and foxes, have a reputation as trickster figures who menace
    humans in Japanese folklore. As such, they fall into the general category of
    bakemono.

21 Ibid., 258–59. The role of *tengu* in the discourse on *fushigi* will be examined
    in considerable detail in the following chapters.

22 J. Victor Koschmann, "Action as Text: Ideology in the Tengu Insurrection," in
    Conflict in Modern Japanese History: The Neglected Tradition, ed. Tetsuo Najita and
    J. Victor Koschmann (Princeton: Princeton University Press, 1982), 83. *Tengu
    ni naru* (to become a *tengu*) is an expression that means "to be a braggart; to
    be boastful."

23 Komatsu discusses the *ijingoroshi* cycle of folktales in part 1 of *Ijinron: minzoku
    shakai no shinsei* [Thesis on strangers: The mentality of Japanese folk societies]
    (Tokyo: Seidosha, 1988), and in part 1 of *Akureiron: ikai kara no messeeji* [Thesis
    on evil spirits: The messages from the other world] (Tokyo: Seidosha, 1989).

24 Fudeyasu's confession is reprinted in Kawamura K., *Genshisuru,* 19–22.

25 Ibid., 15. See also Matsuyama Iwao's account of the rumors that ignited these
    riots, *Uwasa no enkinhō* (Tokyo: Seidōsha, 1993), 9–48.

26 Ibid., 19–20.

27 Nobukuni Koyasu, "Kishinron chūkai: kinsei kishinron no josho toshite"
    [Notes on the Thesis on spirits: A prologue to the modern discourse on
    spirits], *Nihongaku* 8 (February 1987): 159–60.

28 H. D. Harootunian, *Things Seen and Unseen: Discourse and Ideology in Tokugawa
    Nativism* (Chicago: University of Chicago Press, 1988), 199.

29 Haga Noboru, "Kaisetsu" [Commentary], *Hirata Atsutane zenshū: geppō* 2 (De-
    cember 1976): 9.

Chapter 2 Words and Changing Things: Grasping Fushigi *in Meiji Japan*

1 Natsume Sōseki, "Koto no sorane," in *Natsume Sōseki zenshū* (Tokyo: Iwanami, 1965–67), 2:85–123.

2 Inoue dedicated the Tetsugakukan, which is present-day Tōyō University in Tokyo, to "The Four Sages": Kant, Confucius, the Buddha, and Socrates.

3 It is worth noting, however, that hot on the heels of the 1890s hypnosis boom, stories of real Japanese people having telepathic powers were on the rise when Natsume wrote this story. The most famous case involved psychologist (*shin-rigakusha*) and paranormal researcher Fukurai Tomokichi (1869–1952), who in 1910 set up a series of experiments in front of distinguished scholars of various fields at Tokyo Imperial University to test the reputed telepathy (*sen-rigan*) of Mifune Chizuko (1886–1911). For accounts of this and an equally famous case of "thoughtography" (*nensha*), see Matsuyama Iwao, *Uwasa no en-kinhō* (Tokyo: Seidōsha, 1993), 156–67; Yokota Junya, *Meiji fukashigi dō* [The Meiji hall of mystery] (Tokyo: Chikuma shobō, 1995), 27–32; and Lisette Geb-hardt, "Fukurai Tomokichi: Ein japanischer Forscher zwischen Seelenkunde und Spiritismus," unpublished manuscript (1997).

4 Michel Foucault, *The Order of Things: An Archaeology of the Human Sciences* (New York: Vintage, 1973), 132–37.

5 In his citation of Inoue's *Yōkaigaku kōgiroku* in his article "The Tengu," *Trans-actions of the Asiatic Society of Japan* 36, no. 2 (1908): 79, M. W. de Visser in fact translates *yōkaigaku* as "folklore," suggesting a contemporary view of what Inoue was actually doing.

6 Itakura Kiyonobu, *Yōkai hakase, Enryō to yōkaigaku no tenkai* [Enryō, professor of monsters and the development of monsterology] (Tokyo: Kokusho, 1983), 6–7.

7 For a summary of this tendency at the heart of classical philosophy of science, see Gaston Bachelard's introduction to *The New Scientific Spirit,* trans. Arthur Goldhammer (Boston: Beacon Press, 1984).

8 Inoue Enryō, *Yōkaigaku* (Tokyo: Kōjinsha, 1933), 1:2–3. Hereafter, references to this edition appear parenthetically in the text. This is the first of a six-volume reprint of Inoue's lectures on ghosts, goblins, superstitions, and psy-chic phenomena, which was originally published in hardcover as *Yōkaigaku kōgiroku* at the Tetsugakukan in 1896. Itakura, *Yōkai hakase,* 43–44, expresses doubt concerning the integrity of this reprint, given, for example, its mispagi-nation. Because of the near impossibility of acquiring or easily duplicating a copy of the original six-volume set for personal use, I have had to rely on this later edition, which in itself was difficult to obtain. I was able, however, to cross-check portions of this edition with a first-edition copy in the library at

Tōyō University (formerly Inoue's Tetsugakukan) and found no discrepancies in the sections I read.

9 Inoue took extensive notes in English on the works of a number of Western thinkers, from the Greeks to Kant, Hegel, and Spencer. His notes on Spencer's *First Principle of Philosophy (Part 1: The Unknowable)* begin with an eight-point summary of the relationship between religion and science, according to Spencer. Points 4 through 7 are:

> 4. Religion and science are same not in form but in essence.
>
> 5. They have equally certain trace of truth.
>
> 6. There is something in religion and in science, which must be held by each even in the absence of the other; thus something is the point at which they agree.
>
> 7. This something is the most abstract truth contained in religion and science.

Reprinted in Saitō Shigeo, ed., *Inoue Enryō to seiyō shisō* [Inoue Enryō and Western thought] (Tokyo: Tōyō daigaku Inoue Enryō kinen gakujutsu kankō kikin, 1988), 275.

10 For a cross-section of views on Inoue's religious thought, see the essays in section 2 of Shimizu Tadashi, ed., *Inoue Enryō no gakuri shisō* [The theoretical thinking of Inoue Enryō] (Tokyo: Tōyō daigaku Inoue Enryō kinen gakujutsu shinkō kikin, 1989).

11 Inoue plays off the classical folk motif of revealing an apparition's "true form" or *shōtai* (e.g., a hideous serpent being revealed by the hero as the spirit of a jealous lover) with the title of his book *Obake no shōtai* [The true form of monsters] (1914), vol. 6 of *Shinhen yōkai sōsho* (Tokyo: Kokusho, 1983), in which he enumerates various contemporary reports of supernatural phenomena and provides corresponding rational explanations for each.

12 Minosaku Genpara, "Kikai fushigi no kenkyū," *Tōyō gakugei zasshi* 3, no. 42 (25 March 1885): 38. Minosaku specialized in zoology and Western history at Tokyo Imperial University.

13 This list, reprinted in Itakura, *Yōkai hakase,* 24, first appeared in Inoue's "Preface to Lectures on Folklore," of *Tetsugakukan Yearly Lectures* 7 (August 1893).

14 Itakura, *Yōkai hakase,* 27. Inoue's article on the topic appeared in *Tetsugakkai zasshi* in August 1888.

15 The standard system of taxonomy is kingdom, phylum, class, order, family, genus, and species. For a brief explication of the development of natural history as a science of descriptive classification, see Thomas L. Hankins, *Science and the Enlightenment* (Cambridge: Cambridge University Press, 1985), 145–57.

16 Cited in Charles Crittenden, *Unreality: The Metaphysics of Fictional Objects* (Ithaca, NY: Cornell University Press, 1991), 4.

17 Ibid., 22–30.

18 Cited in Itakura, *Yōkai hakase,* 25.

19 Oshima Tatehiko, "Gakuzo no gakumon to minzokugaku" [The discipline of our school's founder and folklore studies], in *Inoue Enryō no gakuri shisō* ed. Shimizu Tadashi (Tokyo: Tōyō daigaku, 1989), 274. A detailed account of Inoue's trips to Yamagata prefecture appears in Utonuma Hiroshi, *Yamagata fushigi kikō: Inoue Enryō no ashiato o tadoru* [Yamagata mystery tour log: Tracing Inoue Enryō's footsteps] (Tokyo: Hōsei daigaku shuppankyoku, 1991).

20 Inoue's name appears, for example in "Shinshuzuihitsu," in *Yanagita Kunio zenshū* (Tokyo: Chikuma shobō, 1989), 24:265–421; "Chimei no kenkyū," in *Yanagita Kunio zenshū,* 6:7–212; and "Yōkai dangi," in *Yanagita Kunio zenshū,* 20:7–290.

21 Oshima, "Gakuzo no gakumon," 270.

22 Inoue berates "educators and theologians" for their unwillingness to consider superstitions worthy of study in *Yōkai kenkyū no kekka* [The results of monster research] (Tokyo: Tetsugakukan, 1897), 14. Yanagita criticizes the narrowminded pedantry of scholars in, among other places, "Obake no koe," in *Yanagita Kunio zenshū,* 6:61.

23 Nishi Akio, "Gakuzo no kengakuseishin taru shin'nyo to yōkaigaku," in *Inoue Enryō no gakuri shisō,* ed. Shimizu Tadashi (Tokyo: Tōyō daigaku, 1989), 39–43.

24 An examination of the yearly bibliographic entries in Inoue Enryō kenkyūkai, ed., *Inoue Enryō kankei bunken nempyō* (Tokyo: Tōyō daigaku Inoue Enryō kenkyūkai, 1987), reveals several essays and published lectures related to *shinrigaku* as well as announcements for Inoue's correspondence course in the subject.

25 Itakura, *Yōkai hakase,* 28–29.

26 Ibid., 29.

27 Inoue, *Yōkai kenkyū no kekka,* 20.

28 Information on Minakata's life and travels in this section has been taken primarily from Tsurumi Kazuko, *Minakata Kumagusu: chikyū ikō no hikakugaku* [Minakata Kumagusu: Comparative studies of global scope] (Tokyo: Kōdansha, 1978); and Kasai Kiyoshi, *Minakata Kumagusu* (Tokyo: Kichigawa Kōbunkan, 1967), and *Minakata Kumagusu: hito to gakumon* [Minakata Kumagusu: The man and his work] (Tokyo: Kichigawa Kōbunkan, 1980). Minakata's daughter's account of home life in Tanabe, Minakata Fumie, *Chichi Minakata Kumagusu o kataru* [Stories of my father, Minakata Kumagusu] (Tokyo: Nihon editaa sukuuru shuppan, 1981), is filled with many amusing stories of her father's eccentricities. For a short introduction to Minakata's eccentric life and eclectic work in English, see Carmen Blacker, "Minakata Kumagusu: A Neglected Japanese Genius," *Folklore* 94, no. 2 (1983): 139–52.

29 From 1893, Minakata contributed to the English journals *Nature* and *Notes and Inquiries* while studying and working in the Reading Room at the British

Museum. After his return to Japan in 1900 he continued sending articles to these journals, reaching a total of 50 articles for *Nature* and 323 for *Notes and Inquiries*. The range of erudition displayed in these articles, dealing principally with natural history and folklore, is astonishing. A summary of this material appears in Blacker, "Minakata Kumagusu." From the 1910s he wrote most notably for *Tōkyō jinrui gakkai zasshi, Taiyō, Nihon oyobi nihonjin,* and Yanagita Kunio's *Kyōdo kenkyū.*

30 Tsurumi, *Minakata Kumagusu,* 205. For details on Toki Hōryū's status in religious circles in Japan and for a summary of his participation in the World Parliament of Religions, see James Ketelaar, *Of Heretics and Martyrs in Meiji Japan: Buddhism and Its Persecution* (Princeton: Princeton University Press, 1990), 136–68.

31 Minakata Kumagusu, *Minakata Kumagusu zenshū* [The complete works of Minakata Kumagusu] (Tokyo: Kangensha, 1951), 9:283. Hereafter, references to this edition appear parenthetically in the text. See his discussions on Buddhism's relation to modern science on 9:32–35, 87–90.

32 This attitude might also be related to Minakata's abhorrence of institutionalized learning. Bored in elementary school, he took to reading on his own tomes of Chinese and Japanese natural history and its lore. He failed his exams at Tokyo Imperial University and was expelled from an agricultural engineering college in Michigan on charges of drunken and disorderly conduct, but afterwards taught himself to read about twenty different languages during his few years in the Reading Room at the British Museum. In Japan he refused to be associated with academic circles in Tokyo (much to the chagrin of Yanagita, who saw Minakata as a valuable, albeit obnoxious, source of information), remaining isolated on the Kii peninsula, where he read, wrote, and collected plant and insect specimens.

33 Tsurumi, *Minakata Kumagusu,* 62.

34 Tsurumi Kazuko, *Minakata Kumagusu,* 81–88, reading it as a scientific model for comparative folk studies derived from Shingon notions of causality, has dubbed the figure "Minakata's Mandala." Also see Tsurumi's *Korosareta mono no yukue: watashi no minzokugaku nooto* [Traces of things done away with: My notes on folk studies] (Tokyo: Haru shobō, 1985), 75–95, for a more detailed analysis of this diagram. Though I agree with Tsurumi's interpretation of this picture as being a key to Minakata's notion of causality in the human sciences, I have found that she tends to gloss over his categories. For example, in *Korosareta mono* (84), when explaining his aligning of disciplines to the four basic categories of *fushigi,* she places mathematics and logic, which Minakata clearly had under *kotofushigi* (9:272, 277), into *rifushigi* because she wants to clear the space of *kotofushigi* for the social sciences, especially folklore. I agree that this arrangement is more logical given Minakata's definitions of *mono,*

kokoro, and *koto* and his location of the human sciences in the realm of *koto,* but I think it is important to work through his setup as he stated it to appreciate the historical scope and complexities of his rethinking the limits of classical science when applied to human culture.

35   As Tsurumi schematizes it in *Korosareta mono* (83–86), in the human world of *koto* one can often see the same effects produced from different causes as well as the same causes producing different effects.

36   Letter to Toki cited in Tsurumi, *Minakata Kumagusu,* 88.

37   Inoue, *Yōkaigaku,* 1:88–89. Inoue seems to have adopted this hydraulic model of the mind from nineteenth-century German psychology, in which he was well read. In the examples shown here, a total value of 300 is given to a normal mind in varying states of intellectual, volitional, and emotive activity. The upper left circle, totaling only 240, represents the mind of an uneducated person.

38   Minakata's proclivity for heavy drinking was notorious. The first time he visited Yanagita at the latter's home he got so drunk that their intended scholarly exchange had to be postponed. At their following meeting Yanagita went out to Minakata's place in Tanabe in Wakayama prefecture and recorded in his journal: "He [Minakata], explaining that 'Since I lose my eyesight when drinking it's too bad you showed up; but so long as I can talk, it will probably be all right,' opened up the cuff of his quilted sleeve and spoke from inside it." Minakata's journal entry for the same day (31 December 1913) simply reads: "Spoke lying prostrate without opening my eyes" (reprinted in Tsurumi, *Minakata Kumagusu,* 155–56). It also became well-known that Minakata, on at least two occasions, got drunk and beat up a museum official working in the British Museum. Inagaki Taruho recites this as well as several other colorful Minakata anecdotes in his essay, "Minakatagaku no mikkyōteki na bō," *Yomiuri shinbun,* 25 May 1970, reprinted in his *Kareedosukoppu* [Kaleidoscope] (Tokyo: Shio shuppansha, 1974).

39   Inoue Enryō, who enjoyed an almost celebrity status among enlightenment thinkers as well as among much of the general populace in Meiji Japan, is mentioned on several occasions in Minakata's correspondence. Earlier in this letter (9:248) Minakata makes reference to Toki Hōryū's own congratulatory address delivered at Inoue's Tetsugakukan.

40   This is not the only topic about which Minakata is in open disagreement with Inoue. In an undated list of questions to Toki (9:137), he points out that he is "seriously opposed to Mr. Inoue Enryō" concerning Inoue's view of there being a strict hierarchical order among all beings. This opposition is likely related to his critique of evolutionism that I will be examining shortly.

41   For a discussion of the vagaries of the word "evolution" as it was used (and not used) by nineteenth-century naturalists, biologists, and sociologists, see

Stephen Jay Gould, *Ontogeny and Phylogeny* (Cambridge: Belknap Press, 1977), 28–32.

42 Minakata personally cultivated large quantities of slime molds for observation, even going so far as keeping a tray of horse manure in his room for them to grow on. When he wasn't growing his own slime molds he was always on the lookout for them. He remarks at the end of one letter to Toki (19 March 1894) that while walking through Hyde Park one afternoon he "discovered a type of rare slime mold on top of some dog shit" (9:231). After he set up house in Tanabe, he trained a series of cats to attack the slugs that would perform nightly raids on the bed of fungus he had growing in his garden.

43 A large portion of this correspondence is reprinted in Tsurumi, *Minakata Kumagusu,* 71–73.

44 Ibid., 75–76, 86.

45 Ibid., 67–69.

46 Rosemary Jackson, *Fantasy: The Literature of Subversion* (London: Methuen, 1981), 35, 171–80.

47 As Minakata enlists dreams to depict this logic of tact, one is tempted to associate it here with Julia Kristeva's reading of Bakhtin's notion of the dialogism in Menippean and carnivalesque discourse as a "poetic logic" or "dream logic" that "implies a categorical tearing from the norm and a relationship of nonexclusive [i.e., both/and] opposites." See Julia Kristeva, "Word, Dialogue, and Novel," in *Desire in Language: A Semiotic Approach to Literature and Art,* ed. Leon S. Roudiez (New York: Columbia University Press, 1980), 70–71. Notable too in her account of the freedom of language in Menippean discourse is that within its tragicomic seriousness "elements of the fantastic" appear, and "phantasmagoria and an often mystical symbolism fuse with macabre naturalism" as it "tends toward the scandalous and eccentric in language" (82–83).

48 Both connotations of tact given above might also be fruitfully considered under the concept of bricolage as Michel de Certeau understands it as a "tactic" of "making do" with what is at hand in order to ensure a favorable outcome. This nuance would emphasize tact as a creative adaptability to changing situations, a kind of savoir faire, in the practice of everyday life, from which Minakata draws the bulk of his examples of tact. But it could also be applied to the tactics needed, for example, by the anthropologist or folklorist in the research of the nonquantifiable aspects of *koto* that mark everyday life and human culture. In this formulation, the ways and means of the object that is studied and the subject who studies it dovetail. See Michel de Certeau, *The Practice of Everyday Life,* trans. Steven F. Randall (Berkeley: University of California Press, 1984), 29–42.

Chapter 3 Modern Science and the Folk

1   Michel Foucault, *Discipline and Punish: The Birth of the Prison,* trans. Alan Sheridan (New York: Vintage, 1979), 138.

2   M. W. de Visser, "The Tengu," *Transactions of the Asiatic Society of Japan* 36, no. 2 (1908): 27–32. The most common form of the goblin called *tengu* is humanoid yet birdlike, with a long nose or beak, often with wings. Frightening but helpful to those who respect them, *tengu* were sometimes believed to be messengers of the gods and were associated with forms of occult mountain asceticism. This symbolic display of power over *tengu* at Nikkō may help explain why the rebel, anti-Iemochi Mito group known as the *Tengu* faction chose to conduct a pilgrimage to Nikkō in May 1864. For an analysis of the action of this group during the so-called Tengu Insurrection, see J. Victor Koschmann, "Action as Text: Ideology in the Tengu Insurrection," in *Conflict in Modern Japanese History: The Neglected Tradition,* ed. Tetsuo Najita and J. Victor Koschmann (Princeton: Princeton University Press, 1982), 81–106.

3   Reprinted in Inoue Enryō, *Meishin to shūkyō* (1916), in *Shinhen yōkai sōsho* (Tokyo: Kokusho, 1986), 7:2. *Meishin to shūkyō* first came out in pamphlet form in March 1916, and in his citation of the national elementary school morals textbook (*Kokutei shōgaku shūshinsho*) Inoue does not specify which edition he has read; he states only that it was from "a few years ago."

4   Mikiso Hane, *Peasants, Rebels, and Outcasts: The Underside of Modern Japan* (New York: Pantheon, 1982), 55–59.

5   Kajiyama Masahi, "Kyōkasho kokuteika o megutte" [Concerning the nationalization of textbooks], in *Teikokugikai to kyōiku seisaku* [The Imperial Diet and education policy], ed. Motoyama Yukihiko (Tokyo: Shibunkaku, 1981), 115–16.

6   Ibid., 117–19.

7   Ibid., 123.

8   From an excerpt of the original text of "A Motion Concerning Elementary School Ethics Textbooks," reprinted in Kajiyama, "Kyōkasho kokuteika," 133.

9   Kaigo Tokiomi, ed., *Nihon kyōkasho taikei* [Japanese textbooks outlines] (Tokyo: Kōdansha, 1961–67), 3:628.

10 Ibid., 3:618. Also Kajiyama, "Kyōkasho kokuteika," 135.

11 Inoue Enryō, *Yōkai kenkyū no kekka* (Tokyo: Tetsugakukan, 1897), 23.

12 Inoue Enryō, *Tenguron* (1916) in *Shinhen yōkai sōsho* (Tokyo: Kokusho, 1986), 2:59.

13 Ibid., 2:76. Elsewhere, Inoue severely admonishes parents who persist in telling their children ghost stories and folk tales, saying that this practice is perhaps the single most disruptive obstacle to the education of the masses in

Japan. In contrast, Yanagita will lament the demise of such storytelling because he sees in it a prime source for a history of unlettered folk.

14   Ibid., 2:80–81.

15   Inoue, *Yōkai kenkyū no kekka,* 13–14.

16   Inoue Enryō, "Kokkagaku to yōkaigaku to no kankei, 1," *Kokkagakkai zasshi* 90 (15 August 1894): 599.

17   Inoue Enryō, "Kokkagaku to yōkaigaku to no kankei, 2," *Kokkagakkai zasshi* 92 (15 October 1894): 811–12.

18   Inoue, *Yōkai kenkyū no kekka,* 10.

19   Inoue, "Kokkagaku to yōkaigaku to no kankei, 2," 815, 822.

20   Inoue Enryō, "Kokkagaku to yōkaigaku to no kankei, 3," *Kokkagakkai zasshi* 96 (15 February 1895): 2.

21   Inoue, "Kokkagaku to yōkaigaku to no kankei, 2," 825.

22   Inoue, "Kokkagaku to yōkaigaku to no kankei, 1," 599.

23   Inoue Enryō, *Yōkaigaku* (Tokyo: Kōjinsha, 1933), 1:26.

24   The rhetorical/political importance of this conception of the nation as a concrete, organic body composed of individual cells and organs working together for a common life in the constitution of the Meiji state is one reason I insist on the translation of *kokutai,* a key ideological category in Meiji political theory, as "national body" rather than the more common "national polity." See Carol Gluck, *Japan's Modern Myths: Ideology in the Late Meiji Period* (Princeton: Princeton University Press, 1985), especially chap. 5, for an outline of the issues, interpretations, and implementations of *kokutai* in Meiji Japan.

25   Kawamura Kunimitsu, *Genshisuru kindai kūkan* (Tokyo: Seikyūsha, 1990), 47–48.

26   The original story is reprinted in its entirety in Kaigo, *Nihon kyōkasho taikei,* 3:164–65.

27   Kawamura K., *Genshisuru,* 55.

28   Ibid., 58.

29   For a discussion in English of the relation between the Meiji state and medicine, see William Johnston, *The Modern Epidemic: A History of Tuberculosis in Japan* (Cambridge, MA: Council on East Asian Studies, 1995), 161–213. For a sense of the folklore as well as the institutional and social history of modern medicine in Meiji, see Tatsukawa Shōji, *Meiji iji ōrai* [The comings and goings of Meiji medicine] (Tokyo: Shinchōsha, 1986), and *Byōki no shakaishi: bunmei ni saguru byōin* [A social history of illness: the search for pathogens in civilization] (Tokyo: NHK Books, 1982), 170–250.

30   Yanagita Kunio, "Miko kō" [On shamans] (1913), in *Yanagita Kunio zenshū* (Tokyo: Chikuma Shobō, 1989), 11:396. See also Ichirō Hori, *Folk Religion in Japan: Continuity and Change* (Chicago: University of Chicago Press, 1983), 203. For an informative account of the blindness of shamans and how that figured

in their modern regulation, see Kawamura Kunimitsu, *Miko no minzokugaku: onna no chikara no kindai* [An ethnology of shamans: the modernity of women's power] (Tokyo: Seikyūsha, 1991), 26–38.

31 Inoue, *Yōkaigaku,* 4:1183, 1262.

32 Ibid., 4:1136.

33 Kawamura K., *Genshisuru,* 74.

34 Ibid., 82–85.

35 Ibid., 92.

36 Ibid., 123.

37 From Deguchi Nao, *Keireki* [My life story] (1902), reprinted in Hori, *Folk Religion,* 239–40.

38 Konjin, as Hori explains (*Folk Religion,* 233), was the most fearful of the *kami* worshipped in *shugendō,* a form of mountain asceticism that had a long and lively tradition in the Okayama region where Kawate lived. The headquarters of Konkōkyō was in Kameoka, not far from Deguchi's hometown.

39 Kawamura K., *Genshisuru,* 154–55.

40 Ibid., 151.

41 Hori, *Folk Religion,* 242.

42 Kawamura K., *Genshisuru,* 211.

43 Chigiri Kōsai, *Tengu kō* [On Tengu] (Tokyo: Nami shobō, 1973), 1:384.

44 Kristin Ross, *The Emergence of Social Space: Rimbaud and the Paris Commune* (Minneapolis: University of Minnesota Press, 1988), 55.

Chapter 4 Modern "Science" of the Folk

1 The scare quotes around science are mine for the discursive effect of Minakata's questioning of the appropriateness of orthodox method and reasoning in the physical sciences to a "science" of humans, the animal that Yanagita would characterize as "the greatest mystery of the universe" (*uchū dai-ichi no fushigi*). The scare quotes around founder are to mark how others have characterized Yanagita.

2 The trails and signposts indicating "Site of *Tōno monogatari* tale number . . ." and "Yanagita was here," ceramic *kappa* dotting riverbanks like the ceramic animals and leprechauns on American front lawns, and noodle shops featuring *minwa no soba,* for example, smack of kitsch exploitation. On the other hand, kitty-corner from one "Yanagita slept here" inn that serves as the center of an exhibit complex called *Mukashibanashi no mura* (folktale village) and next to the town civic center is a first-rate library, research, and museum complex that I found very enjoyable, interesting, and useful for my research.

3 Sasaki's "sentence" in the history of folk studies is fast-approaching the length of a short paragraph. At the time of my initial research in Tōno (spring 1989),

volumes 3 and 4 of Sasaki's complete works and works about him were in the making and have since been published. In fact, the original plan for his complete works, compiled by the Tōno City Museum, was to consist of two volumes of his own works (both of which I was fortunate to acquire) and a final third volume containing his letters as well as scholarly books and essays about him. However, as the third volume went into production the number of works on Sasaki increased beyond the bounds of the intended volume and so a fourth volume had to be planned to accommodate this recent surge in Sasaki research.

4   In a warning he added to the fieldwork notebook of one collector of folk material, Yanagita wrote, "Since there are many old people who believe anything a person says, you must listen to them with that in mind." Reading this statement along with Yanagita's essays that deal with "the efficacy of lies" among the folk, Satō Kenji describes what he sees as a recognition on Yanagita's part of the necessity for a method of reading (i.e., interpreting) the meaning of folk tales at a deeper than surface level. See Satō Kenji, *Dokusho kūkan no kindai: hōhō toshite no Yanagita Kunio* (Tokyo: Kōbundō, 1987), 258. Morse's translation of *seijitsu* appears in Yanagita Kunio, *The Legends of Tōno* (Tokyo: The Japan Foundation, 1975), 5.

5   It was also with that aim in mind that he originally established after his retirement the present-day Tetsugakudō Park in the Nakano area of Tokyo as an open school for the philosophical and social education of the common public. The plan of the Tetsugakudō grounds, still open to the public but without the public lectures that Inoue gave there, is truly incredible. Rather than the traditional figures of Nio-o flanking the entrance, there is a *tengu* and a ghost. Within the compound there are, among other sites, The Park of Materialism, The Garden of Idealism, Epistemology Road, Intuition Path, Experience Hill, Concept Bridge, *Tengu* Pine, The Gate of Common Sense, and The Gate of Philosophical Reason. Each site has attached to it a placard with a description or explanation of the topic named. It is a kind of "Philosophy and *Yōkaigaku* for Beginners." Itakura Kiyonobu calls it "a philosopher's Disneyland" (*Yōkai hakase, Enryō to yōkaigaku no tendai* [Tokyo: Kokusho, 1983], 44).

6   Kikuchi Akio, *Sasaki Kizen: Tōno denshō no hito* (Tōno, 1970), 18.

7   Sasaki also took the pen name Sasaki Tōno, among others. In *Sasaki Kizen* (22) Kikuchi specifies Kyōka's *Kōya hijiri* (1900) as Sasaki's model for a fantasy world where the strange, the inexplicable, and the unexpected can happen. Based on my own reading of *Kōya hijiri* and Sasaki's fiction, I would say that Kikuchi's is a fair comparison. I discuss *Kōya hijiri* and Kyōka's use of the fantastic in chapter 5.

8   A review article of Inoue's "discipline" that appeared years earlier in *Kokumin no tomo* (13 November 1893) had said as much about *yōkaigaku*. The reviewer

points out that because Inoue judges *yōkai* as being "a misapplication of intellect which becomes a delusion," he is not after *yōkai* kenkyū but rather *yōkai benbaku* (refutation) and *yōkai daha* (busting). In short, Inoue Enryō was a ghostbuster.

9   Kikuchi, *Sasaki Kizen,* 26.

10 Reprinted in Yamada Kiyoyoshi, "Mizuno Yōshū to Sasaki Kizen," *Fūen* 9 (1972): 8.

11 Ibid., 10.

12 Ibid., 9.

13 Kikuchi, *Sasaki Kizen,* 4.

14 Ibid., 23–24.

15 Ibid., 30.

16 Ibid., 39.

17 Sasaki was widely recognized as having an uncanny knack for listening to the thickly accented and often garbled tales of old Tōhoku people and transcribing them into a standard Japanese form intelligible to the likes of Yanagita (one of Yanagita's first impressions of Sasaki was his own barely intelligible accent). Yanagita praised him frequently for this ability and clearly identified Sasaki's value with it: Sasaki was one of Yanagita's companions on his second trip to Tōhoku in 1920, during which Sasaki befriended an old charcoal maker whose hours of oral tales Sasaki, with Yanagita's encouragement, transcribed and published in 1922 as *Esashi-guni mukashibanashi* and reprinted in Sasaki Kizen, *Kikimimi sōshi* [The attentive ear copybook] (Tokyo: Chikuma sōsho, 1986), for which Yanagita wrote the preface that describes their encounter with the charcoal maker.

18 Kikuchi, *Sasaki Kizen,* 39–40.

19 Yanagita Kunio, "Jijitsu no kyōmi" [The interest in facts], *Bunshō sekai* 3, no. 14 (1908): 146.

20 Yanagita Kunio et al., "Shōka kidan," [Strange stories while summering], in *Yanagita Kunio taidanshū* (Tokyo: Chikuma sōsho, 1964), 256.

21 Yanagita Kunio, *Minkan denshōron* [Theory of folklore] in *Yanagita Kunio zenshū* (Tokyo: Chikuma shobō, 1989), 28:253–54.

22 Okaya Kōji, "Shijin Yanagita Kunio no imi" [The meaning of Yanagita Kunio the poet], *Kokubungaku: kaisetsu to kyōzai no kenkyū* 27, no. 1 (1982): 81. Of course, others involved in the formation of folk studies would not entirely agree with Yanagita's vision. See Alan S. Christy, "Representing the Rural: Place as Method in the Formation of Japanese Native Ethnology, 1910–1945" (Ph.D. diss., University of Chicago, 1997), for an excellent discussion of the diversity and contention within the field.

23 See, for example, Morse's summary of Yanagita's object of research in "The Search for Japan's National Character and Distinctiveness".

24 The same *tengu* about which, as discussed in chapter 3, Inoue Enryō had published widely. In Yanagita's case, *tengu* were the focus of his investigations, at least until the late 1920s, of the agent that in popular belief was felt to exist invisibly in a "hidden world" (*yūmeikai*) for the purpose of a kind of moral surveillance. See below and Gerald Figal, "The Question of Monsters and Ancestor Worship," in *Select Papers, Volume No. 10: Productions of Culture in Japan* (Chicago: The Center for East Asian Studies, University of Chicago, 1995).

25 Yanagita Kunio, "Tengu no hanashi" (1909), in *Yanagita Kunio zenshū*, 6:184.

26 Yanagita Kunio, "Yūmeidan" [Talks on the hidden world], *Shinkō bunrin* 1, no. 6 (1905): 252.

27 See Christy, "Representing the Rural" (54–64) and Morse, "The Search for Japan's National Character and Distinctiveness" (92), for the activities of the Kyōdokai.

28 *Tengudō*, a popular name for a form of occult mountain asceticism (*shugendō*), could have a derogatory connotation when referring to the selfish practices of Buddhist priests who, out of a desire for personal gain, strayed from "the correct path" and took up occult arts.

29 Yanagita, "Tengu no hanashi," 185–86.

30 Yanagita Kunio, "Hashi-hime" (1918), in *Yanagita Kunio zenshū*, 6:353.

31 Yanagita, "Yūmeidan," 243.

32 Carol Gluck, *Japan's Modern Myths: Ideology in the Late Meiji Period* (Princeton: Princeton University Press, 1985), for example, discusses in some detail the debates concerning the definition of *kokutai* and *kokumin* that took place both inside and outside governmental circles in late Meiji Japan.

33 Yanagita, "Yūmeidan," 242–43.

34 Michel de Certeau, "The Freudian Novel: History and Literature," trans. Brian Massumi, in *Heterologies: Discourses on the Other* (Minneapolis: University of Minnesota Press, 1986), 17.

35 Malcolm Bowie, *Freud, Proust, and Lacan: Theory as Fiction* (Cambridge: Cambridge University Press, 1987), 6.

36 Okaya, "Shijin Yanagita Kunio no imi," 80.

37 Yanagita, "Yūmeidan," 258.

38 Certeau, "The Freudian Novel," 26.

39 Yanagita Kunio, *Tōno monogatari* (1910), in *Yanagita Kunio zenshū*, 4:9.

40 Cited in Yamada Kiyoyoshi, "Yanagita Kunio to Mizuno Yōshū, 1," *Fūen* 7 (1972): 7.

41 Mizuno Yōshū, "Tōno monogatari o yomite," *Yomiuri shinbun*, 18 December 1910.

42 This phrase appears frequently in Tayama's essays of this period and became a trademark of his theory of literary writing although they were not always

carried out in practice. See Iwanaga Yutaka, *Tayama Katai kenkyū* (Tokyo: Hakuyōsha, 1956), 246.

43 Yanagita Kunio, "Shasei to ronbun," *Bunshō sekai* 2, no. 3 (1907): 31.

44 See, for example, Tayama Katai, "Byōsharon" [Theory of description], in *Tayama Katai zenshū* (Tokyo: Katai zenshū kankōkai, 1923–24), 11:117–44.

45 Yanagita Kunio, "Dokusha yori mitaru shizen-ha shōsetsu," *Bunshō sekai* 3, no. 5 (1908): 11.

46 Jacques Derrida, "The Purveyor of Truth," *Yale French Studies* 52 (1975): 89.

47 Clayton Koelb, *The Incredulous Reader: Literature and the Function of Disbelief* (Ithaca, NY: Cornell University Press, 1984), 190.

48 Yanagita, *Tōno monogatari,* 4:25. In his review of *Tōno monogatari* written for *Chūgaku sekai* in July 1910 and collected in *Nihon bungaku kenkyū shiryō sōsho: Yanagita Kunio* (Tokyo: Yūseidō, 1976), 280, Shimazaki Tōson again mentions this comparison. Tale 22 apparently held a particular fascination in literary circles as Mizuno Yōshū also picks up on it for inclusion in his "Kaidan," in *Shumi* 4, no. 6 (May 1909). It is also the tale of Tōno that Mishima Yukio cites in *Shōsetsu to wa nani ka* (Tokyo: Shinchōsha, 1972). For further discussion of this tale, see Ivy, *Discourses of the Vanishing,* 87–92.

49 Yanagita, "Dokusha," 13.

50 Cited in Harold Bloom, *The Anxiety of Influence* (New York: Oxford University Press, 1973), 9.

51 Yanagita, "Shasei to ronbun," 31.

52 Yanagita Kunio, "Genbun no kyori," *Bunshō sekai* 4, no. 13 (1909): 167–72.

53 For further discussion on this point, see Gerald Figal, "Yanagita Kunio Writing in Wonderland: The Limits of Representation in the Representation of Limits" (Master's thesis, University of Chicago, 1987).

54 Mary Louise Pratt, "Fieldwork in Common Places," in *Writing Culture: The Poetics and Politics of Ethnography,* ed. James Clifford and George E. Marcus (Berkeley: University of California Press, 1986), 33.

55 Ibid., 27.

56 Cited in Yoshida Seiichi, *Shizenshugi no kenkyū* (Tokyo: Tōkyōdō, 1958), 2:87. Yanagita's downplaying of conflict with the outcast class (*eta*) is also interesting as perhaps a sign of an incipient class-unconscious cultural conservatism that comes to dominate his later work.

57 See, for example, Tayama, *Tayama Katai zenshū,* 11:110–11.

58 Tōson, "Tōno monogatari," 280.

59 Uchida Ryūzō, *Yanagita Kunio to jiken no kiroku* (Tokyo: Kōdansha sensho metier, 1995), 79–80.

60 James Clifford, "On Ethnographic Authority," in *Writing Culture,* ed. James Clifford and Gerald E. Marcus (Berkeley: University of California Press, 1986), 112–13.

244 *Notes to Chapter Four*

61 For discussions of this see, for example, Takayanagi Shun'ichi's review article of Morse's translation of *Tōno monogatari*, "In Search of Yanagita Kunio," *Monumenta Nipponica* 31, no. 2 (summer 1976): 165–78, and Iwamoto Yoshiteru, *Mō hitotsu no Tōno monogatari* [One more tale of Tōno] (Tokyo: Tōsui shobō, 1983), 112–19.

62 Certeau, "The Freudian Novel," 17. This is Certeau's reading of Tzvetan Todorov's *The Fantastic: A Structural Approach to a Literary Genre,* trans. Richard Howard (Ithaca, NY: Cornell University Press, 1975). Although a groundbreaking work to the study of fantastic literature, Todorov's approach is historically sterile when it comes to the analysis of the cultural, social, and political conditions and implications surrounding "fantastic" texts. Rosemary Jackson's *Fantasy: The Literature of Subversion* (London: Methuen, 1981), makes an admirable attempt to fill this lack.

63 On the inadequacies of "great man" historiography, see for example, "Jijitsu no kyōmi." For more on Yanagita's dissatisfaction with the Naturalist School, see also his essays "Kanri no yomu shōsetsu," *Bunshō sekai* 2, no. 11 (October 1907): 26–30, and "Shinkyuryō jidai no bungei," *Mumei tsūshin* 10 (October 1909): 125–26.

64 Yanagita Kunio, "Obake no koe" (1931), in *Yanagita Kunio zenshū,* 6:61.

65 Yanagita Kunio, "Yōkai ko-i: gengo to minzoku no kankei" (1934), in *Yanagita Kunio zenshū,* 6:40–58.

66 Ibid., 6:45.

67 Even though he did not take a degree in the social sciences proper, which could in fact have everything to do with his defensive attitude toward other disciplines, he could still offer as sanction for his texts on folklore the paratextual prestige of well-traveled professional in his field of specialization, agricultural policy.

68 Yanagita Kunio, *Senzo no hanashi* (1945), in *Yanagita Kunio zenshū,* 13:150.

69 Yanagita, "Yūmeidan," 252.

70 Ivy, *Discourses of the Vanishing,* 79. Uchida, *Yanagita Kunio to jiken no kiroku,* 79.

71 Yanagita discusses this aspect of *Tōno monogatari* in an interview cited in Iwamoto, *Mō hitotsu no Tōno monogatari,* 103–4.

72 Yamada Kiyoyoshi, "Yanagita Kunio to Mizuno Yōshū, 2," *Fūen* 8 (1972): 6.

73 Todorov, *The Fantastic,* 82.

74 Yoshimoto Takaaki, *Kyōdō gensōron,* cited in Takayanagi, "In Search of Yanagita Kunio," 177.

75 Such commentaries by Japanese scholars are too numerous to enumerate as this characterization of Yanagita's development has become commonly accepted knowledge. Nagaike Kenji provides a short synopsis of this break in Yanagita's interests in "Kaisetsu," in *Yanagita Kunio zenshū,* 4:507–18.

76 Akasaka Norio is one who has recently popularized this view in his essay

"Minakata Kumagusu, mata wa yamabito e no wakare—*Yanagita Kunio-Minakata Kumagusu ōfuku shokan o yomu*" [Minakata Kumagusu, or farewell to mountain people—Reading *The Yanagita Kunio-Minakata Kumagusu Correspondence*] (*Gendaishi techō,* July 1987), reprinted as "Minakata Kumagusu—Yamabito e no wakare," in *Kyōkai no hassei* (Tokyo: Sunagoya shobō, 1989), 241–55.

77 Akasaka, "Minakata Kumagusu—Yamabito e no wakare," 252. Minakata suggests that, for example, if one considered the mentally deranged who ran off from their village into the mountains to live as "mountain people," then so-called *yamabito* did exist. See Minakata's 23 December 1916 letter to Yanagita reprinted in Minakata Kumagusu and Yanagita Kunio, *Minakata Kumagusu senshū bekkan: Yanagita Kunio-Minakata Kumagusu ōfuku shokan* (Tokyo: Heibonsha, 1985), 440.

78 Minakata and Yanagita, *Yanagita Kunio-Minakata Kumagusu ōfuku shokan,* 442.

79 Certeau, "The Freudian Novel," 33.

80 See H. D. Harootunian, *Things Seen and Unseen: Discourse and Ideology in Tokugawa Nativism* (Chicago: University of Chicago Press, 1988), especially chap. 7.

81 Yanagita, "Yūmeidan," 247. Yanagita mistakes the name of Hirata's text. It is actually *Kokon yōmiko* [On marvels past and present]. In fact, Hirata wrote this text principally to denigrate Buddhism and therefore purposefully focused on stories of evil Buddhists who had turned into *tengu* after death, but he did not consider such *tengu* as "true *tengu.*" For a summary of Hirata's view of the hidden world as it pertained to *tengu,* see Chigiri Kōsai, *Tengu kō* (Tokyo: Nami shobō, 1973), 1:323–73, and *Tengu no kenkyū* (Tokyo: Tairiku, 1975), 255–61.

82 Yanagita, "Yūmeidan," 246–47.

83 Yanagita Kunio, *Teihon Yanagita Kunio shū* (Tokyo: Chikuma shobō, 1964), 23:389–91, contains a passage in which Yanagita reminisces over this early education. In nearly all his future references to the workings of the hidden world Yanagita prefaces his explanation with an acknowledgment of Matsuura as the source of his knowledge.

84 See, for example, Miyata Noboru's discussion of Yanagita's definition of monsters in *Yōkai no minzokugaku: Nihon no mienai kūkan* (Tokyo: Iwanami shoten, 1988), 3–4.

85 Yanagita Kunio, "Shōka kidan," in *Yanagita Kunio taidanshū* (Tokyo: Chikuma sōsho, 1964), 259–60.

86 Yanagita, *Senzo no hanashi,* 167.

87 Ibid., 168.

88 Yanagita Kunio and Kuwabara Takeo, "Nihonjin no dōtoku ishiki" [The moral consciousness of the Japanese], in *Yanagita Kunio taidanshū,* 239.

89 Ibid.

90 Lacan's distinction between "aim" and "goal," summarized by Slavoj Žižek, *Looking Awry: An Introduction to Jacques Lacan through Popular Culture* (Cam-

bridge: MIT Press, 1991), is relevant here: "A goal, once reached, always re-
treats anew. Can we not recognize in this paradox the very nature of the
psychoanalytical notion of *drive,* or more properly the Lacanian distinction
between its *aim* and *goal*? The goal is the final destination, while the aim is
what we intend to do, i.e., the way itself. Lacan's point is that the real purpose
of the drive is not its goal (full satisfaction) but its aim: the drive's ultimate
aim is simply to reproduce itself as drive, to return to its circular path, to
continue its path to and from the goal. The real source of enjoyment is the
repetitive movement of this closed circuit" (5). It is in this sense of circuit
that the economy of affects enfigured by the hidden world and driving folk
studies should be understood here.

91   I credit Stefan Tanaka for inspiring this formulation of the relationship among
heterogeneity, alterity, otherness, and history. See his *Japan's Orient: Rendering
Pasts into History* (Berkeley: University of California Press, 1995), for a penetrating discussion of the formation of modern Japanese historiography and
national identity during the Meiji period.

Chapter 5 *Transforming the Commonplace:* Fushigi *as Critique*

1   Tzvetan Todorov, *The Fantastic: A Structural Approach to a Literary Genre,* trans.
Richard Howard (Ithaca, NY: Cornell University Press, 1975), 25.

2   Rosemary Jackson, *Fantasy: The Literature of Subversion* (London: Methuen,
1981), 36. Original italics.

3   P. M. Pasinetti, "Erasmus, *The Praise of Folly,*" in *The Norton Anthology of World
Masterpieces,* 4th ed., ed. Maynard Mack et al. (New York: Norton, 1979),
1:1209.

4   Izumi Kyōka, "Romanchikku to shizenshugi" (1908), in *Kyōka zenshū* (Tokyo:
Iwanami, 1940–42), 28:684–85.

5   It should be noted that the word I have translated here literally as "flavor" is
aji, which is the same word I translated as "taste" in the title of Kyōka's essay
"Tasogare no aji" [The taste of twilight], which opened the prologue of this
text. The connotation in this present context suggests "taste" or "flavor" in
the sense of a practical knowledge or enriching experience. Kyōka's use of
this word is a way of signifying truth or meaning that escapes empirical demonstration but is nonetheless felt to exist.

6   Yanagita Kunio, "Shasei to ronbun," *Bunshō sekai* 2, no. 3 (1907): 31.

7   Izumi Kyōka, "Jijitsu no kontei, sōzō no junshoku: jijitsu to sōzō" (1909), in
Kyōka zenshū, 28:730–33. The nuance of the word *jijitsu* in both Kyōka's and
Yanagita's critical usage is somewhat difficult to get across in a single English
word. When used in reference to the Naturalists and in contradistinction to

"imagination" it connotes "facts" in the sense of empirically verifiable items of an actual reality, thus my translation "factual reality." The term *genjitsu,* which they both also use, designates "actual reality" proper, and the word *shinjitsu,* which Yanagita occasionally uses, is best understood, I believe, as "truth derived from actual reality."

8 Izumi Kyōka, "Jijitsu to chakusō" (1909), in *Kyōka zenshū,* 28:748.

9 For an interesting discussion of Yanagita's linguistic method, see Yoshikuni Igarashi, "Imagining History: Discourses of Cultural Politics in Japan, 1930s and 1960s" (Ph.D. diss., University of Chicago, 1994), 136–53.

10 Izumi Kyōka, "Yo no taido" (1908), in *Kyōka zenshū,* 28:693–94.

11 Yanagita Kunio, "Shoko Kyōka kan," in *Bungei dokuhon: Izumi Kyōka* (Tokyo: Kawade shobō shinsha, 1988), 69.

12 Izumi Kyōka, "Tōno no kibun" [Strange news from Tōno] (1910), in *Kyōka zenshū,* 28:462, 465.

13 In "Rampu no kaiten" [The turn of the lamp], in *Shikō no monshōgaku* [The heraldry of thought] (Tokyo: Kawade bunko, 1985), Shibusawa Tatsuhiko analyzes Kyōka's story "Kusameikyū" in relation to the tale of Tōno (number 22) that Mishima Yukio features in his essay *Shōsetsu to wa nani ka* [What is narrative fiction?] (Tokyo: Shinchōsha, 1972).

14 Izumi Kyōka, "Byōsha no shinka" [The true value of description] (1909), in *Kyōka zenshū,* 28:733.

15 Kyōka, "Yo no taido," 28:697. It is curious that he uses the old name of Tokyo here when he is referring to a train in Tokyo. However, such a circumlocution, suggesting a temporal twisting, seems perfectly normal coming from Kyōka's pen.

16 Quoted in Nagaike Kenji, "Kaisetsu" [Commentary], in *Yanagita Kunio zenshū* (Tokyo: Chikuma shobō, 1989), 4:509.

17 A *hyaku monogatari* (one hundred tales) was a ghost-story-telling game popularized during the Edo period. By the mid–seventeenth century its form was established among samurai as a playful test of courage, but by the early nineteenth century it had become a widespread entertainment for commoners. The game began with a group of people gathering after sundown to the pale blue light of one hundred lit wicks covered with blue paper shades. Each person in turn would tell a tale of supernatural horror and at the end of each tale one wick would be extinguished. As the tales progressed the room would become dimmer, until after the one hundredth tale the room would go dark. At that moment it was believed that real ghouls would appear in the darkness, conjured up by the terrifying tale-telling. For a brief analysis of the *hyaku monogatari* game and its relationship to the belief in and pictorial representations of the *hyakki yakō* (night parade of one hundred demons) in the

Edo period, see Midori Deguchi, "One Hundred Demons and One Hundred Supernatural Tales," in *Japanese Ghosts and Demons: Art of the Supernatural,* ed. Stephen Addiss (New York: George Braziller, 1985), 15–23.

18 Taking its name from the French restaurant in Azabu where the group usually met after being organized around 1902 in Yanagita's home, the Ryūdokai included at this time the likes of Tayama Katai, Shimazaki Tōson, and Kunikida Doppo. Its membership and focus changed over the years, and it was from this group that the Ibsen Society and key players in the Japanese naturalist movement eventually emerged during the first decade of the twentieth century.

19 Nagaike, "Kaisetsu," 4:510.

20 Izumi Kyōka, "Kaidankai: jo" (1909), in *Kyōka zenshū,* 28:628.

21 Yanagita Kunio, *Tōno monogatari* (1910), in *Yanagita Kunio zenshū,* 4:25.

22 Ibid., 4:24–25. I have made minor modifications to Ronald Morse's translation appearing in *The Legends of Tōno* (Tokyo: Japan Foundation, 1975), 25–26.

23 Nagaike, "Kaisetsu," 4:511–12.

24 Mishima, *Shōsetsu to wa nani ka,* 79.

25 Shibusawa, "Rampu no kaiten," 13.

26 Kyōka, "Tōno no kibun," 28:464.

27 Izumi Kyōka, "Kai-i to hyōgenho" (1909), in *Kyōka zenshū,* 28:713.

28 I was relieved to find out that I was not the only person confused over whether or not this piece was a eulogy (it actually had me double-checking dates on Kyōka as well as of the essay). Nakamura Akira attests to the likelihood of such confusion in "Kyōka to Yanagita: Kyōka no Hokkai minzokugaku," *Bungaku* 51, no. 6 (1983): 46.

29 Okaya Kōji, "Shijin Yanagita Kunio no imi," *Kokubungaku: kaisetsu to kyōzai no kenkyū* 27, no. 1 (1982): 80.

30 Yanagita, "Shoko Kyōka kan," 69. *Tamayori-hime* (literally "jewel-possessed princess") refers to a female demigoddess figure associated with shamans in folk beliefs. Yanagita wrote an essay on the topic in 1917 in which he explains that *tama* in this context indicates the spirit of a deity and *yori* is the act of a human (in this case, a young woman) being possessed by this spirit. Originally, he says, the term *tamayori* specifically referred to a concretization (as opposed to a symbol) of the power of a deity, but then was applied to shamans as well.

31 The "round shining jewel" turning for ages that Yanagita evokes is very close to the final scene of Kyōka's story "Kusameikyū" (1908) in which a *Tamayori-hime*-like enchantress is displaying numerous shining handballs before the sleeping Akira (whose name means "bright"). Even more startling is the appearance in "Kusameikyū" of a "turning lamp" that is described almost identically to the turning charcoal scuttle in *Tōno.* That coincidence (?) is the point of departure for Shibusawa's discussion of Kyōka's tale and provides the title of his essay, "Rampu no kaiten" (The turn of the lamp).

Kyōka's story has, as Shibusawa demonstrates, three narratives spatially arranged in concentric circles to suggest the falling of Akira, the story's hero, into a "retrogressive dream," a kind of "reverse transcendence" by which he overcomes historical time. In Shibusawa's interesting but somewhat heavy-handed mythicopsychological reading, this retrogression leads to a return to the womb, represented by the mysterious enchantress and the haunted house at the center of this maze of time. In contrast to Theseus, who slays the Minotaur and escapes the labyrinth with the help of Ariadne's thread, Akira finds a dreamy repose in threads of prenatal memories ("Rampu no kaiten," 24–26).

Taken at face value, this reading amounts to little more than an escapist fairy tale, but the circular operation of time in this complex story and the recurrent motifs related to its spatiotemporal concentricity suggest provocative connections between Kyōka's and Yanagita's handling of time. For example, Shibusawa comments that rather than the time of the story converging on the center of Akira's dream, his dream expands and envelops the time of the story. In some of his more stretched interpretive turns, whether it be his theory of *yamabito* as traces of an aboriginal race in Japan or his southern route origin of the Japanese, Yanagita too can be said to have been spinning his "dream" — his imagination and desire — over an expanse of ages to grasp times past.

32 Makita Shigeru, "World Authority on Folklore: Yanagita Kunio," *Japan Quarterly* 20, no. 3 (1973): 288.

33 Yanagita Kunio, "Minzokugaku kara minzokugaku e" [From folk studies to ethnology], in *Minzokugaku ni tsuite: Dai-ni Yanagita Kunio Taidanshū* (Tokyo: Chikuma, 1965), 65–67.

34 Nishimura expresses this view in "Minzoku dai-ikkan shokan" [Impressions of the first volume of *Minzoku*], *Minzoku*, 2, no. 1 (1926): 124. He elucidates his position further in "Setsuwa, densetsu, shinwa tai rekishi" [Legends, folktales, and myths versus history], *Minzoku* 2, no. 3 (1927): 139–43.

35 Yanagita Kunio, "Matsuō Kenji no monogatari," *Minzoku*, 2, no. 2 (1927): 59. The preface to this essay was Yanagita's first response to Nishimura's critique of the first volume of *Minzoku*. Yanagita's full rebuttal is printed after Nishimura's essay in *Minzoku*, 2, no. 3 (1927): 141–43.

36 Robert Darton, *The Great Cat Massacre and Other Episodes in French Cultural History* (New York: Vintage, 1984), 6.

37 Yanagita Kunio, *Meiji Taishōshi sesō hen* (Tokyo: Kōdansha, 1976), 1:4. It is also interesting that Yanagita proceeds to compare his comparative method to that of natural history although lacking in the latter's precise description, the tediousness of which he feels his readers would not appreciate.

38 A gathering of writers, including Yanagita and Kyōka, on the evening of 19 June 1928 produced the "Symposium on Ghosts and Ghost Tales" published in *Shufu no tomo* [The housewife's friend] (August 1928) and reprinted

in *Nihon bungaku kenkyū shiryō sōsho: Izumi Kyōka* (Tokyo: Yūseidō, 1980). A similar symposium, conducted by Kikuchi Kan, was held the previous year and published in the August 1927 edition of Kikuchi's journal *Bungei shunjū* [Chronicle of literary arts], just two months after the publication of the discussions about fantastic phenomena and folk imagination that Yanagita took part in with Akutagawa and Kikuchi. (It is reprinted in *Kyōka zenshū,* vol. 29.) For better or worse, the discussions involving Kyōka really did amount to little more than convivial exchanges of eerie stories based on personal experiences or those of acquaintances. As entertaining as these stories are, there is little in the way of analysis of the broader topic of the fantastic in modern everyday life in Japan, the context in which these stories are ostensibly set. A photo of the 1928 meeting (reprinted in *Bungei dokuhon: Izumi Kyōka*), held in what appears to be the banquet room of the Kagetsu in Shinbashi, attests to the conviviality of the occasion, endemic to such symposia among writers and academics in Japan both then and now.

39   On this point it is interesting to note that after his first encounter with Sasaki, Yanagita confessed that at first he could hardly understand Sasaki's thick regional accent.

40   Yanagita Kunio, *Yama no jinsei* (1917, 1925), in *Yanagita Kunio zenshū,* 4:79–254. The main part of *Yama no jinsei* consists of essays that Yanagita wrote for *Asahi Gurafu* from January to June 1925. The final section that he appended to these essays is a copy of a lecture entitled "Yamabito kō" [On mountain people] that he gave at the 1917 Japanese History and Geography Society Conference.

41   Yanagita, *Yama no jinsei,* 4:89.

42   Kasahara Nobuo, "Mori, aruiwa gensō kūkan" [The forest, or fantastic space], in *Bungei dokuhon: Izumi Kyōka* (Tokyo: Kawade shobō shinsha, 1988), 102.

43   One example is a story Sasaki provided about a woman in Tōno (4:94–95).

44   For a discussion of the problem of gender and nationalism in Yanagita's writing, see Mariko Asano Tamanoi, "Gender, Nationalism, and Japanese Native Ethnology," *positions: east asia cultures critique* 4 no. 1 (spring 1996): 59–86.

45   Yanagita Kunio, "Imo no chikara" (1925), in *Yanagita Kunio zenshū,* 11:25.

46   In "Miko kō" (1913), in *Yanagita Kunio zenshū,* 11:338, Yanagita writes at great length on the connections between shamanistic training and the mountain asceticism (*shugendō*) practiced by *yamabushi.* In some cases it is reported that *miko* "took *yamabushi* as husbands" (the circumlocution suggests sex more than marriage). The practice of these *shugen-miko* was banned by the government at the start of the Meiji period. On blind *miko,* see the discussion on 11:396 and Kawamura Kunimitsu, *Miko no minzokugaku: onna no chikara no kindai* (Tokyo: Seikyūsha, 1991), 26–58.

47   Akasaka offers an interesting analysis of the fictionality of *jōmin* in the context of Yanagita's shift from the heterogeneity of vagabonds, *yamabito,* and

other discriminated groups to the homogeneity of rice-cultivating, ancestor-worshiping, sedentary plains people, the *jōmin*. See his essay "Yanagita Kunio —Genzō toshite no jōmin" [Yanagita Kunio—*jōmin* as phantom], in *Kyōkai no hassei* (Tokyo: Sunagoya shobō, 1989), 220–24.

48   Yanagita Kunio, "Yukiguni no haru" (1926), in *Yanagita Kunio zenshū*, 2:11–27.

49   *Kōya hijiri* appeared in February 1900 in *Shinshōsetsu* [New fiction]. I will be referring to the annotated version found in *Kōya hijiri, Uta andon* (Tokyo: Obunsha, 1970). An English translation of *Kōya hijiri* by Charles Shirō Inouye appears in *Japanese Gothic Tales* (Honolulu: University of Hawaiʻi Press, 1996), 21–72.

50   For a predominantly psychological and archetypal analysis of *Kōya hijiri,* see Susan J. Napier, *The Fantastic in Modern Japanese Literature: The Subversion of Modernity* (London: Routledge, 1996), 27–36.

51   Bloodletting with leeches was still a popular form of treatment in Europe during the first half of the nineteenth century. Until statistical results demonstrated the method's lack of effectiveness, the French leech market boomed. In 1820 France exported more than one million leeches abroad; in 1827 it imported more than thirty-three million. See Georges Canguilham, *Ideology and Rationality in the History of the Life Sciences,* trans. Arthur Goldhammer (Cambridge, MA: MIT Press, 1988), 56. The near fatal attack of the leeches on the priest can be read as a cruel satire of the practice. It is also worth mentioning here that Kyōka makes a subtle jab at the military (or perhaps only at the mentality of precision behind the geometry of cartography) when the priest describes the Army map he has been using as being of no help at all on this path full of unexpected happenings.

52   The symptoms of the disease in the story are described as "pussy, red, and infected eyes" caused by heads of rice entering the eyes during harvest time. Although not necessarily the more serious clinical trachoma, which is caused by a strain of the rickettsia microorganism, it is likely that in its propaganda the Education Ministry knowingly lumped equally common though less serious eye afflictions under the name of the feared *torahoomu*. The point is that this common eye ailment among rice harvesters is made out to be something treatable only by the "expert" in modern medicine. This coincidence of eye diseases appearing in medical and educational discourse as well as in Kyōka's story of the same period is in itself interesting.

53   "Monster Bird" is a possible translation for "Kechō," but "Metamorphosing Bird" is probably closer to a literal translation as well as to its meaning in the context of the story. In the climactic scene it is hinted that the "winged princess" who saves the boy is actually his transformed mother. Humans are also continually being perceived and understood by the schoolboy in the story in terms of other animals. Additionally, the *Kōjien* entry for *kechō* indicates that

kechō-fū refers to a style of joking, riddle-like wordplay that employs *kake-kotoba* ("pivot-words" or puns) and metaphors, suggesting a metamorphosis of words. Certainly the schoolboy's questioning of the rational categories that his teacher espouses is founded on this poetic logic.

54 Maeda Ai and Yamaguchi Masao comment on the identity of this bridge-keeper as a *hashi-hime* figure in their discussion, "Kyōkai senjō no bungaku: Kyōka sekai no genkyō" [Literature on the borderlines: The sources of Kyōka's world], *Kokubungaku: kaishaku to kyōzai no kenkyū* 30, no. 7 (1985): 17.

55 Izumi Kyōka, "Kechō" (1897), in *Kyōka zenshū*, 3:116.

56 Kasahara Nobuo in "Yūkasuru jikan" [Dissolving time], *Kokubungaku: kaishaku to kanshō* 182, no. 8 (August 1974): 156–69 and Yamada Yūsaku in "Miseijuku to yume" [Immaturity and dreams], *Bungaku* 51, no. 6 (June 1983): 120–26, both analyze this narrative structure of "Kechō" and its consequences.

57 Orikuchi Shinobu, "Kyōka to no isseki" [An evening with Kyōka], in *Orikuchi Shinobu zenshū* (Tokyo: Chūoronsha, 1957), 28:192.

58 Two other short stories by Kyōka that are set in classrooms deserve brief mention here. Both are set in Kyōka's hometown of Kanazawa and are purportedly based on Kyōka's own unusual experiences as a schoolboy. The first one is entitled "Bakemono nendaiki" [Monster chronicles] (1895), in *Kyōka zenshū*, 27:5–26, which is narrated by Kyōka as a dorm student at a school that has a building with a strange history behind it (involving an Edo-period love murder and ghostly revenge). He reveals that his sole purpose in enrolling at this particular school is to investigate the rumors of mysterious happenings (*fushigi*) going on there. He was not there for "English, geometry, or Chinese classics," nor to "eradicate monsters," nor to "research them with the academic knowledge" he had accumulated. "It was only for the curiosity of saying in everyday language that I saw something frightening."

The second school-related story set in Kanazawa is "Kaidan Onna no wa" [The ring of women, a ghost story] (1900), in *Kyōka zenshū*, 27:40–51. This story opens at twilight (*tasogare*) in a decrepit house used as a *juku* (cram school). Here too English, math, and Chinese are what the narrator is supposed to be studying, but he spends his time in his room stealthily reading novels, which were strictly prohibited in the *juku*. One evening while reading, as if it were conjured by his reading, he hears a sound like rain pitter-pattering, but it isn't raining. He investigates and finds that it is the sound of a woman's feet, and only her feet, approaching his room . . .

59 Yanagita Kunio, "Ono ga inochi no hayazukai" [Express messenger of one's own life] (1911), in *Yanagita Kunio zenshū*, 6:124.

60 In some versions a *yamabushi* hears of the transaction between the woman and the traveler and intercepts the traveler. He then reads the message to him (on

the assumption that the peasant cannot read), warns him not to deliver the message as is, and then rewrites something benign for him.

61 Yanagita, "Ono ga inochi," 6:128.

62 Yanagita Kunio, "Hashi-hime" (1918), in *Yanagita Kunio zenshū*, 6:357–58.

63 Tsubouchi Shōyō, *Shōsetsu shinzui* (Tokyo: Iwanami, 1963), 60.

64 Ibid., 63.

65 Kawamura Jirō, "Dōshisareta kūkan" [Eye-popping space], in *Ginga to jigoku: gensō bungakuron* [The milky way and hell: On fantastic literature] (Tokyo: Kōdansha, 1985), 66.

66 Kyōka, "Romanchikku to shizenshugi," 28:687.

67 Kawamura Jirō, "Dōshisareta kūkan: Izumi Kyōka," in *Ginga to jigoku*, 61.

Chapter 6 Supernatural Ideology

1 Lionel Trilling, *The Liberal Imagination* (New York: Doubleday and Anchor, 1953), 277.

2 Kawada, *The Origins of Ethnography in Japan: Yanagita and His Times,* trans. Toshikoi Kishida-Ellis (London: Kegan Paul International, 1993), chaps. 1, 2.

3 The Minakata boom of the 1990s strikes me as particularly fascinating because its form and content closely ally it with the *bakemono* boom. Not only has there been renewed scholarly interest that has led to a torrent of new publications and popular public exhibitions of his work—he has crossed over into mass media in the form of several comic books (two written by none other than famed *bakemono* researcher and artist Mizuki Shigeru), which highlight his unusual life and "ecological" thought; an ambitious but uncompleted film project by Yamamoto Masashi entitled *Kumagusu;* a ·CD-ROM in production called *Minakata Kumagusu Mandala;* and a serious-minded homepage on the World Wide Web.

4 Cited in Kawamura Kunimitsu, *Genshisuru kindai kūkan* (Tokyo: Seikyūsha, 1989), 38.

5 Ibid., 39.

6 Ibid., 183–84.

7 Ibid., 188.

8 For a concise description of the 1910 *shūshin* revision, see Wilbur M. Fridell, *Japanese Shrine Mergers, 1906–1912: State Shintō Moves to the Grassroots* (Tokyo: Sophia University Press, 1973), 112. For more detail, see Fridell, "Government Ethics Textbooks in Late Meiji Japan," *Journal of Asian Studies* 29, no. 4 (1970): 823–34.

9 Fridell, *Japanese Shrine Mergers,* 33–34.

10 Fridell, in ibid., 76, states that Nakamura was the House representative from

the neighboring Mie prefecture, site of the most intense mergers, but separate sources dealing with Nakamura's relationship with Minakata Kumagusu state that he represented Minakata's prefecture of Wakayama. More on this connection shortly.

11   On the same page, Fridell comments that it "is remarkable how few instances of outright resistance have been reported in a matter which so assuredly violated popular socio-religious sentiments and traditions." He need only have pursued the Yanagita connection a bit further to have uncovered the vast involvement among Yanagita, Minakata, and Representative Nakamura in reporting many instances of outright resistance toward the shrine merger policy. That large newspapers did not go out of their way to report provincial incidents of resistance is not too remarkable.

12   Minakata Kumagusu, "Jinja gappei hantai iken" [An opinion opposing shrine mergers], reprinted in *Minakata Kumagusu,* by Tsurumi Kazuko (Tokyo: Kōdansha, 1978), 249–89. The work was originally published in four parts in *Nihon oyobi nihonjin* [Japan and the Japanese] 580, 581, 583, and 584 (April, May, and June 1912). Minakata's figures appear on page 252. Fridell's figures for Mie (89 percent) closely match Minakata's. Fridell did not do a case study of Wakayama.

13   Nakase Hisaharu, "Kaisetsu," in *Chichi Minakata Kumagusu o kataru,* by Minakata Fumie (Tokyo: Nihon editaa sukuuru shuppan, 1981), 147–48. This volume contains several documents dealing with Minakata's opposition to the shrine merger policy that are edited and commented on by Nakase and Yoshikawa Toshihiro.

14   Nakase Hisaharu and Hasegawa Kōzō, eds., *Minakata Kumagusu arubamu* (Tokyo: Yatsuzaka shobō, 1991), 126–27.

15   Minakata, "Jinja gappei hantai iken," 252.

16   Ibid., 254. Photos of his notebook—with notes written in French, English, and Japanese—are included in Nakase and Hasegawa, *Minakata arubamu,* 131.

17   Tsurumi, *Minakata Kumagusu,* 157.

18   Amid a correspondence debating the purview of *kyōdo kenkyū* (community studies), which Yanagita advertised as "rural economy," Minakata accusingly wrote to Yanagita in a letter dated 14 May 1914: "You wrote in the inaugural issue that *Kyōdo Kenkyū* would be a journal of rural economy. But I don't understand why there is so little rural economy here. If this is a study of rural formations, then it must be accompanied by studies of rural politics. This journal should be debating more issues such as the pros and cons of the recent shrine mergers or the advantages and disadvantages of all kinds of for-profit enterprises in the regions" (Minakata Kumagusu and Yanagita Kunio, *Minakata Kumagusu senshū bekkan: Yanagita Kunio–Minakata Kumagusu ōfuku shokan,* [Tokyo: Heibonsha, 1985], 372). For an analysis of this dispute, see Alan S.

Christy, "Representing the Rural: Place as Method in the Formation of Japanese Native Ethnology, 1910–1945" (Ph.D. diss., University of Chicago, 1997), 70–75.

19 Minakata, "Jinja gappei hantai iken," 249–50.

20 Kenneth Strong, *Ox Against the Storm: A Biography of Tanaka Shōzō (1841–1913)* (Vancouver: University of British Columbia Press, 1977). For a brief English overview of Tanaka's career, see Victor Carpenter, "Tanaka Shōzō: Champion of Local Autonomy," in *Japan Examined: Perspectives on Modern Japanese History,* ed. Harry Wray and Hilary Conroy (Honolulu: University of Hawai'i Press, 1983), 112–19.

21 Tsurumi, *Minakata Kumagusu,* especially chap. 3.

22 Yanagita Kunio, *Minkan denshōron,* cited in Yoshikuni Igarashi, "Imagining History: Discourses of Cultural Politics in Japan, 1930s and 1960s" (Ph.D. diss., University of Chicago, 1994), 97. Although arguing against the reduction of Yanagita to *nihonjinron* nationalist, Igarashi does point out where Yanagita invites such readings.

23 Stressing the discursive nature of Yanagita's writings, Igarashi rightly warns against assuming an earlier "radical Yanagita" and a later "nationalistic Yanagita" ("Imagining History," 148–49). Still, insofar as disciplinization of his discourse entailed delimiting a focus of study, his folk studies necessarily became more bounded and familiarized, in a sense, less "radical" if not "nationalistic." For an assessment of Yanagita's reformist and conservative tendencies, see J. Victor Koschmann, "Folklore Studies and the Conservative Anti-Establishment in Modern Japan," in *International Perspectives on Yanagita Kunio and Japanese Folklore Studies,* ed. J. Victor Koschmann, Ōiwa Keibō, and Yamashita Shinji (Ithaca, NY: Cornell University East Asia Program, 1985), 131–64.

24 Igarashi, "Imagining History," chaps. 3–5. On forms of amateur postwar historiography inspired by democratic movements, folk studies, and challenges to conventional historiography, see Gerald Figal, "How to *jibunshi*: Making and Marketing Self-Histories of Shōwa among the Masses in Postwar Japan," *Journal of Asian Studies* 55, no. 4 (November 1996): 902–33.

25 Carol Gluck provides a convenient contemporaneous overview of the historiographical trends of which Irokawa was a part in "The People in History: Recent Trends in Japanese Historiography," *Journal of Asian Studies* 38, no. 1 (November 1978): 25–50.

26 Irokawa Daikichi, *The Culture of the Meiji Period,* translation edited by Marius Jansen (Princeton: Princeton University Press, 1985), vii.

27 Igarashi, "Imagining History," 136–53.

28 Irokawa Daikichi, *Shōwashi sesō hen* (Tokyo: Shōgakukan, 1990), 11.

29 Marilyn Ivy, *Discourses of the Vanishing: Modernity, Phantasm, Japan* (Chicago: University of Chicago Press, 1995), 18.

30 Irokawa Daikichi, *Meiji no bunka* (Tokyo: Iwanami shoten, 1970), 2–5; *The Culture of the Meiji Period*, 3–4.

31 T. Fujitani provides an excellent account of the manufacturing of this dual aspect of the Meiji emperor in *Splendid Monarchy: Power and Pageantry in Modern Japan* (Berkeley: University of California Press, 1996), 95–194.

32 Tanizaki Jun'ichirō, *In Praise of Shadows* [*In'ei raisan*] trans. Thomas J. Harper (New Haven, CT: Leete's Island Books, 1977), 31; originally published in *Keizai ōrai* (December 1933 and January 1934).

33 Komatsu Kazuhiko and Naitō Masatoshi, *Oni ga tsukutta kuni, Nihon* (Tokyo: Kōbunsha, 1985), 211.

34 Cornel West, "The New Cultural Politics of Difference," in *Out There: Marginalization and Contemporary Cultures,* ed. Russell Ferguson, Martha Gever, Trinh T. Minh-ha, and Cornel West (Cambridge, MA: MIT Press, 1990), 29.

35 Stefan Tanaka, *Japan's Orient: Rendering Pasts into History* (Berkeley: University of California Press, 1995), provides a trenchant analysis of the formation of modern Japanese historiography in the context of discourses on national identity situated between the East and the West. See also Christy's discussion of native ethnology's close relations with Japanese colonialism in the definition of a Japanese ethnos, "Representing the Rural," especially chap. 5.

36 E. Patricia Tsurumi, "Colonizer and Colonized in Taiwan," in *Japan Examined: Perspectives on Modern Japanese History,* ed. Harry Wray and Hilary Conroy (Honolulu: University of Hawai'i Press, 1983), 215.

37 Han-Kyo Kim, "Japanese Colonialism in Korea," in *Japan Examined: Perspectives in Modern Japanese History,* ed. Harry Wray and Hilary Conroy (Honolulu: University of Hawai'i Press, 1983), 225–26.

38 The reference is to the 1942 "Comprehensive Cultural Conference Symposium: Overcoming the Modern," in which the majority of the participating intellectuals viewed Japan as standing in a privileged position outside of the problems of modernity in the West and thus justified to critique—even attack—it. For the proceedings, see Kawakami Tetsutarō et al., *Kindai no chōkoku* (Tokyo: Toyambō, 1979). For a sample of the new demonic images of Westerners, see John Dower's analysis of wartime propaganda in *War without Mercy: Race and Power in the Pacific War* (New York: Pantheon Books, 1986), 191–290.

39 On the process of turning Okinawans into Imperial Japanese subjects from late Meiji to early Shōwa, see Alan S. Christy, "The Making of Imperial Subjects in Okinawa," *positions: east asia cultures critique* 1, no. 3 (winter 1993): 607–39.

40 Hearn's use of Hirata Atsutane in his explanation of ancestor worship and the operation of the supernatural sanctions of spirits existing invisibly around the living in the everyday world is uncannily similar to that of Yanagita. See especially the chapter "The Ancient Cult" in Lafcadio Hearn, *Japan: An At-*

tempt at Interpretation (Rutland, VT: Tuttle, 1981); originally published by the Macmillan Co. in 1904.

41 Ibid., 5–19.

42 Peter N. Dale, *The Myth of Japanese Uniqueness* (New York: St. Martin's Press, 1990), 25. This book is a good, albeit vituperative, survey of the texts, tropes, and strategies of *nihonjinron*. See also Kosaku Yoshino, *Cultural Nationalism in Contemporary Japan: A Sociological Enquiry* (New York: Routledge, 1992).

GLOSSARY

aburatori	油取り
aikoku-chūkō	愛国忠孝
aikyōshin	愛郷心
Aizawa Seishisai	会沢正志斎
Akutagawa Ryūnosuke	芥川竜之介
Amaterasu	天照
Andō Kametarō	安藤亀太郎
Andō Shōeki	安藤昌益
Ansei	安政
Awa	阿波
Azabu	麻布
bakemono	化け物
bakeru	化ける
bakufu	幕府
bakumatsu	幕末
Bashō	芭蕉
bonjin	凡人
bujin	武人
bunka	文化
bunmei kaika	文明開花
buraku	部落
bushidō	武士道
butsuri	物理
Chiba	千葉
chiryoku	知力
chūi	注意
chūkan	中間

chūkanteki	中間的
chūkō-aikoku	忠孝愛国
Chūshingura	忠臣蔵
Daifushigi	大不思議
Dainichi Nyorai	大日如来
danketsu	団結
Deguchi Nao	出口なお
Deguchi Onisaburō	出口王仁三郎
dōri	道理
Ekōin	回向院
en	縁
Engi-shiki	延喜式
eta	穢多
Fudeyasu Shigetarō	筆保卯太郎
fūdoki	風土記
Fujita Tōko	藤田東湖
fujōri	不常理
fukachiteki	不可知的
fukashigi	不可思議
Fukchiyama	福知山
Fukuzawa Yūkichi	福沢勇吉
fushigi	不思議
Fushigi Kenkyūkai	不思議研究会
fushigi na genshō	不思議な現象
fushigi na hanashi	不思議な話
gakusha	学者
geka	外科
genbun-itchi	原文一致
genjitsu	現実
genri	原理
gense	現世
gensō bungaku	幻想文学
gikai	偽怪
gikō	技巧
gokoku-airi	護国愛理
gōshi	合祀
gūmin	偶民

gunryaku	軍略
gyōsei-son	行政村
Hakusan	白山
hashi-hime	橋姫
Hayachine	早池峰
Heian	平安
heimen byōsha	平面描写
henji	変事
henka	変化
henryaku	変略
henshikigaku	変式学
Hida	飛騨
Hirata Atsutane	平田篤胤
Hirata Tōsuke	平田東助
Honjo	本所
hotoke	仏
hyakki yakō	百鬼夜行
hyaku monogatari	百物語
hyōimōsō	憑依妄想
Ibaraki	茨城
ibutsu	異物
igaku	医学
ijin	異人
ijingoroshi	異人殺し
ijō	異常
ijō-shinri	異常心理
inga	因果
Inoue Enryō	井上円了
Inoue Tetsujirō	井上哲次郎
inyō	陰陽
Ise	伊勢
ishi	意志
Ishigami	石神
isson issha	一村一社
Iwate	岩手
Izumi Kyōka	泉鏡花
jijitsu	事実

jinja gappei	神社合併
jinja seiri	神社整理
jiri	事理
jitsukai	実怪
jōmin	常民
jukuren	熟練
jutsu	術
kagaku	科学
Kagawa	香川
kaibutsu	怪物
kaidan	怪談
Kaidankai	怪談会
kai-i bendan	怪異弁談
kaika	怪火
kakai	假怪
kami	神
Kamiguni	神国
kami-kakushi	神隠し
kaname-ishi	要石
kanjō	感情
kansha	官社
Kantō	関東
kappa	河童
Katō Hiroyuki	加藤弘之
kawatare	彼は誰
Kawate Bunjirō	川手文治郎
kazoku kokka	家族国家
Kechō	化鳥
kendō	権道
kesshi	決死
ketsutori	血取り
ketsuzei ikki	血税一揆
ki	気
kibun	気分
Kii	紀伊
kikaiteki	機械的
Kikuchi Kan	菊池寛

kishin	鬼神
Kita Ikki	北一輝
kohyōbyō	狐憑病
Koizumi Yakumo	小泉八雲
Kokkagakkai zasshi	国家学会雑誌
kokkagaku	国家学
kokoro	心
kokoro no hataraki	心の働き
kokorofushigi	心不思議
kokugaku	国学
kokumin	国民
kokutai	国体
Kokutei shūshin kyōkasho	国定修身教科書
Konjin	金神
Konkōkyō	金光教
kosshi	骨子
koto	事
kotofushigi	事不思議
kotori	子取り
kuchiyose	口寄せ
kūsō	空想
Kyōbushō	教部省
kyōdō gensō	共同幻想
Kyōdokai	郷土会
kyōdōtai	共同体
kyōdotai	郷土体
kyōikugaku	教育学
magureatari	紛れ当たり
meigo	迷悟
Meiji	明治
Meireki	明暦
meishin	迷信
"Meishin o ochiruna"	迷信をおちるな
"Meishin o sakeyo"	迷信を避けよ
meishin-taiji	迷信退治
Mie	三重
miko	巫女

Minakata Kumagusu	南方熊楠
minsha	民社
minshūshi	民衆史
minzokugaku (ethnology)	民族学
minzokugaku (folk studies)	民俗学
minzokugakusha	民俗学者
Miroku	弥勒
misemono	見せ物
Mito	水戸
Mizuno Yōshū	水野葉舟
Monbushō	文部省
mono	物
monofushigi	物不思議
Mori Arinori	森有礼
Morioka	盛岡
mōsō	妄想
Motoda Eifu	元田永孚
Motora Yūjirō	元良勇次郎
Motoyama Keisen	元山桂川
mugikō	無技巧
muishiki no denshō	無意識伝承
mukakusha	無各社
naika	内科
Nakamura Keijirō	中村啓次郎
namahagi	生剥ぎ
namazu-e	鯰絵
nenkingaku	粘菌学
nensha	念写
Nihonbashi	日本橋
nihonjinron	日本人論
Niigata	新潟
Nikkō	日光
ninjō	人情
Nio-o	仁王
nishiki-e	錦絵
Nishimura Shinji	西村真次
Nitobe Inazō	新渡戸稲造

obake	お化け
Obake hakase	お化け博士
obake yashiki	お化け屋敷
Okayama	岡山
Ōmotokyō	大本教
Orikuchi Shinobu	折口信夫
Osatake Takeki	尾佐竹猛
rakugo	落語
rifushigi	理不思議
rigai no ri	理外の理
rigaku	理学
Rikkoku-shi	六国史
rinne	輪廻
risō	理想
Rokkoushi	六角牛
ronbun	論文
Ryōgoku	両国
Ryūdōkai	竜道会
Saigyō	西行
San'yūtei Enchō	三遊亭円朝
Sasaki Kizen (Kyōseki)	佐々木喜善（鏡石）
seijigaku	政治学
seikatsu gaikei	生活外形
seikatsu ishiki	生活意識
seikatsu kaisetsu	生活解説
seiryaku	政略
seisai	制裁
seishikigaku	正式学
seishin	精神
seishinbyō	精神病
seishinshi	精神史
seitō no jōri	正当の常理
Sendai	仙台
sennin	仙人
senrigan	千里眼
senzo	先祖
shaseibun	写生文

shichi	四知
shijitsu	史実
Shimazaki Tōson	島崎籐村
Shimōsa	下総
Shingon	真言
shinjitsu	真実
shinka	進化
shinkai	真怪
shinkai-risō	真怪理想
shinkeibyō	神経病
shinkō	信仰
shin'nyo	真如
shi-nō-kō-shō	士農工商
shinonome	東雲
shinri	心理
shinrigaku	心理学
shinsui	神水
shintai	神体
Shintō	神道
shi-shōsetsu	私小説
shizenshugi	自然主義
Shizenshugi-ha	自然主義派
shōgun	将軍
shōtai	正体
Shōwa	昭和
shugendō	修験道
shūkyōgaku	宗教学
shūshin	修身
Shūshin Kyōkasho Chōsa I-inkai	修身教科書調査委員会
shūshū	収集
sōzō	想像
sugomi	凄味
suiten	萃点
sūryōteki	数量的
taika	退化
Taishō	大正
Takamatsu	高松

Takizawa Bakin	滝沢馬琴
Tamayori-hime	玉依姫
Tanabe	田辺
Tanaka Shōzō	田中正造
tanuki	狸
tasogare	黄昏（誰ぞ彼は）
Tayama Katai	田山花袋
tengu	天狗
tengu sōdō	天狗騒動
tengudō	天狗道
Tengu-tō	天狗党
Tenpō	天保
Tetsugakkai zasshi	哲学会雑誌
Tetsugakukan	哲学館
Tochigi	栃木
Tōhoku	東北
Toki Hōryū	土宜法竜
Tokugawa Ieyasu	徳川家康
Tokugawa Ieyoshi	徳川家慶
Tokugawa Nariaki	徳川斉昭
Tokushima	徳島
Tōno	遠野
Tōno monogatari	遠野物語
torahoomu	トラホーム
torahoomu mizu	トラホーム水
Tottori	鳥取
Tsubouchi Shōyō	坪内逍遥
Tsuchibuchi	土淵
ukiyo-e	浮世絵
Ushigome	牛込
Utagawa Kuniyoshi	歌川国吉
Wakayama	和歌山
Yakushi	薬師
yamabito	山人
yamabushi	山伏
Yamaguchi	山口
yama-hime	山姫

yamaonna	山女
yamaotoko	山男
Yamato-damashii	大和魂
yamauba	山姥
Yanagita Kunio	柳田国男
yariate	やりあて
yashikirō	屋敷牢
Yashima	八島
Yasukuni Jinja	靖国神社
yōkai	妖怪
yōkai sōdō	妖怪騒動
yōkaigaku	妖怪学
yonaoshi	世直し
yose	寄席
yuisho	由緒
yukionna	雪女
yūmei(kai)	幽冥（界）
yūmeikyō	幽冥教
yūrei	幽霊

BIBLIOGRAPHY

Akamatsu Keisuke. *Hi-jōmin no minzoku bunka: seikatsu minzoku to sabetsu mukashi-banashi.* Tokyo: Asahi shoten, 1986.

Akasaka Norio. *Kyōkai no hassei.* Tokyo: Sunagoya shobō, 1989.

———. *Yama no seishinshi: Yanagita Kunio no hassei.* Tokyo: Shōgakukan, 1991.

———. *Yanagita Kunio no yomikata: mō hitotsu no minzokugaku wa kanō ka.* Tokyo: Chikuma shinsho, 1994.

Aso, Noriko. "New Illusions: The Emergence of a Discourse on Traditional Japanese Arts and Crafts, 1868–1945." Ph.D. diss., University of Chicago, 1997.

Bachelard, Gaston. *The New Scientific Spirit.* Translated by Arthur Goldhammer. Boston: Beacon, 1984.

Bakhtin, Mikhail M. *The Dialogic Imagination.* Edited by Michael Holquist. Translated by Caryl Emerson and Michael Holquist. Austin: University of Texas Press, 1981.

———. *Rabelais and His World.* Translated by Helene Iswolsky. Bloomington: Indiana University Press, 1984.

Blacker, Carmen. "Minakata Kumagusu: A Neglected Japanese Genius." *Folklore* 94, no. 2 (1983): 139–52.

Bloom, Harold. *The Anxiety of Influence.* New York: Oxford University Press, 1973.

Bowie, Malcolm. *Freud, Proust, and Lacan: Theory as Fiction.* Cambridge: Cambridge University Press, 1987.

Canguilham, Georges. *Ideology and Rationality in the History of the Life Sciences.* Cambridge, MA: MIT Press, 1988.

Certeau, Michel de. "The Freudian Novel: History and Literature." In *Heterologies: Discourses on the Other,* translated by Brian Massumi. Minneapolis: University of Minnesota Press, 1986. 17–34.

———. *The Practice of Everyday Life.* Translated by Steven F. Randall. Berkeley: University of California Press, 1984.

Chigiri Kōsai. *Tengu kō.* 2 vols. Tokyo: Nami shobō, 1973.

———. *Tengu no kenkyū.* Tokyo: Tairiku, 1975.

Christy, Alan S. "Representing the Rural: Place as Method in the Formation of Japanese Native Ethnology, 1910–1945." Ph.D. diss., University of Chicago, 1997.

———. "The Making of Imperial Subjects in Okinawa." *positions: east asia cultures critique* 1, no. 3 (winter 1993): 607–39.

Clifford, James. "On Ethnographic Allegory." In *Writing Culture,* edited by James Clifford and George E. Marcus. Berkeley: University of California Press, 1986. 98–121.

———. "On Ethnographic Authority." *Representations* 1, no. 2 (1983): 118–46.

———. *The Predicament of Culture: Twentieth-Century Ethnography, Literature, and Art.* Cambridge, MA: Harvard University Press, 1988.

Clifford, James, and George E. Marcus, eds. *Writing Culture: The Poetics and Politics of Ethnography.* Berkeley: University of California Press, 1986.

Costa Lima, Luiz. *Control of the Imaginary: Reason and Imagination in Modern Times.* Translated by Ronald W. Sousa. Minneapolis: University of Minnesota Press, 1988.

Crapanzano, Victor. "Hermes' Dilemma: The Masking of Subversion in Ethnographic Description." In *Writing Culture,* edited by James Clifford and George E. Marcus. Berkeley: University of California Press, 1986. 51–76.

Crittenden, Charles. *Unreality: The Metaphysics of Fictional Objects.* Ithaca, NY: Cornell University Press, 1991.

Dale, Peter N. *The Myth of Japanese Uniqueness.* New York: St. Martin's Press, 1990.

Darton, Robert. *The Great Cat Massacre and Other Episodes in French Cultural History.* New York: Vintage, 1984.

Deguchi, Midori. "One Hundred Demons and One Hundred Tales." In *Japanese Ghosts and Demons: Art of the Supernatural,* edited by Stephen Addiss. New York: George Braziller, 1985. 15–23.

Derrida, Jacques. "Cogito and the History of Madness." In *Writing and Difference,* translated by Alan Bass. Chicago: University of Chicago Press, 1978. 31–63.

———. "The Purveyor of Truth." *Yale French Studies* 52 (1975): 31–113.

———. "Structure, Sign, and Play in the Discourse of the Human Sciences." In *Writing and Difference,* translated by Alan Bass. Chicago: University of Chicago Press, 1978. 278–93.

de Visser, M. W. "The Tengu." *Transactions of the Asiatic Society of Japan* 36, no. 2 (1908): 25–99.

Dower, John. *War without Mercy: Race and Power in the Pacific War.* New York: Pantheon, 1986.

Fabian, Johannes. *Time and the Other: How Anthropology Makes Its Object.* New York: Columbia University Press, 1983.

Field, Norma. *In the Realm of a Dying Emperor: A Portrait of Japan at Century's End.* New York: Pantheon, 1991.

Figal, Gerald. "The Folk and the Fantastic in Japanese Modernity: Dialogues on

Reason and Imagination in Late Nineteenth- and Early Twentieth-Century Japan." Ph.D. diss., University of Chicago, 1992.

———. "How to *jibunshi:* Making and Marketing Self-histories of Shōwa among the Masses in Postwar Japan." *Journal of Asian Studies* 55, no. 4 (November 1996): 902–33.

———. "The Question of Monsters and Ancestor Worship." In *Select Papers, Volume No. 10: Productions of Culture in Japan.* Chicago: The Center for East Asian Studies, University of Chicago, 1995.

———. "Yanagita Kunio Writing in Wonderland: The Limits of Representation in the Representation of Limits." Master's thesis, University of Chicago, 1987.

Foucault, Michel. *The Archaeology of Knowledge and the Discourse on Language.* Translated by A. M. Sheridan Smith. New York: Pantheon, 1972.

———. *The Birth of the Clinic: An Archaeology of Medical Perception.* Translated by A. M. Sheridan Smith. New York: Vintage, 1975.

———. *Discipline and Punish: The Birth of the Prison.* Translated by Alan Sheridan. New York: Vintage, 1979.

———. *Language, Counter-memory, Practice.* Translated by Donald F. Bouchard and Sherry Simon. Ithaca, NY: Cornell University Press, 1977.

———. *Madness and Civilization: A History of Insanity in the Age of Reason.* Translated by Richard Howard. New York: Pantheon, 1965.

———. *The Order of Things: An Archaeology of the Human Sciences.* New York: Vintage, 1973.

Fridell, Wilbur M. "Government Ethics Textbooks in Late Meiji Japan." *Journal of Asian Studies* 29, no. 4 (1970): 823–34.

———. *Japanese Shrine Mergers, 1906–1912: State Shintō Moves to the Grassroots.* Tokyo: Sophia University Press, 1973.

Fujitani, T. *Splendid Monarchy: Power and Pageantry in Modern Japan.* Berkeley: University of California Press, 1996.

Gebhardt, Lisette. "Fukurai Tomokichi: Ein japanischer Forscher zwischen Seelenkunde und Spiritismus." Unpublished manuscript, 1997.

Gluck, Carol. *Japan's Modern Myths: Ideology in the Late Meiji Period.* Princeton: Princeton University Press, 1985.

———. "The People in History: Recent Trends in Japanese Historiography." *Journal of Asian Studies* 38, no. 1 (November 1978): 25–50.

Gould, Stephen Jay. *Ontogeny and Phylogeny.* Cambridge: Belknap Press, 1977.

Haga, Noboru. "Kaisetsu." *Hirata Atsutane zenshū: geppō* 2 (December 1976): 1–4.

Hane, Mikiso. *Peasants, Rebels, and Outcasts: The Underside of Modern Japan.* New York: Pantheon, 1982.

Hankins, Thomas L. *Science and the Enlightenment.* Cambridge: Cambridge University Press, 1985.

Harootunian, H. D. "Disciplining Native Knowledge and Producing Place: Yanagita Kunio, Origuchi Shinobu, Takata Yasuma." In *Culture and Identity: Japanese Intellectuals during the Interwar Years,* edited by J. Thomas Rimer. Princeton: Princeton University Press, 1990. 99–127.

———. *Things Seen and Unseen: Discourse and Ideology in Tokugawa Nativism.* Chicago: University of Chicago Press, 1988.

Hashizume Shinya. *Meiji no meikyū toshi: Tōkyō-Osaka no yūraku kūkan.* Tokyo: Heibonsha, 1990.

Hearn, Lafcadio. *Exotics and Retrospectives.* 1898. Rutland, VT: Tuttle, 1982.

———. *Japan: An Attempt at Interpretation.* 1904. Rutland, VT: Tuttle, 1981.

———. *Kwaidan: Stories and Studies of Strange Things.* 1904. Rutland, VT: Tuttle, 1989.

Hirakawa Sukehiro. "Gensō kūkan no tōsai." In *Gensō kūkan no tōsai: Furansu bungaku toshite mita Izumi Kyōka,* edited by Kanazawa Daigaku Furansu Bungakkai. Kanazawa: Jūgatsusha, 1990. 7–31.

Hirano Imao, ed. *Inoue Enryō Yōkaigaku kōgi.* Tokyo: Libro, 1983.

Hori, Ichirō. *Folk Religion in Japan.* Chicago: University of Chicago Press, 1983.

Igarashi, Yoshikuni. "Imagining History: Discourses of Cultural Politics in Japan, 1930s and 1960s." Ph.D. diss., University of Chicago, 1994.

Inagaki Taruho. "Minakatagaku no mikkyōteki na bō." In *Kareedosukoppu.* Tokyo: Shio shuppansha, 1974.

Inoue Enryō. "Kokkagaku to yōkaigaku to no kankei, 1." *Kokkagakkai zasshi* 90 (15 August 1894): 589–600.

———. "Kokkagaku to yōkaigaku to no kankei, 2." *Kokkagakkai zasshi* 92 (15 October 1894): 811–26.

———. "Kokkagaku to yōkaigaku to no kankei, 3." *Kokkagakkai zasshi* 96 (15 February 1895): 1–8.

———. *Meishin to shūkyō.* 1916. Vol. 7 of *Shinhen yōkai sōsho.* Tokyo: Kokusho, 1986.

———. *Obake no shōtai.* 1914. Vol. 6 of *Shinhen yōkai sōsho.* Tokyo: Kokusho, 1986.

———. *Tenguron.* 1916. Vol. 2 of *Shinhen yōkai sōsho.* Tokyo: Kokusho, 1986.

———. *Yōkaigaku.* 6 vols. Tokyo: Kōjinsha, 1933. Originally published as *Yōkaigaku kōgiroku* (1896).

———. *Yōkai kenkyū no kekka.* Tokyo: Tetsugakukan, 1897.

Inoue Enryō kenkyūkai, ed. *Inoue Enryō kankei bunken nempyō.* Tokyo: Tōyō daigaku Inoue Enryō kenkyūkai, 1987.

Irokawa Daikichi. *Meiji no bunka.* Tokyo: Iwanami shoten, 1970.

———. *The Culture of the Meiji Period.* Translation edited by Marius B. Jansen. Princeton: Princeton University Press, 1985.

———. *Shōwashi sesō hen.* Tokyo: Shōgakukan, 1990.

Itakura Kiyonobu. *Yōkai hakase, Enryō to yōkaigaku no tenkai.* Tokyo: Kokusho, 1983.

Ivy, Marilyn. *Discourses of the Vanishing: Modernity, Phantasm, Japan.* Chicago: University of Chicago Press, 1995.

Iwamoto Yoshiteru. *Mō hitotsu no Tōno monogatari*. Tokyo: Tōsui shobō, 1983.

Iwanaga Yutaka. *Tayama Katai kenkyū*. Tokyo: Hakuyōsha, 1956.

Izumi Kyōka. *Kōya hijiri, Uta andon*. Tokyo: Obunsha, 1970.

———. *Kyōka zenshū*. 31 vols. Tokyo: Iwanami, 1940–42.

Izumi Kyōka, Yanagita Kunio, et al. "Izumi Kyōka zadankai." 1927. In *Kyōka zenshū*. Tokyo: Iwanami, 1940–42. 29:228–64.

Izumi Kyōka, Yanagita Kunio, et al. "Yūrei to kaidan no zadankai." 1928. In *Nihon bungaku kenkyū shiryō sōsho: Izumi Kyōka*. Tokyo: Yūseidō, 1980. 281–93.

Jackson, Rosemary. *Fantasy: The Literature of Subversion*. London: Methuen, 1981.

Johnston, William. *The Modern Epidemic: A History of Tuberculosis in Japan*. Cambridge, MA: Council on East Asian Studies, 1995.

Kaigo Tokiomi, ed. *Nihon kyōkasho taikei*. 27 vols. Tokyo: Kōdansha, 1961–67.

Kajiyama Masahi. "Kyōkasho kokuteika o megutte." In *Teikokugikai to kyōiku seisaku*, edited by Motoyama Yukihiko. Tokyo: Shibunkaku, 1981. 115–67.

Karatani Kōjin. *Origins of Modern Japanese Literature*. Durham, NC: Duke University Press, 1993.

Kasahara Nobuo. "Mori, aruiwa gensō kūkan." In *Bungei dokuhon: Izumi Kyōka*. Tokyo: Kawade shobō shinsha, 1988. 94–103.

———. "Yūkasuru jikan." *Kokubungaku: kaishaku to kanshō* 182, no. 8 (August 1974): 156–69.

Kasai Kiyoshi. *Minakata Kumagusu*. Tokyo: Kichigawa Kōbunkan, 1967.

———. *Minakata Kumagusu: hito to gakumon*. Tokyo: Kichigawa Kōbunkan, 1980.

Kawada, Minoru. *The Origins of Ethnography in Japan: Yanagita and His Times*. Translated by Toshiko Kishida-Ellis. London: Kegan Paul International, 1993.

Kawakami Tetsutarō et al. *Kindai no chōkoku*. Tokyo: Toyambō, 1979.

Kawamura Jirō. *Ginga to jigoku: gensō bungakuron*. Tokyo: Kōdansha, 1985.

Kawamura Kunimitsu. *Genshisuru kindai kūkan*. Tokyo: Seikyūsha, 1990.

———. *Miko no minzokugaku: onna no chikara no kindai*. Tokyo: Seikyūsha, 1991.

Ketelaar, James. *Of Heretics and Martyrs in Meiji Japan: Buddhism and Its Persecution*. Princeton: Princeton University Press, 1990.

Kikuchi Akio. *Sasaki Kizen: Tōno denshō no hito*. Tōno, 1970.

Kim, Han-Kyo. "Japanese Colonialism in Korea." In *Japan Examined: Perspectives on Modern Japanese History*, edited by Harry Wray and Hilary Conroy. Honolulu: University of Hawai'i Press, 1983.

Koelb, Clayton. *The Incredulous Reader: Literature and the Function of Disbelief*. Ithaca, NY: Cornell University Press, 1984.

Komatsu Kazuhiko. *Akureiron: ikai kara no messeeji*. Tokyo: Seidosha, 1989.

———. *Hyōrei shinkō ron: Yōkai kenkyū no kokoromi*. Tokyo: Arina shobō, 1989.

———. *Ijinron: minzoku shakai no shinsei*. Tokyo: Seidosha, 1988.

———. *Yōkaigaku shinkō: yōkai kara miru nihonjin no kokoro*. Tokyo: Shōgakukan, 1994.

Komatsu Kazuhiko and Aramata Hiroshi. *Yōkai sōshi: ayashiki monotachi no shōsoku.* Tokyo: Kōsakusha, 1987.

Komatsu Kazuhiko, Maeda Ai, and Miyata Noboru. "Ijin to yōkai." *Shizen to bunka, tokushū: Ijin to Yōkai* 16 (spring 1987): 5–67.

Komatsu Kazuhiko and Mizuki Shigeru. "Yōkaidangi aruiwa takai e no manazashi." *Yurika* 16, no. 8 (August 1984): 114–30.

Komatsu Kazuhiko and Naitō Masatoshi. *Oni ga tsukutta kuni, Nihon.* Tokyo: Kōbunsha, 1985.

Koschmann, J. Victor. "Action as Text: Ideology in the Tengu Insurrection." In *Conflict in Modern Japanese History: The Neglected Tradition,* edited by Tetsuo Najita and J. Victor Koschmann. Princeton: Princeton University Press, 1982. 81–106.

———. "Folklore Studies and the Conservative Anti-Establishment in Modern Japan." In *International Perspectives on Yanagita Kunio and Japanese Folklore Studies,* edited by J. Victor Koschmann, Ōiwa Keibō, and Yamashita Shinji. Ithaca, NY: Cornell University East Asia Program, 1985. 131–64.

Koschmann, J. Victor, Ōiwa Keibō, and Yamashita Shinji, eds. *International Perspectives on Yanagita Kunio and Japanese Folklore Studies.* Ithaca, NY: Cornell University East Asia Program, 1985.

Koyasu Nobakuni. "Kishinron chūkai: kinsei kishinron no josho toshite." *Nihongaku* 8 (February 1987): 156–65.

Kristeva, Julia. "Word, Dialogue, and Novel." In *Desire in Language: A Semiotic Approach to Literature and Art,* edited by Leon S. Roudiez. New York: Columbia University Press, 1980. 64–91.

LaCapra, Dominick. "Bakhtin, Marxism, and the Carnivalesque." In *Rethinking Intellectual History: Texts, Contexts, Language.* Ithaca, NY: Cornell University Press, 1983. 291–324.

Langess, L. L., and Gelya Frank. "Fact, Fiction, and the Ethnographic Novel." *Anthropology and Humanism Quarterly* 3 (1978): 18–22.

Maeda Ai. *Kindai dokusha no seiritsu.* Tokyo: Iwanami shoten, 1993.

Maeda Ai and Yamaguchi Masao. "Kyōkai senjō no bungaku: Kyōka sekai no genkyō." *Kokubungaku: kaishaku to kyōzai no kenkyū* 30, no. 7 (1985): 8–24.

Makita Shigeru. "World Authority on Folklore: Yanagita Kunio." *Japan Quarterly* 20, no. 3 (1973): 283–93.

Marcus, George, and Richard Cushman. "Ethnographies as Texts." *Annual Review of Anthropology* 11 (1982): 25–69.

Markus, Andrew L. "The Carnival of Edo: *Misemono* Spectacles from Contemporary Accounts." *Harvard Journal of Asian Studies* 45, no. 2 (December 1985): 499–541.

Matsui Ryūgo. *Minakata Kumagusu: issai chi no yume.* Tokyo: Asahi sensho, 1991.

Matsui Ryūgo, Tsukikawa Kazuo, Nakase Hisaharu, and Kirimoto Tōta, eds. *Minakata Kumagusu o shiru jiten.* Tokyo: Kōdansha gendai shinsho, 1993.

Matsuyama Iwao. *Uwasa no enkinhō.* Tokyo: Seidōsha, 1993.

Michener, James A. *The Floating World.* Honolulu: University of Hawai'i Press, 1983.

Minakata Fumie. *Chichi Minakata Kumagusu o kataru.* Tokyo: Nihon editaa sukuuru shuppan, 1981.

Minakata Kumagusu. "Jinja gappei hantai iken." In *Minakata Kumagusu: chikyū ikō no hikakugaku,* by Tsurumi Kazuko. Tokyo: Kōdansha, 1978. 249–89.

———. *Minakata Kumagusu zenshū.* 10 vols. Tokyo: Kangensha, 1951.

Minakata Kumagusu and Yanagita Kunio. *Minakata Kumagusu senshū bekkan: Yanagita Kunio—Minakata Kumagusu ōfuku shokan.* Tokyo: Heibonsha, 1985.

Minosaku Genpara. "Kikai fushigi no kenkyū." *Tōyō gakugei zasshi* 3, no. 42 (25 March 1885): 33–38.

Mishima Yukio. *Shōsetsu to wa nani ka.* Tokyo: Shinchōsha, 1972.

Miyata Noboru. *Yōkai no minzokugaku: Nihon no mienai kūkan.* Tokyo: Iwanami Shoten, 1988.

———. "Kyōka to yōtai." *Kokubungaku: k Kaishaku to Kyōzai no Kenkyū* 30, no. 7 (June 1986): 63–67.

Mizuno Yōshū. "Kaidan." *Shumi* 4, no. 6 (May 1909).

———. "Tōno monogatari o yomite." 1910. In *Nihon bungaku kenkyū shiryō sōsho: Yanagita Kunio.* Tokyo: Yūseidō, 1976. 285–87.

Morse, Ronald A. "The Search for Japan's National Character and Distinctiveness: Yanagita Kunio (1875–1962) and the Folklore Movement." Ph.D. diss., Princeton University, 1974.

Morson, Gary Saul, and Caryl Emerson. *Mikhail Bakhtin: Creation of a Prosaics.* Stanford: Stanford University Press, 1990.

Nagaike Kenji. "Kaisetsu." In *Yanagita Kunio zenshū.* 32 vols. Tokyo: Chikuma shobō, 1989. 4:507–518.

Najita, Tetsuo, and J. Victor Koschmann, eds. *Conflict in Modern Japanese History: The Neglected Tradition.* Princeton: Princeton University Press, 1982.

Nakamura Akira. "Kyōka to Yanagita: Kyōka no Hokkai minzokugaku." *Bungaku* 51, no. 6 (1983): 41–48.

Nakase Hisaharu and Hasegawa Kōzō, eds. *Minakata Kumagusu arubamu.* Tokyo: Yatsuzaka shobō, 1991.

Napier, Susan J. *The Fantastic in Modern Japanese Literature: The Subversion of Modernity.* London: Routledge, 1996.

Natsume Sōseki. "Koto no sorane." 1905. In *Natsume Sōseki zenshū.* 16 vols. Tokyo: Iwanami, 1965–67. 2:85–123.

Nishi Akio. "Gakuzo no kengaku—seishin taru shin'nyo to yōkaigaku." In *Inoue Enryō no gakuri shisō,* edited by Shimizu Tadashi. Tokyo: Tōyō daigaku, 1989. 5–44.

Nishimura Shinji. "Minzoku dai-ikkan shokan." *Minzoku* 2, no. 1 (1926): 121–27.

———. "Setsuwa, densetsu, shinwa tai rekishi." *Minzoku* 2, no. 3 (1927): 139–43.

Okaya Kōji. "Shijin Yanagita Kunio no imi." *Kokubungaku: kaisetsu to kyōzai no ken-kyū* 27, no. 1 (1982): 70–84.

Okura Takeharu. *Inoue Enryō no shisō.* Tokyo: Azekura shobō, 1986.

Olsen, Lance. *Ellipse of Uncertainty: An Introduction to Postmodern Fantasy.* New York: Greenwood Press, 1986.

Orikuchi Shinobu. "Kyōka to no isseki." 1942. In *Orikuchi Shinobu zenshū.* Tokyo: Chūoronsha, 1957. 28:188–93.

Oshima Tatehiko. "Gakuzo no gakumon to minzokugaku." In *Inoue Enryō no gakuri shisō,* edited by Shimizu Tadashi. Tokyo: Tōyō daigaku, 1989. 263–307.

Ouwehand, Cornelius. *Namazu-e and Their Themes.* Leiden: Brill, 1964.

Pratt, Mary Louise. "Fieldwork in Common Places." In *Writing Culture: The Poetics and Politics of Ethnography,* edited by James Clifford and George E. Marcus. Berkeley: University of California Press, 1986. 27–50.

Ross, Kristin. *The Emergence of Social Space: Rimbaud and the Paris Commune.* Minneapolis: University of Minnesota Press, 1988.

Saitō Shigeo, ed. *Inoue Enryō to seiyō shisō.* Tokyo: Tōyō daigaku Inoue Enryō kinen gakujutsu kankō kikin, 1988.

San'yūtei Enchō. *Shinkei Kasane ga fuchi.* In *Enchō zenshū,* edited by Suzuki Kōzō. 12 vols. Tokyo: Sekai bunko, 1963–64. 1:1–397.

Sasaki Kizen. *Kikimimi sōshi.* Tokyo: Chikuma sōsho, 1986.

———. *Sasaki Kizen zenshū.* Vols. 1–2. Tōno: Tōno shiritsu hakubutsukan, 1986.

Sasaki Miyoko and Morioka Heinz. "*Rakugo:* Popular Narrative Art of the Grotesque." *Harvard Journal of Asian Studies* 41, no. 2 (December 1981): 417–59.

Satō Kenji. *Dokusho kūkan no kindai: hōhō toshite no Yanagita Kunio.* Tokyo: Kōbundō, 1987.

Shibusawa Tatsuhiko. "Rampu no kaiten." In *Shikō no monshōgaku.* Tokyo: Kawade bunko, 1985. 9–27.

———. *Shikō no monshōgaku.* Tokyo: Kawade bunko, 1985.

Shimazaki Tōson. "Tōno monogatari." In *Nihon bungaku kenkyū shiryō sōsho: Yanagita Kunio.* Tokyo: Yūseidō, 1976. 279–80.

Shimizu Tadashi, ed. *Inoue Enryō no gakuri shisō.* Tokyo: Tōyō daigaku Inoue Enryō kinen gakujutsu shinkō kikin, 1989.

Sibley, William F. "Naturalism in Japanese Literature." *Harvard Journal of Asian Studies* 28 (1968): 157–69.

Sōma Tsuneo. *Yanagita Kunio to bungaku.* Tokyo: Yōyōsha, 1994.

Strong, Kenneth. *Ox against the Storm: A Biography of Tanaka Shōzo (1841–1913).* Vancouver: University of British Columbia Press, 1977.

Takagi Hirosuke, ed. *Inoue Enryō kankei bunken nempyō.* Tokyo: Tōyō daigaku Inoue Enryō kenkyūkai, 1987.

Takahashi Yasuo. *Kokoro ni fushigi ari: Minakata Kumagusu, hito to shisō.* Tokyo: JICC, 1992.

Takayanagi Shun'ichi. "In Search of Yanagita Kunio." *Monumenta Nipponica* 31, no. 2 (summer 1976): 165–78.

Tamanoi, Mariko Asano. "Gender, Nationalism, and Japanese Native Ethnology." *positions: east asia cultures critique* 4, no. 1 (spring 1996): 59–86.

Tanaka, Stefan. *Japan's Orient: Rendering Pasts into History.* Berkeley: University of California Press, 1995.

Tanizaki Jun'ichirō. *In Praise of Shadows* [*In'ei raisan,* 1933]. Translated by Thomas J. Harper. New Haven, CT: Leete's Island Books, 1977.

Tatsukawa Shōji. *Byōki no shakaishi: bunmei ni saguru byōin.* Tokyo: NHK Books, 1982.

———. *Meiji iji ōrai.* Tokyo: Shinchōsha, 1986.

Tayama Katai. *Tayama Katai zenshū.* Tokyo: Katai zenshū kankōkai, 1923–24.

Todorov, Tzvetan. *The Fantastic: A Structural Approach to a Literary Genre.* Translated by Richard Howard. Ithaca, NY: Cornell University Press, 1975.

Trilling, Lionel. *The Liberal Imagination.* New York: Doubleday and Anchor, 1953.

Tsuboi Hirofumi. *Imo to Nihonjin: minzoku bunkaron no kadai.* Tokyo: Miraisha, 1979.

Tsubouchi Shōyō. *Shōsetsu shinzui.* 1885–86. Tokyo: Iwanami, 1963.

Tsurumi, E. Patricia. "Colonizer and Colonized in Taiwan." In *Japan Examined: Perspectives on Modern Japanese History,* edited by Harry Wang and Hilary Conroy. Honolulu: University of Hawai'i Press, 1983.

Tsurumi Kazuko. *Korosareta mono no yukue: watashi no minzokugaku nooto.* Tokyo: Haru shobō, 1985.

———. *Minakata Kumagusu: chikyū ikō no hikakugaku.* Tokyo: Kōdansha, 1978.

Tyler, Stephen A. "Ethnography, Intertextuality and the End of Description." *American Journal of Semiotics* 3, no. 4 (1985): 83–98.

Uchida Ryūzō. *Yanagita Kunio to jiken no kiroku.* Tokyo: Kōdansha sensho metier, 1995.

Utonuma Hiroshi. *Yamagata fushigi kikō: Inoue Enryō no ashiato o tadoru.* Tokyo: Hōsei daigaku shuppankyoku, 1991.

Vlastos, Stephen. *Peasant Protests and Uprisings in Tokugawa Japan.* Berkeley: University of California Press, 1986.

Volosinov, V. N. *Marxism and the Philosophy of Language.* Translated by Ladislav Matejka and I. R. Titunik. Cambridge, MA: Harvard University Press, 1973.

Webster, Steven. "Ethnography as Storytelling." *Dialectical Anthropology* 8 (1983): 185–205.

West, Cornel. "The New Cultural Politics of Difference." In *Out There: Marginalization and Contemporary Cultures,* edited by Russell Ferguson, Martha Gever, Trinh T. Minh-ha, and Cornel West. Cambridge, MA: MIT Press, 1990. 19–36.

White, Hayden. *Tropics of Discourse: Essays in Cultural Criticism.* Baltimore: Johns Hopkins University Press, 1978.

Wilson, George M. *Patriots and Redeemers in Japan: Motives in the Meiji Restoration.* Chicago: University of Chicago Press, 1992.

Wray, Harry, and Hilary Conroy, eds. *Japan Examined: Perspectives on Modern Japanese History.* Honolulu: University of Hawai'i Press, 1983.

Yamada Kiyoyoshi. "Mizuno Yōshū to Sasaki Kiyoshi." *Fūen* 9 (1972): 8–12.

———. "Yanagita Kunio to Mizuno Yōshū, 1." *Fūen* 7 (1972): 6–9.

———. "Yanagita Kunio to Mizuno Yōshū, 2." *Fūen* 8 (1972): 6–8.

Yamada Yūsaku. "Miseijuku to yume." *Bungaku* 51, no. 6 (1983): 120–26.

Yanagita Kunio. "Dokusha yori mitaru shizen-ha shōsetsu." *Bunshō sekai* 3, no. 5 (1908): 10–14.

———. "Genbun no kyori." *Bunshō sekai* 4, no. 13 (1909): 167–72.

———. "Jijitsu no kyōmi." *Bunshō sekai* 3, no. 14 (1908): 146–47.

———. "Kanri no yomu shōsetsu." *Bunshō sekai* 2, no. 11 (October 1907): 26–30.

———. *The Legends of Tōno.* Translated by Ronald Morse. Tokyo: Japan Foundation, 1975.

———. "Matsuō Kenji no monogatari." *Minzoku* 2, no. 2 (1927): 59.

———. *Meiji Taishōshi sesō hen.* Vol. 1. Tokyo: Kōdansha, 1976.

———. "Minzokugaku kara minzokugaku e." In *Minzokugaku ni tsuite: Dai-ni Yanagita Kunio Taidanshū.* Tokyo: Chikuma, 1965.

———. "Randoku no kuse." *Bunshō sekai* 2, no. 6 (1907): 41–44.

———. "Shasei to ronbun." *Bunshō sekai* 2, no. 3 (1907): 30–32.

———. "Shinkyuryō jidai no bungei." *Mumei tsūshin* 10 (October 1909): 125–26.

———. "Shoko Kyōka kan." In *Bungei dokuhon: Izumi Kyōka.* Tokyo: Kawade shobō shinsha, 1988. 68–70.

———. *Teihon Yanagita Kunio shū.* 31 vols. 5 suppls. Tokyo: Chikuma shobō, 1962–71.

———. *Yanagita Kunio taidanshū.* Tokyo: Chikuma sōsho, 1964.

———. *Yanagita Kunio zenshū.* 32 vols. Tokyo: Chikuma shobō, 1989.

———. "Yūmeidan." *Shinkō bunrin* 1, no. 6 (1905): 242–58.

Yanagita Kunio and Kuwabara Takeo. "Nihonjin no dōtoku ishiki." 1958. Reprinted in *Yanagita Kunio taidanshū.* Tokyo: Chikuma sōsho, 1964. 221–45.

Yanagita Kunio, Osatake Takeki, Akutagawa Ryūnosuke, and Kikuchi Kan. "Shōka kidan." 1927. Reprinted in *Yanagita Kunio taidanshū.* Tokyo: Chikuma sōsho, 1964. 247–84.

"Yōkai Tetsugaku." *Kokumin no tomo,* 13 November 1893, 47–48.

Yokota Junya. *Meiji fukashigi dō.* Tokyo: Chikuma shobō, 1995.

Yoshida Seiichi. *Shizenshugi no kenkyū.* Vol. 2. Tokyo: Tōkyōdō, 1958.

Yoshimoto Takaaki. *Kyōdō gensōron.* Tokyo: Kawade shobō, 1968.

———. *Yanagita Kunio ron shūsei.* Tokyo: JICC, 1990.

Yoshino, Kosaku. *Cultural Nationalism in Contemporary Japan: A Sociological Enquiry.* London: Routledge, 1992.

Žižek, Slavoj. *Looking Awry: An Introduction to Jacques Lacan through Popular Culture.* Cambridge, MA: MIT Press, 1991.

INDEX

Hashi-hime (bridge princess), 115,
194; Kyōka's depiction of 185–92;
Yanagita on, 190–92
Hearn, Lafcadio, 77, 155, 220–21,
256–57 n.40
Heimen byōsha (flat description). See
Shaseibun
Heterogeneity: Kyōka's depiction of,
162; Yanagita's interest in, 162, 172
Hidden world, the. See *Yūmei*
Hirata Atsutane, 217; anti-Buddhist
polemics, 36, 84; on the hidden
world, 143, 146, 151; on spirits and
monsters, 35–36, 142; on *tengu,* 84,
245 n.81
History: Certeau on, 118–19; folk
studies and, 134, 151, 163–64, 172–74,
207–9, 214; Irokawa and, 210–12;
Sasaki's interest in, 109; Yanagita's
views of, 116–17, 130, 137, 158,
170–71, 244 n.63; *yōkaigaku* and, 48
Hyaku monogatari (ghost story–telling
game), 166, 247–48 n.17

Identity: *fushigi* as source of, 209–22;
Kyōka's exploration of, 2–3, 157; and
monsters, 5–6; of national citizenry,
3, 16, 218; *nihonjinron* and, 14, 198,
212–16, 221. *See also* Japanese Spirit
Ideology: education and, 77–79; folk
studies and, 130; Inoue and, 90; and
the Meiji emperor, 15, 199–203, 215,
219; and the Meiji state, 3–5, 10,
16, 77–79, 90–91, 96, 103, 197–99;
supernatural aspects of, 52, 197–222
Igarashi, Yoshikuni, 210, 227 n.23, 255
nn. 22, 23
Ijin (stranger/foreigner), 26, 33
Imagination, 3, 17, 31, 71, 86, 152;
among the Japanese folk, 113, 177;
Kyōka's promotion of, 161–66, 171,

174, 179; modern reason versus, 4,
195; and reality, 158–62; and reason
in "Kechō," 184, 189–90; role in folk
studies, 111–14, 131–38, 168–71, 192,
215; status of, in fiction, 123, 158,
193–94; suppression of, 4; and tact,
71; Yanagita's use of, 131–38, 171, 195
Imperial Rescript on Education, 80,
198
Inoue, 16, 105, 199–200; and Buddhism, 40–43, 49; compared with
Minakata, 52–56, 59–60; criticism
of scholars, 47, 87, 233 n.22, diagram
of mind, 59; and Fushigi Kenkyūkai
(Mystery Research Society), 44–
46, 193; and Kant's thought, 43, 50;
lectures on *yōkai* (monsters), 83; on
meishin (superstition), 16; as member
of Shūshin Kyōkasho I-inkai (Ethics
Textbook Survey Committee), 82–
83, 186; Minakata's criticism of,
67, 72, 235 n.40; as *obake hakase*
(professor of monsters), 83; and
philosophy, 39–50; popularity of,
235 n.39; as promoter of *bunmei kaika*
(civilization and enlightenment),
40–44, 52–53, 90, 155; as promoter
of *yōkaigaku* (monsterology), 8,
41–52, 84, 87–92, 103, 108; and
psychology, 39–50; and reason, 67;
and Spencer's thought, 43, 232 n.9;
on *tengu,* 83–87; and Tetsugakudō,
240 n.5; and Tetsugakukan, 39, 49,
109, 166; Yanagita's criticism of,
116–17, 155
Inoue Testujirō, 82
Insanity. *See* Mental illness
Intruder, The (Maeterlinck): Yanagita's
impressions of, 123–25, 167–69
Irokawa Daikichi, 210–14
Ise Shrine, 200–203

239 n.2; Tōson's review of, 128–29; translation of, 226 n.16

Torahoomu. See Trachoma

Tōson. *See* Shimazaki Tōson

Trachoma, 98; in ethics lessons, 93–95; in *Kōya hijiri,* 183, 251 n.52; neologism for, 94

Transformation, 5, 14, 16, 150; culture and, 70–71; dreams and, 52; evolution and, 69–70; monsters and, 14, 141, 170, 182

Truth, 65, 91; depicted in writing, 123, 175, 212; of folk tales, 127–28, 134, 172–73; not identified with reality, 123–25; Naturalists' view of, 158–60, 163; scientific, 121, 156; status in folk studies, 107, 121, 131–35, 155, 167. *See also* Fact; Reality

Tsubouchi Shōyō: on fiction writing, 193; as member of Fushigi Kenkyūkai, 44

Tsurumi Kazuko: on Minakata, 71; on Minakata's Mandala, 234–35 n.34

Twilight: and *chūkan* (the in-between), 1–3, 156–57; definition of, 223 n.2; identity and, 2–5, 219; imagination and, 4; Kyōka's concept of, 1–6, 17, 186; monsters at, 4–6

Uchida Ryūzo, 9–10, 12, 227 nn. 20, 21; on preface of *Tōno monogatari,* 134; on Yanagita's style in *Tōno monogatari,* 129

Utagawa Kuniyoshi, 29–30

West, Cornell, 217–18

Western medicine. *See* Medicine

Yamabito (mountain people), 10, 16, 194, 220, 245 n.77, 250–51 n.47; Yanagita on, 138–41, 172–73, 179

Yamabushi (mountain ascetic), 26, 144, 151, 182, 250 n.46, 252–53 n.60

Yama-hime (mountain princess): Kyōka's depiction of, 180–85; Yanagita on, 178–79

Yanagita Kunio: application of *genbun-itchi,* 126; concept of *jōmin,* 9, 209, 225–26 n.12; critique of *gakusha* (scholars), 47, 131, 233 n.22; critique of Hirata Atsutane, 36; critique of Naturalist School, 123–25, 155–65; critique of rural policy, 198; critique of *yōkaigaku,* 116–17, 155, 191; debate over folk tales with Nishimura, 134, 172–73; discussion of hidden world with Kuwabara, 148–49; discussions with Akutagawa, 32, 113, 145–46; on folk study methodology, 113; and formation of folk studies (*minzokugaku*), 8–9, 12–17, 32, 106, 112–17, 130–52, 215, 219–20; and *fushigi,* 5–6, 16–17, 104; on *hashi-hime,* 190–92; and Inoue, 46–47; on *kami-kakushi,* 177–78; and Kyōka, 5–6, 155–80; on Kyōka's writing, 155, 170; linguistic analysis, 130–31, 143–44, 164; as literary fiction writer, 118–20, 126–31, 151–57, 167–70; and Minakata, 68, 106, 139–41, 235 n.38; as *minzokugakusha,* 132–35; as model for postwar historians, 210–14; on monsters, 5–6, 114–17, 130–31; and Nitobe, 114–15; opposition against shrine mergers, 204; on place-names, 164; as poet, 119–21, 136–37, 141–42; and Sasaki, 106–12, 128, 133, 241 n.17; on shamans (*miko*), 178–79, 250 n.46; on *shaseibun,* 122–23, 160–61; temporality in work of, 120, 171–75, 248–49 n.31; on *tengu,* 83, 114–17, 179, 242 n.24; *Tōno mono-*

Gerald Figal is Assistant Professor of History at the University of Delaware.

Library of Congress Cataloging-in-Publication Data
Figal, Gerald A.
Civilization and monsters : spirits of modernity in Meiji Japan /
Gerald Figal.
p.   cm. — (Asia-Pacific)
Includes bibliographical references and index.
ISBN 0-8223-2384-2 (cl. : alk. paper)
ISBN 0-8223-2418-0 (pa. : alk. paper)
1. Japan—Civilization—1868-1912.   2. Japanese literature—
Meiji period, 1868-1912.   3. Folklore—Japan.   I. Title.   II. Series.
DS822.3   .F54   1999
398.2′0952′09034—dc21   99-25983   CIP